Samuel Johnson

LIFE OF MILTON

Samuel Johnson

LIFE OF MILTON

[Edited with Complete Introduction, Biography, Author's Background, Complete Text, Select Criticism and Bibliography]

Anshu Mallika Sawhney
M.A. English, Delhi University
M. Phil., Himachal Pradesh University

ANMOL PUBLICATIONS PVT. LTD.
NEW DELHI - 110 002 (INDIA)

ANMOL PUBLICATIONS PVT. LTD.

H.O.: 4374/4B, Ansari Road, Darya Ganj,
New Delhi-110 002 (India)
Ph.: 23278000, 23261597

B.O.: No. 1015, Ist Main Road, BSK IIIrd Stage
IIIrd Phase, IIIrd Block
Bangalore - 560 085 (India)
Visit us at: www.anmolpublications.com

Life of Milton

First Published, 2009

PRINTED IN INDIA

Printed at Mehra Offset Press, Delhi.

Contents

Preface *vii*

1. Introduction 1
2. Samuel Johnson the Man and His Masterpiece 5
3. Samuel Johnson Biography 12
4. More on Johnson 22
5. Samuel Johnson Works 28
6. Time Line 29
7. The Restoration Period and the 18th Century 40
8. John Milton: Biography 51
9. Milton's Youthful Works and Poetic Ambitions 60
10. Life of Milton 64
11. Explanatory Notes 133
12. The Essential Elements of the Preface 142

Bibliography 253

Preface

Samuel Johnson was born on September 18, 1709 and died on 13 December 1784. His father was a poor book seller, Michael Johnson. He was born in Lichfield and enrolled in Lichfield Grammar School. In the year 1728, he got enrolled as a fellow commoner in Pembroke College, Oxford. He was nineteen only. He left Oxford without completing his degree to Lichfield.

One of his most renowned works, A Dictionary of the English Language had been written between 1745 to 1755. A few popular works of 1747 Plan for a Dictionary of the English Language, 1750-1752 The Rambler, 1753-1754 The Adventurer, 1755 Preface to a Dictionary of the English Language, 1758-1760 The Idler (1758-1760), 1765 Preface to the Plays of William Shakespeare, 1770 The False Alarm, 1771 Thoughts on the Late Transactions Respecting Falkland's Islands, 1774 The Patriot , 1775 Taxation No Tyranny etc.

Author

Chapter 1

Introduction

Perhaps because his works are little read today, we tend to see Samuel Johnson (through the medium of Boswell's great biography) primarily as a personality, as a conversationalist, as a great and eccentric character. He was, however, first and foremost a man of letters: he was a superb poet, a great moralist and critic, a remarkable lexicographer, a novelist, a journalist, a biographer, a playwright, an essayist, a satirist, a bibliographer, an autobiographer, a diarist, a journalist, a book reviewer, an editor, a scholar, a translator, a sermon writer, and a writer on travel and politics. He wrote his philosophical poems, essays, and classical tragedies, his satires in the classical tradition, his fiction and his criticism in a style which was at once polished, witty, urbane, heavy, Latinate, and ponderous. He was the literary dictator of his era, and he remains the central figure of what is still called the Age of Johnson — the period between 1750 and 1798 when a still-dominant Neoclassicism was slowly giving way before the incipient Romantic Movement.

After a long period of obscurity, of poverty, of hardship and disappointment, he emerged in his later years as a famous and beloved personality, loved as much for his eccentricities, for his mythic qualities—he was an enormous, uncouth, shambling man, with, all his life, a provincial accent, his face scarred by smallpox and by scrofula, full of quirks and quarrels and convulsive starts and tremors, slovenly in appearance, indolent, generous, melancholy, peevish, and arrogant, a great drinker of tea, a great admirer of ladies, a great monopolizer of conversation—as for his remarkable intellectual brilliance.

He presided over and dominated the famous Literary Club, formed in 1764, which created or influenced contemporary literary tastes and styles: its members included Edmund Burke, Oliver Goldsmith, Bishop Percy, David Garrick, Edward Gibbon, Adam Smith, and James Boswell, all important figures in them. After his death his conservatism, his stylistic mannerisms, his didacticism, and his rationalism all went out of fashion, and—with a few notable exceptions among literary artists and critics during the nineteenth century—it has been only in recent years that the real quality and depth of his thought—which had become obscured in his endearing Boswellian persona—have once again begun to be appreciated. He has only one real theme, but it is a noble one, one of the great themes of literature, as it was the theme of his own life: he writes about man's unceasing search for happiness, about the inevitable hopelessness of that search, and about his refusal, in spite of his awareness of the fact that he is doomed to fail, to give up his quest.

Johnson's Religion

Johnson was deeply but not necessarily conventionally religious: he struggled within himself most of his life to sustain his belief in God in the face of enormous pressures, disappointments, and psychological calamities. On the surface, and in much of his work, he appeared to be an orthodox, conventional, conservative adherent of revealed religion, of the Church of England, but the conventional Anglican explanations for the existence of evil in the world failed to satisfy him, and in any case his characteristic reluctance to believe without evidence, his fear of credulity, his dislike of mysteries, continually undermined his attempts to accept conventional beliefs.

He was remarkable, privately, for his tolerance; maintaining that the differences between Christian sects (Protestants and Roman Catholics, for example) were trivial, and due primarily to political rather than religious differences.

His religious difficulties began at a very early age. His mother, when he was only three, told him of "a fine place filled with happiness called Heaven" and "a sad place, called Hell." Many years later he recalled that (as one might expect) this account did not impress him very deeply: it is significant, however, that he remembered it at all. After the age of nine, and through his adolescence, he stopped going to church. One part of him remained a skeptic for the rest of his life, and, as his private journals show, even after he had regained his faith he struggled continually (and privately) with fears, guilt, and disbelief: in The Vanity of Human Wishes, written when he was forty, he returns to a traditional religious theme as well as a personal preoccupation and insists that we cannot find genuine or permanent happiness in this world, and that we must therefore turn to religious belief and a faith in the existence of a better world after death if we are to endure our existence here. It was a belief; however, which he himself had difficulty maintaining.

The happiness derived from such belief was in any case a limited one, but the only alternative to religious faith, as Johnson saw it, was a dull apathy, a stoical disengagement from life. He was troubled, too—a better word would be tormented—by a fear of death and by a deeper fear that he might in spite of his best efforts be so guilty, so sinful, that he merited damnation. And beneath that fear was another, even deeper—the fear that God might not exist at all, that death might bring annihilation, mere nothingness, the loss of personal identity. He struggled all his life—in the end, successfully—not so much to overcome these fears as to coexist with them.

In public he was much more conventional, much more characteristically paternalistic. He maintained in print, for example, that religion was a valuable asset to society and to mankind and that Anglicanism, as the English state religion, ought therefore to be carefully protected: "Permitting men to preach any opinion contrary to the doctrine of the established church," he wrote, "tends, in a certain degree, to lessen the authority of the church, and, consequently, to lessen the influence of religion." In private, though, his religious beliefs were much less doctrinaire, and much more complicated.

Samuel Johnson and Philosophy

Johnson's works are the productions of a mind which was profoundly pessimistic and innately melancholy: he was desperately conservative in religion and politics because he believed that only the maintenance of order protected individuals and whole human societies from despair; and that authority and tradition were not ends in themselves but rather means of upholding and sustaining order.

He despised the French philosophies, remarking, of Voltaire and Rousseau, that "It is too difficult to settle the proportion of iniquity between them." When his reason conflicted with his fear of disorder, that fear often won out, and manifested itself in an outburst of temper or a refusal to pursue the subject further. When Boswell suggested that it was impossible to refute Bishop Berkeley's assertion that matter did not exist, Johnson reacted in characteristic fashion: "I shall never forget," wrote Boswell, "the alacrity with which Johnson answered, striking his foot with mighty force against a large stone, till he rebounded from it, 'I refute it thus.'"

A friend wrote that "His religion... made his extraordinary talents of Mind continually at War with each other," but when he came upon scientific evidence which suggested that the biblical account of the creation of the earth could not be taken literally, he rejected it out of hand. Overall, Johnson had a conservative belief in the necessity of order, and in the dangers of disorder.

Chapter 2

Samuel Johnson the Man and His Masterpiece

As an English Language major, it was to learn more about Samuel Johnson the lexicographer, as well as his Dictionary of the English Language, that I initially decided on taking the individual author course which bears his name (as well as that of his now-famous biographer). However, as the course progressed and I found the Dictionary to have maintained its place of prominence in my admiration for this great man, I nevertheless perceived the task of writing about it as something more than daunting: like the mountain climber who possesses neither rope nor piton, I was ill-equipped to take on a meaningful examination of that monolithic work. It was not until learning of Frederick Pottle's three-point formula of literary criticism that I realized I had at my disposal the perfect method with which to confront and examine Johnson's Dictionary. Therefore, I shall proceed in this brief monograph to examine the questions of just what Samuel Johnson was trying to achieve with his Dictionary, how well he achieved it, and, finally, whether it was worth it.

Before going into Johnson's intentions, however, it is important to give a little background first, in order to place Johnson's achievement in its proper historical perspective. The first work designed specifically for the use of English-speaking people to find listings and definitions of English words was Robert Cawdrey's A Table Alphabetical (1604). This work was formulated for the purpose of defining only difficult words in the language and was by no means intended to be comprehensive. Others were to follow, including Bullokar's An English Expositour (1616), Cockerams's English Dictionarie (1623), Blount's Glossographia (1656), Phillip's New World of English Words (1658), Cocker's English Dictionary (1704), and, finally, Nathan Bailey's two offerings, the Universal Etymological English Dictionary (1721) and the Dictionarium Britannicum (1730). The latter, containing some 48,000 entries, was to be Johnson's basis for his own dictionary. (While Johnson's Dictionary contains only 40,000 words, one might well wonder what became of the other 8,000 contained in Bailey; Johnson addresses these omissions in the preface to the Dictionary, going to great lengths to enumerate the various types of words he considered inappropriate, including technical terms, foreign words, and, the bane of his linguistic existence, "cant words.")

It is significant to note that by continental standards, mid-eighteenth century England was far behind the times, linguistically speaking. The Tuscan dictionary of the Accademia della Crusca, the standing Italian dictionary, had appeared in 1612, and the dictionary of the Academie Francaise was out as of 1694. It is even more amazing to consider that one man set out to do the work that had taken whole national think-tanks decades to achieve. (Johnson's well-know quip about the ratio of Englishmen to Frenchmen would prove to be more than mere boast, as generations of Englishmen were soon to find out. Indeed, upon completion, David Garrick was quoted as exclaiming that Johnson had "beat forty Frenchmen and will beat forty more!")

In addressing the question of Johnson's intentions regarding his Dictionary, we must first debunk one of many popular misconceptions held by the general public, as well as linguistic and literary scholars who should know better, namely that Johnson was trying to "fix" the English language. Indeed, while his original Plan of an English Dictionary of 1747 is full of prescriptive sentiment, indicating that he was determined to set English in stone once and for all, in fact, through the very process of writing the mighty tome, Johnson became far more modern in his awareness of language. While it was, no doubt, his personal dream to have his fellow Englishmen speak and write correctly, the lesson of his own dictionary taught him the difference between stability and stagnation, as well as imparting a deeper understanding of the living, fluid quality of his native tongue.

He declared as much in the preface to the Dictionary when he wrote, "Those who have been persuaded to think well of my design will require that I should fix our language, and put a stop to those alterations which time and chance have hitherto been suffered to make in it without opposition. With this consequence I will confess that I flattered myself for a while; but now begin to fear that I have indulged expectation which neither reason nor experience can justify." This is not to say that he had thrown up his hands and fallen in with what in modern parlance would be termed the "descriptive school." He remained extremely conservative in his views on language, as he stated in the very same preface that, "Much less ought our written language to comply with the corruptions of oral utterance, or copy that which every variation of time or place makes different from itself, and imitate those changes which will again be changed, while imitation is employed in observing them."

As we have seen, Johnson's intention in writing his Dictionary was an evolving one, changing over the course of the writing itself. The final version of it can be seen in the preface to the abridged edition, published in 1756, wherein he states, "I lately published a Dictionary like those compiled by the academies of Italy and France, for the use of such as aspire to exactness of criticism, or elegance of style." It is this two-fold intention, the creation of a dictionary to serve the pursuits of criticism and style that has, as I shall endeavor to prove in the summation of this paper, been gloriously and effectively realized.

At this point, I think it important to look in on Johnson's garret at Number 17 Gough Square to get an idea of just how the Dictionary took shape. One might assume that Johnson simply grabbed his copy of Bailey's Dictionarium Britannicum and started revising. In fact, the initial preparation was quite different and, not to be too redundant, classically Johnsonian: He read. Johnson pored over all the works of the great English authors; Shakespeare, Milton, Watts, Spenser, Baker, Pope, Hooker, Boyle, Dryden, Addison, Bacon, Swift, Locke, and many more, men of science as well as men of letters, and wherever he found a passage that seemed to illustrate a particular word, he marked it, citing the word's first letter in the margin, and passed the book to one of his six amanuenses. (A facsimile of a page so marked is attached to the end of this paper.) The amanuensis would then copy the quotations onto slips of paper, cross off the letter from the margin of the marked page, and paste the quotation slip onto a larger sheet of paper allotted to the word in question.

The idea was to have a barrage of quotations for each word with which to supplement a given definition. In this way, the reader would be provided with a specific definition (or, as was often the case, a list of definitions), as well as having the opportunity of seeing the word used in context; not only that, but the reader could enjoy the luxury of seeing how a given word had been utilized by one of the great writers of the sixteenth and seventeenth centuries.

This was Johnson's unique contribution to lexicography: the addition of illustrative quotations, some 114,000 in all. (It should be noted that the modern use of quotations, such as in the Oxford English Dictionary, has become more a method of showing the historical evolution of a given word, while Johnson's intention was more that of displaying an exactness and excellence of usage.) Once the bulk of quotations had been compiled, the making of master word lists was taken up, consulting Bailey as well as others. Definitions were composed, etymologies appended and additional quotes added.

The enormity of the task is beyond belief, and one might think that spending nine years with six amanuenses, five of whom were Scots, would have been too much for the supposedly Scot-hating Johnson. Here again we find the truth underlying the myth, in this case the erroneous conception of a prejudiced Samuel Johnson. The amanuenses Johnson employed were Shiels, the two Macbean brothers, Stewart,

Maitland, and Peyton, the latter being the single Englishman. Over time, Johnson came to look on these men as not just mere employees, but as dependents, supporting Stewart, who died during the process, Shiels, who died shortly afterward, as well as literally burying Peyton.

The much-quoted joke definition for "oats" was designed more as a good-natured jibe toward the Scots on his team than some arrogant slap at Scotland in general. This is not to imply that Johnson and his assistants enjoyed a non-stop, rosy joviality; there was plenty of backbiting, gossiping, time-wasting and trips to the pub when the boss was away. But the fact remains that Johnson treated these men, Scots though they were, with the same kindness he reserved for all common people.

Much criticism has been leveled at Johnson for the supposed inferiority of his etymologies, and, here again; it is my intention to correct the record. Amongst his early detractors was William Smellie, the first editor of the Encyclopaedia Britannica, who expressed his own misgivings in the entry for "dictionary" in the original 1768 edition. Then, in 1775, John Whitaker, himself a decidedly bad etymologist [4], attacked Johnson's etymologies of Celtic derivatives. 1786 saw Horne Tooke, in The Diversions of Purley, taking aim at Johnson for violating his (Tooke's) own bizarre theory that there should be only one meaning per word.(This torch was picked up and carried as late as 1836 by Tooke's literary disciple, Charles Richardson, in his A New Dictionary of the English Language.) In 1807,, for reasons of his own, Noah Webster climbed on the Johnson-bashing bandwagon. Macaulay called him a "wretched etymologist." Even the supreme acolyte, James Boswell, stated, "The etymologies, though they exhibit learning and judgement, are not, I think, entitled to the first praise amongst the various parts of this immense work." Wherefore this veritable plethora of condemnation?

Before answering this question, we must look into the mind of Samuel Johnson, for, as he had for everything else, he had formulated his own philosophy regarding etymology. For one thing, since Latin was still much in use, he saw little need to fill in every variation between a Latin derivative and its English counterpart. Secondly, his brevity in etymological entries stemmed from a combination of his own staunch nationalism and an empirical, Occam's Razor-type approach which precluded undue concern for the various continental forms of the Latin derivatives.

It is important to note that much of the earlier criticism came from direct comparisons of Johnson's Dictionary and Bailey's Dictionarium Britannicum; however, the latter's so-called "etymologies" were in fact no more, in most cases, than wholesale listings of every possible form of a given word from all of the various continental languages, with little concern for what Johnson would have termed "concatenation." (Even the use of the term "etymological" in the title of Bailey's earlier work was more a selling point and an excuse to publish a new dictionary than a genuine innovation in the science of lexicography.) In addition, whenever Johnson felt that such concatenations were significant, his usual brevity was breached and a more complete etymology was provided. Finally, it must be realized that Johnson's Dictionary was, in fact, written some 250 years ago, and it is inappropriate to judge it by modern standards of language study; taken in context, it remains the outstanding work of its century.

Having looked at a bit of lexicographical history, Johnson's evolving intentions for his Dictionary, his methods of execution, his innovative use of quotations, his working relationship with his crew of amanuenses, and his theory of etymology, as well as clearing up a few popular misconceptions, it remains for us to ask the final question: Was it worth it? The answer is a resounding and unequivocal YES. Samuel Johnson's Dictionary remained the authoritative work in its field for a century after its publication and set the standard by which subsequent dictionaries would be judged. Its importance cannot be understated.

To the dilettante, the occasional, much-quoted joke definitions found sprinkled throughout the work, together with the more eccentric characterizations provided by Boswell, might make the Dictionary, as well as its author, seem silly and inconsequential; it is only through depth of examination that we begin to see the real merit of such a phenomenal achievement, and appreciate Johnson for the intellectual giant that he was.

Samuel Johnson was a man of his age. As John Wain puts it, "The eighteenth-century aim was a language which would not seem obsolete in two generations, and this aim was brilliantly achieved." Today we can read Johnson with complete comprehension, and it is this fact which says more for his achievement than any other. Further, this continuity of language carries a greater significance: the continuity of culture. The Dictionary provided for the critic and the stylist of Johnson's day a greatly improved instrument with which to pursue their literary and, as a consequence, cultural goals, a tool to serve the pursuit and ultimate mastery of the English language. It is for this reason that we revere him, respect him, and will not forget him.

Chapter 3

Samuel Johnson Biography

Samuel Johnson was born on September 18, 1709 (N.S.) in the country town of Lichfield in Staffordshire, the son of Michael Johnson, aged 50, a bookseller and stationer, and his wife Sara, aged 37. The elder Johnson was prone, as his son would be, to bouts of melancholy, but he was a man of some local repute—at the time of Johnson's birth, he was Sheriff of the city. Johnson, a sickly child, was not expected to live: in 1711, at the age of two, he was taken, nearly blind, partially deaf, suffering from scrofula and a tubercular infection, to be touched for the "King's Evil" by Queen Anne, the last of the Stuarts to rule England. No miraculous cure, however, took place.

In 1716 Johnson, sensitive, clumsy, and precocious, entered the Lichfield Grammar School which was headed by the scholarly but brutal John Hunter, who beat his students, as he said, "to save them from the gallows." Later in life Johnson would insist that had he not been beaten he would have done nothing, but under Hunter's tutelage he learned Latin and Greek and began to write poetry. In 1725 at the age of sixteen, a very provincial Johnson came for a six-month visit with his cousin, Cornelius Ford, a sophisticated and somewhat rakish former Cambridge don, and became aware for the first time of the existence of the larger intellectual and literary world represented by Cambridge and London.

In 1726, Johnson left school and went to work in his father's bookshop, which was failing: he spent the next two years were unhappy ones, but during this time he continued—avidly if unsystematically—to study English and classical literature. In 1728, with a small legacy of forty pounds left to his mother upon the death of a relative, he was—very unexpectedly—able to enter Pembroke College at Oxford. At Oxford, however, he was unable to keep himself adequately supplied with food or clothing—a problem which he would have for many years—and though he occasionally displayed considerable erudition symptoms of the melancholia which would haunt him for the remainder of his life were already beginning to manifest themselves. He paid, in consequence, little attention to his studies, and in 1789, extremely depressed and too poor to continue, he left Oxford without taking a degree. Johnson's Latin translation of Pope's "Messiah," written at Oxford, was published in 1731, but by that time Johnson, poor, in debt, depressed, partially blind, partially deaf, scarred by scrofula and smallpox, found himself (understandably enough) fearing for his sanity. In December of that year his father died, a virtual bankrupt.

In 1732, Johnson found employment as an usher at Market Bosworth Grammar School. On a visit to Birmingham, he made the acquaintance of Henry Porter and his wife Elizabeth. The following year, lying in bed during another lengthy visit to a friend in Birmingham, Johnson dictated an abridged English version of a French translation of a travel book—A Voyage to Abyssinia—, which had been written by a seventeenth-century Portuguese Jesuit. It became his first published book, and he earned five guineas by it. In 1735, aged twenty-five, Johnson married his "Tetty," the by-now-widowed Elizabeth Porter, aged forty-six. With his wife's dowry of £700, Johnson established, in the following year, an ill-fated private academy at Edial, near Lichfield: boarding pupils included David Garrick, who would become the most famous actor of his day, and one of Johnson's closest friends. By 1737, the academy had proved a failure, and Johnson, determined to make his fortune by writing, left for London, accompanied by Garrick.

In 1738, living in London in extreme poverty, Johnson began to write for Edward Cave's The Gentleman's Magazine, and published his "London," an imitation of Juvenal's satire on the decadence of ancient Rome, for which he **receives ten** guineas. He also made the acquaintance of Richard Savage, another impoverished poet of dubious reputation. A year later, Samuel Johnson, who had never met Johnson but who had admired his "London," attempted to get him an M. A. degree from Trinity College in Dublin so that he could become headmaster at a school: the attempt, however, failed, and Johnson was forced to continue his life of poverty and literary drudgery in (metaphorically speaking) Grub Street.

Between 1740 and 1743, he edited parliamentary debates for the Gentleman's Magazine: when, years later, he was complimented for his impartial approach to his task, he stated, characteristically, that though he "saved appearances tolerably well," he nevertheless "took care that the WHIG DOGS should not have the best of it."

In 1744, Richard Savage ended a miserable existence in a Bristol jail. Johnson was moved to write a Life of Savage—remarkable for its honest portrayal of the strenghs and weaknesses of his friend's character—which became the first of Johnson's prose works to attract the attention of the reading public. 1745 saw the publication of Johnson's "Miscellaneous Observations on the Tragedy of Macbeth." The following year he signed a contract with a group of publishers and (alotting himself, intially, three years) undertook the enormous task of compiling an English dictionary which would be analogous to that which had been produced, in French, by the forty members of the French Academy. He addressed his "Plan of a Dictionary" to the Earl of Chesterfield, who would prove to be a most unsatisfactory patron. In 1748, with six assistants, Johnson moved into a large house in Fleet Street and began work upon his dictionary. In 1749 his great but melancholy "The Vanity of Human Wishes" appeared, and Garrick produced Johnson's tragedy Irene at Drury Lane: though Johnson made a small profit, the play proved unsuccessful.

Between 1750 and 1752, writing two a week, he produced the more than two hundred Rambler essays. In 1752, his wife Tetty died. Two years later Johnson returned to Oxford, where he became acquainted with Thomas Warton, the future Poet Laureate. The following year, with Warton's help, Johnson received an M. A. degree from Oxford. In the same year his great Dictionary of the English Language was finally completed and published, and, though he was still very poor, his literary reputation was finally established. During this period he made new friends of the much younger Joshua Reynolds, Bennet "Lanky" Langton, and Topham Beauclerk.

In 1756, Johnson produced his "Proposals for a New Edition of Shakespeare," which would not, however, appear until 1765, and continued his activities as a journalist, editing, writing prefaces, and contributing articles to journals. Briefly arrested for debt, he was bailed out by Samuel Richardson. Between 1758 and 1760, he wrote another series of essays, The Idler, for a weekly periodical. In 1759 his mother Sarah died, and, in a somber mood, he wrote the moral fable Rasselas to pay, as he said, for her funeral.

In 1762, upon the succession to the throne of George III, Johnson was provided (much to his satisfaction, but much, also, to his embarrassment, for he was an unrepentant old Tory, and, with Whig abuses in mind, had defined "pension" in his dictionary as "pay given to a state hireling for treason to his country") with a pension of £300 per year. For the first time in his life he was not forced to scrape for money, and though his personal appearance was still remarkably and unavoidably uncouth he became one of the most prominent literary lions in polite society: when several young ladies, encountering him at a literary soiree, surrounded him "with more wonder than politeness," and contemplated his odd figure "as if he had been some monster from the deserts of Africa," Johnson is said to have remarked "Ladies, I am tame; you may stroke me." In 1763, he met James Boswell (aged twenty-two) for the first time, and after he got over the fact that Boswell was Scottish (Johnson abhorred the Scots—hence his famous definition, in his dictionary, of "oats": "A grain, which in England is generally given to horses, but in Scotland supports the people") the two got on very well together. 1764 brought the formation of the Literary Club, whose members included Johnson, Reynolds, and Edmund Burke, as well as (eventually) David Garrick and Boswell.

In 1765, Johnson's edition of Shakespeare's Plays, with its

splendid and perceptive preface, was finally published, and he received an honorary LL.D. from Trinity College in Dublin. He also met the wealthy Henry and Hester Thrale, with whom he would spend much of his time during the next sixteen years, talking brilliantly but writing little‹"No one but a blockhead," he once remarked, "writes but for money."

In 1769 Boswell, by now an Edinburgh lawyer, married, and remained in Scotland until 1772. Between 1770 and 1775, Johnson produced a series of fiercely but characteristically opinionated political pamphlets. In August of 1773, though he had always despised Scotland, Johnson undertook his memorable trip to the Hebrides with Boswell. In July of 1774, Johnson went to Wales with the Thrales. During that same year Oliver Goldsmith, one of the few contemporaries whom Johnson genuinely admired, died, and Johnson felt a tremendous sense of loss.

In 1775, Johnson published his A Journey to the Western Islands of Scotland. During the same year he received an honorary LL.D. from Oxford, and visited to France (which he finds worse than Scotland) with the Thrales. He reacted furiously to the American Revolution, characterizing the rebellious colonists as "a race of convicts." In 1776 he travelled with Boswell to Oxford, Ashbourne, and Lichfield, where he stood bareheaded in the rain in the market-place before the stall which had housed his father's bookshop, in order to atone for a "breach of filial piety" committed fifty years before.

In 1778 he made the acquaintance of Fanny Burney, aged twenty-four, and soon to be the sucessful authoress of Evelina. In the following year David Garrick, Johnson's old pupil and close friend, died, and he was again shaken. In 1781, after Johnson's The Lives of the English Poets had been published, Henry Thrale died. Johnson consoled his widow and, though he ought perhaps to have known better, contemplated marrying her. In 1783, however, his health began to fail, and he suffered a stroke. The following year, partially recovered, he broke with Mrs. Thrale when she announced her intention of marrying Gabriele Piozzi. Johnson, frail and troubled by gout, asthma, dropsy, and a tumour, found that his his lifelong fear of death had begun to preoccupy him, but he faced it bravely, as he had faced all adversities. On December 13 he died, aged seventy-five: he was buried in Westminster Abbey, with approriate ceremony, on December 20.

Samuel Johnson was born on September 18, 1709 (N.S.) in the country town of Lichfield in Staffordshire, the son of Michael Johnson, aged 50, a bookseller and stationer, and his wife Sara, aged 37. The elder Johnson was prone, as his son would be, to bouts of melancholy, but he was a man of some local repute—at the time of Johnson's birth, he was Sheriff of the city. Johnson, a sickly child, was not expected to live: in 1711, at the age of two, he was taken, nearly blind, partially deaf, suffering from scrofula and a tubercular infection, to be touched for the "King's Evil" by Queen Anne, the last of the Stuarts to rule England. No miraculous cure, however, took place.

In 1716 Johnson, sensitive, clumsy, and precocious, entered the Lichfield Grammar School which was headed by the scholarly but brutal John Hunter, who beat his students, as he said, "to save them from the gallows." Later in life Johnson would insist that had he not been beaten he would have done nothing, but under Hunter's tutelage he learned Latin and Greek and began to write poetry. In 1725 at the age of sixteen, a very provincial Johnson came for a six-month visit with his cousin, Cornelius Ford, a sophisticated and somewhat rakish former Cambridge don, and became aware for the first time of the existence of the larger intellectual and literary world represented by Cambridge and London.

In 1726, Johnson left school and went to work in his father's bookshop, which was failing: he spent the next two years were unhappy ones, but during this time he continued—avidly if unsystematically—to study English and classical literature. In 1728, with a small legacy of forty pounds left to his mother upon the death of a relative, he was—very unexpectedly—able to enter Pembroke College at Oxford. At Oxford, however, he was unable to keep himself adequately supplied with food or clothing—a problem which he would have for many years—and though he occasionally displayed considerable erudition symptoms of the melancholia which would haunt him for the remainder of his life were already beginning to manifest themselves. He paid, in consequence, little attention to his studies, and in 1789, extremely depressed and too poor to continue, he left Oxford without taking a degree. Johnson's Latin translation of Pope's "Messiah," written at Oxford, was published in 1731, but by that time Johnson, poor, in debt, depressed, partially blind, partially deaf, scarred by scrofula and smallpox, found himself (understandably enough) fearing for his sanity. In December of that year his father died a virtual bankrupt.

In 1732, Johnson found employment as an usher at Market Bosworth Grammar School. On a visit to Birmingham, he made the acquaintance of Henry Porter and his wife Elizabeth. The following year, lying in bed during another lengthy visit to a friend in Birmingham, Johnson dictated an abridged English version of a French translation of a travel book—A Voyage to Abyssinia—which had been written by a seventeenth-century Portuguese Jesuit. It became his first published book, and he earned five guineas by it.

In 1735, aged twenty-five, Johnson married his "Tetty," the by-now-widowed Elizabeth Porter, aged forty-six. With his wife's dowry of £700, Johnson established, in the following year, an ill-fated private academy at Edial, near Lichfield: boarding pupils included David Garrick, who would become the most famous actor of his day, and one of Johnson's closest friends. By 1737 the academy had proved a failure, and Johnson, determined to make his fortune by writing, left for London, accompanied by Garrick.

In 1738, living in London in extreme poverty, Johnson began to write for Edward Cave's The Gentleman's Magazine, and published his "London," an imitation of Juvenal's satire on the decadence of ancient Rome, for which he receives ten guineas. He also made the acquaintance of Richard Savage, another impoverished poet of dubious reputation. A year later, Samuel Johnson, who had never met Johnson but who had admired his "London," attempted to get him an M. A. degree from Trinity College in Dublin so that he could become headmaster at a school: the attempt, however, failed, and

Johnson was forced to continue his life of poverty and literary drudgery in (metaphorically speaking) Grub Street.

Between 1740 and 1743, he edited parliamentary debates for the Gentleman's Magazine: when, years later, he was complimented for his impartial approach to his task, he stated, characteristically, that though he "saved appearances tolerably well," he nevertheless "took care that the WHIG DOGS should not have the best of it."

In 1744, Richard Savage ended a miserable existence in a Bristol jail. Johnson was moved to write a Life of Savage—remarkable for its honest portrayal of the strengths and weaknesses of his friend's character—which became the first of Johnson's prose works to attract the attention of the reading public. 1745 saw the publication of Johnson's "Miscellaneous Observations on the Tragedy of Macbeth." The following year he signed a contract with a group of publishers and (allotting himself, initially, three years) undertook the enormous task of compiling an English dictionary which would be analogous to that which had been produced, in French, by the forty members of the French Academy. He addressed his "Plan of a Dictionary" to the Earl of Chesterfield, who would prove to be a most unsatisfactory patron.

In 1748, with six assistants, Johnson moved into a large house in Fleet Street and began work upon his dictionary. In 1749 his great but melancholy "The Vanity of human wishes" appeared, and Garrick produced Johnson's tragedy Irene at Drury Lane: though Johnson made a small profit, the play proved unsuccessful. Between 1750 and 1752, writing two a week, he produced the more than two hundred Rambler essays. In 1752, his wife Tetty died. Two years later Johnson returned to Oxford, where he became acquainted with Thomas Warton, the future Poet Laureate. The following year, with Warton's help, Johnson received an M. A. degree from Oxford. In the same year his great Dictionary of the English Language was finally completed and published, and, though he was still very poor, his literary reputation was finally established. During this period he made new friends of the much younger Joshua Reynolds, Bennet "Lanky" Langton, and Topham

Beauclerk. In 1756, Johnson produced his "Proposals for a New Edition of Shakespeare," which would not, however, appear until 1765, and continued his activities as a journalist, editing, writing prefaces, and contributing articles to journals. Briefly arrested for debt, he was bailed out by Samuel Richardson. Between 1758 and 1760, he wrote another series of essays, The Idler, for a weekly periodical. In 1759, his mother Sarah died, and, in a somber mood, he wrote the moral fable Rasselas to pay, as he said, for her funeral.

In 1762, upon the succession to the throne of George III, Johnson was provided (much to his satisfaction, but much, also, to his embarrassment, for he was an unrepentant old Tory, and, with Whig abuses in mind, had defined "pension" in his dictionary as "pay given to a state hireling for treason to his country") with a pension of £300 per year. For the first time in his life he was not forced to scrape for money, and though his personal appearance was still remarkably and unavoidably uncouth he became one of the most prominent literary lions in polite society: when several young ladies, encountering him at a literary soiree, surrounded him "with more wonder than politeness," and contemplated his odd figure "as if he had been some monster from the deserts of Africa," Johnson is said to have remarked "Ladies, I am tame; you may stroke me."

In 1763 he met James Boswell (aged twenty-two) for the first time, and after he got over the fact that Boswell was Scottish (Johnson abhorred the Scots—hence his famous definition, in his dictionary, of "oats": "A grain, which in England is generally given to horses, but in Scotland supports the people") the two got on very well together. 1764 brought the formation of the Literary Club, whose members included Johnson, Reynolds, and Edmund Burke, as well as (eventually) David Garrick and Boswell.

In 1765, Johnson's edition of Shakespeare's Plays, with its splendid and perceptive preface, was finally published, and he received an honorary LL.D. from Trinity College in Dublin. He also met the wealthy Henry and Hester Thrale, with whom he would spend much of his time during the next sixteen years, talking brilliantly but writing little."No one but a blockhead," he once remarked, "writes but for money." In 1769 Boswell, by now an Edinburgh lawyer, married, and remained in Scotland until 1772. Between 1770 and 1775 Johnson produced a series of fiercely but characteristically opinionated political pamphlets. In August of 1773, though he had always despised Scotland, Johnson undertook his memorable trip to the Hebrides with Boswell. In July of 1774, Johnson went to Wales with the Thrales. During that same year Oliver Goldsmith, one of the few contemporaries whom Johnson genuinely admired, died, and Johnson felt a tremendous sense of loss.

In 1775, Johnson published his A Journey to the Western Islands of Scotland. During the same year he received an honorary LL.D. from Oxford, and visited to France (which he finds worse than Scotland) with the Thrales. He reacted furiously to the American Revolution, characterizing the rebellious colonists as "a race of convicts." In 1776 he travelled with Boswell to Oxford, Ashbourne, and Lichfield, where he stood bareheaded in the rain in the market-place before the stall which had housed his father's bookshop, in order to atone for a "breach of filial piety" committed fifty years before.

In 1778 he made the acquaintance of Fanny Burney, aged twenty-four, and soon to be the sucessful authoress of Evelina. In the following year David Garrick, Johnson's old pupil and close friend, died, and he was again shaken. In 1781, after Johnson's The Lives of the English Poets had been published, Henry Thrale died. Johnson consoled his widow and, though he ought perhaps to have known better, contemplated marrying her.

In 1783, however, his health began to fail, and he suffered a stroke. The following year, partially recovered, he broke with Mrs. Thrale when she announced her intention of marrying Gabriele Piozzi. Johnson, frail and troubled by gout, asthma, dropsy, and a tumour, found that his his life-long fear of death had begun to preoccupy him, but he faced it bravely, as he had faced all adversities. On December 13 he died, aged seventy-five: he was buried in Westminster Abbey, with approriate ceremony, on December 20.

Chapter 4

More on Johnson

Samuel Johnson and Politics: An Introduction

Politically, Johnson was a conservative and a Tory, though the eighteenth-century Tory was not necessarily the frequently caricatured and insistently conservative member of the political establishment (and alter ego of the liberal Whig) whom we would encounter in England in the nineteenth or even the twentieth century. Johnson's own political statements, made over the course of his life, are frequently mutually contradictory, in part because his views altered with time and events (he was always a rebel, always a supporter of the underdog), in part because he always sought to be truthful even if it meant being inconsistent, and in part (though this may seem paradoxical) because he loved to argue, and frequently argued both sides of a question (though on different occasions) with equal dexterity and with (apparently) equal sincerity.

W. Jackson Bate identifies a common principle in all of Johnson's political thought, and calls it "protective subordination," or "subordination for the sake of protection"—a principle which we can also detect in his religious thought. Johnson believed that mankind, though capable of good, is also inherently sinful, and that a state of nature—in which mankind would be deprived, that is, of a paternalistic government which could benevolently impose order and regulation, and in so doing protect the weak and the poor from the exploitation of the strong and the wealthy—would be a state of savagery. In what sense is this neoclassical sentiment? Johnson was therefore, on occasion, fiercely protective of the prerogatives of government—he violently condemned, for example, the American Revolution and its underlying principles. On the other hand, when he saw government as tyrannical rather than paternal, he could be equally fierce—as he was in his "London"—in his condemnation of its betrayal of its responsibilities.

During the 1730's and 1740's he wrote pamphlets denouncing what he saw as a tyrannical and corrupt government; in the 1750's he denounced the hidden imperialist and economic factors which lay behind Britain's entry into the Seven Year's War; in the 1770's his concern with political morality led him to denounce, in various works, political jingoism, false patriotism, American complaints about British "oppression." Always he sought the truth, and party labels always meant a great deal less to him than an individual's sense of charity, of responsibility for the spiritual and material well-being of his fellow man. To his mind wisdom, not political rhetoric was the key: in important matters, Johnson said, "a wise Tory and a wise Whig, I believe, will agree." What they could or should agree upon, Johnson believed, were the sentiments he expressed in "The Vanity of Human Wishes" and in Rasselas.

Johnson- Literary Career

"No man but a blockhead," said Johnson, "ever wrote except for money." The doctrine is, of course, perfectly outrageous, and specially calculated to shock people who like to keep it for their private use, instead of proclaiming it in public. But it is a good expression of that huge con-tempt, for the foppery of high-flown sentiment which, as is not uncommon with Johnson, passes into something which would be cynical if it were not half humorous. In this case it implies also the contempt of the professional for the amateur. Johnson despised gentlemen who dabbled in his craft, as a man whose life is devoted to music or painting despises the ladies and gentlemen who treat those arts as fashionable accomplishments. An author was, according to him, a man who turned out books as a brick- layer turns out houses or a tailor coats. So long as he supplied a good article and got a fair price, he was a fool to grumble, and a humbug to affect loftier motives.

Johnson was not the first professional author, in this sense, but perhaps the first man who made the profession respectable. The principal habitat of authors, in his age, was Grub Street — a region which, in later years, has ceased to be ashamed of it, and has adopted the more pretentious name Bohemia. The original Grub Street, it is said, first became associated. with authorship during the increase of pamphlet literature, produced. by the civil wars. Fox, the martyrologist, was one of its original inhabitants. Another of its heroes was a certain Mr. Welby, of whomthe sole record is, that he "lived there forty years without being seen of any." In fact, it was a region of holes and corners, calculated. to illustrate that great advantage of London life, which a friend of Boswell's described by say- ing, that a man could there be always "close to his bur- row." The "burrow" which received the luckless wight, was indeed no pleasant refuge. Since poor Green, in the earliest generation of dramatists, bought his "groat's worth of wit with a million of repentance," too many of his brethren had trodden the path which led to hopeless misery or death in a tavern brawl.

The history of men, who had to support themselves by their pens, is a record of almost universal gloom. The names of Spenser, of Butler, and of Otway, are enough to remind us that even warm contemporary recognition was not enough to raise an author above the fear of dying in want of necessaries. The two great dictators of literature, Ben Johnson in the earlier and Dryden in the later part of the century, only kept their heads above water by help of the laureate's pittance, though reckless imprudence, encouraged by the precarious life, was the cause of much of their sufferings. Patronage gave but a fitful resource, and the author could hope at most but an occasional crust, flung to him from better provided tables.

In the happy days of Queen Anne, it is true; there had been a gleam of prosperity. Many authors, Addison, Congreve,

Swift, and others of less name, had won by their pens not only temporary profits but permanent places. The class which came into power at the Revolution was willing for a time, to share some of the public patronage with men distinguished for intellectual eminence. Patronage was liberal when the funds came out of other men's pockets. But, as the system of party government developed, it soon became evident that this involved a waste of power.

There were enough political partisans to absorb all the comfortable sinecures to be had; and such money as was still spent upon literature, was given in return for services equally degrading to giver and receiver. Nor did the patronage of literature reach the poor inhabitants of Grub Street. Addison's poetical power might suggest or justify the gift of a place from his elegant friends; but a man like De Foe, who really looked to his pen for great part of his daily subsistence,

was below the region of such prizes, and was obliged in later years not only to write inferior books for money, but to sell himself and act as a spy upon his fellows. One great man, it is true, made an independence by literature. Pope received some 8000 for his translation of Homer, by the then popular mode of subscription — a kind of compromise between the systems of patronage and public support. But his success caused little pleasure in Grub Street. No love was lost between the poet and the dwellers in this dismal region. Pope was its deadliest enemy, and carried on an internecine warfare with its inmates, which has enriched our language with a great satire, but which wasted his powers upon low objects, and tempted him into disgraceful artifices.

The life of the unfortunate victims, pilloried in the Dunciad and accused of the unpardonable sins of poverty and dependence, was too often one, which might have extorted sympathy even from a thin-skinned poet and critic.

Samuel Johnson, His Influence and Reputation

Both the scope of Johnson's reading and the tenacity of his memory were prodigious. It would be difficult to name a major author, either what his contemporaries called an an

Ancient or a Modern, with whose works he was not familiar, though he was perhaps most influenced by Shakespeare, Donne, Dryden, and Pope. He was a fine classical scholar, and he was, perhaps, the best-read man, so far as modern literature was concerned, of his day.

He did not dabble in literature, but wallowed in it, ponderously; and yet he was able to bring all of his learning, all of his accumulated knowledge, aptly and appropriately to bear upon whatever subject he had in hand, whether he was writing an original work or an imitation of a work by a classical author. He was the central figure of the literary period still referred to as the Age of Johnson, and yet because he was essentially a miscellaneous writer (though all of his important works in various genres share certain themes and concerns) he received a great deal of criticism during his lifetime, and even more criticism after it. During his lifetime he did not mind it much: "It is advantageous to an author," he wrote, "that his book should be attacked as well as praised. Fame is a shuttlecock. If it be struck only at one end of the room, it will soon fall to the ground. To keep it up, it must be struck at both ends."

Johnson's shuttlecock, of course, has been kept in the air ever since. Succeeding generations, familiar with him less from their acquaintance with his own work than through Boswell's great Biography, read him "through Boswell's spectacles," and reacted according to their own tastes and predelictions: Jane Austen would continue to admire both Johnson and his works, while Carlyle would profess admiration for the one, transforming Johnson into a Carlylean Hero, and disdain for the other. The Romantics rejected all of what they believed to be Johnson's most important assumptions concerning man, nature, and human existence: Blake, Coleridge, Hazlitt, and De Quincey all attacked him.

Coleridge derided "The Vanity of Human Wishes" (text) as "bombast and tautology." Jeremy Bentham referred to him as "that pompous preacher of melancholic moralities." Lytton Strachey, as late as 1906, could write with smug equanimity, of Johnson's Lives of the Poets, that "as serious criticism, they can hardly appear to the modern reader to be very far removed from the futile. Johnson's aesthetic judgements are almost invariably subtle, or solid, or bold; they have always some good quality to recommend them — except one: they are never right." With a few significant exceptions, it was not until the twentieth century and the explosion of scholarly criticism that his works were read seriously again: it was T. S. Eliot, in 1930, who wrote that "London" and "The Vanity of Human Wishes" were "amongst the greatest verse satires of the English or any other language."

Chapter 5

Samuel Johnson Works

- The Idler
- "London"
- "The Vanity of Human Wishes"
- The Rambler
- 172. The effect of sudden riches upon the manners
- 180. The study of life not to be neglected for the sake of books
- 182. The history of Leviculus, the fortune-hunter
- 183. Envy
- 184. The subject of essays often suggested by chance
- 196. Human opinions mutable. The hopes of youth fallacious.
- Rasselas
- The Adventurer
- 50. On Lying.
- 84. Folly of false pretences to importance. A journey in a stage coach.
- 108. On the uncertainty of human things.
- Lives of the Poets
- Dictionary

Chapter 6

Time Line

Year	Age	Major/Well Known Writings	Events
1709			Samuel Johnson born (September 18 —the tercentenary is coming) in Lichfield, England, to Michael Johnson (bookseller, age 52), and Sarah Johnson *nee* Ford (age 40). He is their first child, and they are proud parents. It is Michael's pre-appointed duty, as Sheriff of Lichfield, to lead the citizens of the town around the town's borders a couple days later, and he is generous to all in doing so. Johnson is put out to a wetnurse

		whose milk was tubercular Bate correctly describes the results as "disastrous." J's eyes are infected, and he contracts scrofula; he is almost blind in his left eye, and his right eye is also affected. He is deaf in one ear. His face is also scarred.
1712	2	Brother Nathaniel born (October).
1725	15	Johnson spends time living with his older 1st cousin, the Rev. Cornelius Ford. Ford had a huge influence on Johnson. In the words of Pat Rogers *(The Samuel Johnson Encyclopedia)*, "the worldly Ford first opened the young man's eyes to a world of sophistication which he had never seen as a boy in Lichfield. It is probable that SJ acquired his first knowledge of the London literary scene from his cousin during

		a prolonged stay in 1725-26."
1726 -28	16 -18	Johnson returns home, and reads a lot. A Lot. Discovers Petrarch and The Classics.
1728	18	Johnson enters Oxford University (Pembroke College).
1729	19	Johnson experiences deep depression, described by Boswell as "overwhelmed with an horrible hypochondria dejection, gloom, and despair." Johnson leaves Oxford without a degree; exit is due to a lack of funds.
1731	21	J's father Michael dies in December.
1732	22	Works as usher in a school at Market-Bosworth.
1733	23	Spends time living in Birmingham, with Edmund Hector (a schoolfellow and lifelong friend). He contributes a few essays to a local publisher, and meets a number of people, includingElizabeth Porter, whom he will eventually marry. He works on his translation of Lobo,

			with a lot of assistance from Hector.
1734	24		J returns to Lichfield. Writes a letter (November) to Edward Cave, London magazine publisher (*Gentleman's Magazine*), offering the services of someone he knows well, uh, er, probably J himself, now that you mention it, who would make sundry contributions to his publication.
1735	25	J's translation of Lobo's Voyage to Abyssinia published.	J marries Elizabeth "Tetty" Porter, age 46, in July. She is the widow of a mercer he met in Birmingham in 1733. J tries his hand as a schoolmaster in Edial. The effort is unsuccessful. David Garrick is one of his students. "From Mr. Garrick's account he did not appear to have been profoundly revere-nced by his pupils," says Boswell. "His oddities of manner, and uncouth gesticulations, could not but be the subject of merriment to them."
1736-37	26-27		While working as a schoolmaster, J works on his play *Irene*.

1737	27		Brother Nathaniel dies, perhaps a suicide. J goes to London with Garrick, seeking fame and fortune (the education industry providing neither), and leaving his wife in Lichfield for the time being. J makes further proposals to Cave. In the summer he returns to Lichfield and Tetty, and to finish *Irene*. Later this year they both move to London.
1738	28	*London;Life Of Sarpi.*	J gets work as a hack writer for Cave's *Gentleman's Magazine.* J gets ten guineas from publisher Robert Dodsley for *London*. On reading *London,* Alexander Pope is impressed.
1739	29	*Complete Vindication of the Licensers of the Stage; Marmor Norfolciense;* Life of Boerhaave.	
1740	30	Start of the Parliamentary Debates; *Life of Admiral Drake; Life of Admiral Blake; Life of Barretier.*	
1744	34	Life Of Savage	
1745	35	Miscellaneous Observations on the	

		Tragedy of Macbeth, part of a planned edition of Shakespeare's plays. The project was aborted after a publisher of another edition threatened to sue for copyright infringement.	
1746	36		J is approached by a consortium of booksellers, and begins work on the *Dictionary*.
1747	37	Plan for a Dictionary of the English Language	
1748	38	Vision of Theodore the Hermit	
1749	39	The Vanity of Human Wishes; *Irene* opens.	Founds the Ivy Lane Club (not to be confused with The Club, founded in 1764).
1750	40	Start of *The Rambler* essays.	
1751	41	*Life of Cheynel*	
1752	42	End of *The Rambler* essays.	Wife Tetty dies. (They had no children, but she had a daughter from her previous marriage.)
1753	43	Contributes essays to *The Adventurer* series.	Considers remarrying. Bate and others have concluded that the object of his affection

			was a woman named Claire Hill Boothby (1708-56). However, "any thought of marriage was quickly dropped," says Bate.
1754	44	*Life of Edward Cave*	Johnson receives an honorary degree from Oxford University (an M.A.), which will appear on the title page of his *Dictionary*.
1755	45	The famous Letter to Lord Chesterfield; *A Dictionary of the English Language*, 1st edition.	
1756	46	2nd edition of the *Dictionary*.	In March, Johnson is arrested for debt, and released with the help of Richardson.
1758	48	Start of *The Idler* essays; *On the Bravery of the Common English Soldier*.	Money continues to be a problem, and Johnson avoids being arrested for debt again with another loan from a friend.
1759	49	Rasselas, Prince of Abyssinia	J's mother Sarah dies.
1760	50	End of *The Idler* essays.	
1762	52		J receives an annual pension from the crown. He greeted the offer with apprehension—he had earlier characterized pensioners in his *Dictionary* as state hirelings and traitors to the country. However, he is assured that the pension is for his *past* efforts, not work to be done in the future.

1763	53	The Life Of Ascham Account of the Imposture of the	On May 16, J meets Boswell (age 23), in Thomas Davies bookshop, Cock-Lane Ghost. London. Biography will not be the same.
1764	54		The Club is formed, with J as a charter member. The list of eventual members is impressive: among them are Joseph Banks, Boswell, Edmund Burke, Charles Burney, Charles James Fox, Garrick, Edward Gibbon, Richard Brinsley Sheridan ,Adam Smith, and William Windham.
1765	55	Johnson's edition of Shakespeare's plays.	J meets Hester (1741-1821) and Henry (1728?29?-1781)Thrale. J is very depressed when they meet him, and they take him in. J's visits with them, exposure to their family life in Streatham, and their friendship mean a lot to him, and his spirits are considerably lifted.
1766	56	The Fountains	
1767	57		During a February visit to the library of King George III, Johnson encounters George III himself. During the conversation, the King "expressed a desire to have the literary biography of his country ably executed," says Boswell.

1770	60	The False Alarm	
1771	61	Thoughts on the Late Transactions Respecting Falklands Islands	
1773	63	4th edition of his *Dictionary* .	J and Boswell tour Scotland, August 18 - November 22.
1774	64	The first *"Collected Edition"* of J's works published. (The genesis of the edition is curious: Davies, in financial difficulties, started it without J's authorization, rounding out the second volume [of an intended 2 volumes] with the works of others; the whole idea incenses J, but his temper is dissipated on seeing Davies' financial straits, and they publish more.) The Patriot	J visits Wales with the Thrales.
1775	65	A Journey to the Western Islands of Scotland; Taxation No Tyranny	Visits France with the Thrales.
1781	71	The Lives of the Poets; the full title is. *Prefaces Biographical and Critical to the Works of the most eminent English Poets*	Friend Henry Thrale dies J is one of four executors o f his estate.

1784	74		The Thrale Brewery is sold, providing Hester with somewhat of a release. She marries Gabriel Piozzi, an Italian musician. This upsets J, who has become extraordinarily fond of Hester over the years. J dies on December 13. (We have Hawkins account ofJohnson's last years and George Steevens' account of Johnson's funeral.
1785			Boswell's *Journal of a Tour to the Hebrides* appears in September. Some are shocked by the explicit, detailed retelling of conver-sations.
1786			Mrs. Piozzi's *Anecdotes of the Late Samuel Johnson* publi-shed.
1787			Sir John Hawkins' *Life of Samuel Johnson, LL.D.* published. I've posted an extract covering Johnson's Last Years.
1788		*Sermons Left For Publication By John Taylor, LL.D.* (Sermon 4) These - sermons are generally accepted as having been written by Johnson. Johnson's name first appeared on an 1812 edition.	

Hester Piozzi's Letters To And From the Late Samuel Johnson published. This is the first edition of his letters, and includes her letters to him as well as his to her.

1791 Boswell's *Life of Samuel Johnson, LL.D.* published. This is pretty much the only endeavor at which Boswell is successful. Boswell will die in 1795.

Chapter 7

The Restoration Period and the 18th Century

This period extends from 1660, the year Charles II was restored to the throne, until about 1789. The prevailing characteristic of the literature of the Renaissance had been its reliance on poetic inspiration or what today might be called imagination.

The inspired conceptions of Marlowe, Shakespeare, and Milton, the true originality of Spenser, and the daring poetic style of Donne all support this generalization. Furthermore, although nearly all these poets had been far more bound by formal and stylistic conventions than modern poets are, they had developed a large variety of forms and of rich or exuberant styles into which individual poetic expression might fit.

In the succeeding period, however, writers reacted against both the imaginative flights and the ornate or startling styles and forms of the previous era. The quality of the later age is suggested by its writers' admiration for Ben Johnson and his disciples; the transparent and apparently effortless poetic medium of the "school of Ben," along with its emphasis on good taste, moderation, and the Greek and Latin classics as models, appealed profoundly to the new generation.

Thus, the restoration of Charles II ushered in a literature characterized by reason, moderation, good taste, deft management, and simplicity. The historical parallel between the early imperialism of Rome and the restored English monarchy, both of which had replaced republican institutions, was not lost on the ruling and learned classes. Their appreciation of the literature of the time of the Roman emperor Augustus led to a widespread acceptance of the new English literature and encouraged grandeur of tone in the poetry of the period, the later phase of which is often referred to as Augustan. In addition, the ideals of impartial investigation and scientific experimentation promulgated by the newly founded Royal Society of London for Improving Natural Knowledge (established in 1662) were influential in the development of clear and simple prose as an instrument of rational communication.

Finally, the great philosophical and political treatises of the time emphasize rationalism. Even in the earlier 17th century, Francis Bacon had moved in this direction by advocating reasoning and scientific investigation in Advancement of Learning (1605) and The New Atlantis (1627). Essay Concerning Human Understanding (1690), by John Locke, is the product of a belief in experience as the exclusive basis of knowledge, a view pushed to its logical extreme in An Enquiry Concerning Human Understanding (1748) by David Hume. Locke himself continued to profess faith in divine revelation, but this residual belief was weakened among the similarly rationalist Deists, who tended to base religion on what reason could find in the world God had created around humans.

In political thought, the arbitrary acceptance of the monarch's divine right to rule (a conception popular in the Renaissance) had so nearly succumbed to skeptical criticism that Thomas Hobbes in his Leviathan (1651) found it necessary to defend the idea of political absolutism with a rationally conceived sanction.

According to him, the monarch should rule not by divine right but by an original and indissoluble social contract in order to secure universal peace and material gratification. Similarly rationalistic, but opposed to this rigorous subordination of all organs of the state to central control, were Locke's two Treatises on Government (1690), in which he stated that the authority of the governor is derived from the always revocable consent of the governed and that the people's welfare is the only proper object of that authority.Perhaps the greatest historical work in English is The History of the Decline and Fall of the Roman Empire (6 volumes, 1776-1788), by Edward Gibbon. Notable for its stately, balanced style, it is permeated with rationalistic skepticism and distrust of emotion, particularly religious emotion.

The successive stages of literary taste during the period of the Restoration and the 18th century are conveniently referred to as the ages of Dryden, Pope, and Johnson, after the three great literary figures that, one after another, carried on the so-called classical tradition in literature. The age as a whole is sometimes called the Augustan age, or the classical or neoclassical period.

Age of Dryden

The poetry of John Dryden possesses a grandeur, force, and fullness of tone that were eagerly received by readers still having something in common with the Elizabethans. At the same time, however, his poetry set the tone of the new age in achieving a new clarity and in establishing a self-limiting, somewhat impersonal canon of moderation and good taste. His polished heroic couplet (a unit of two rhyming lines of iambic pentameter, generally end-stopped), which he inherited from less accomplished predecessors and then developed, became the dominant form in the composition of longer poems.

In a number of critical works Dryden defined the stylistic restraint, compression, clarity, and common sense that he exemplified in his own poetry and that he showed to be lacking in much of the poetry of the preceding age, particularly in the exuberant and mechanically complex metaphorical wit of the older metaphysical school.

His reputation rests primarily on satire. This form became the dominant poetic genre of the age, both because of the religious and political factionalism of the times and because mocking denunciation of the ludicrousness or rascality of the opposition comes naturally to an age with so strong a public sense of norms of behavior. Absalom and Achitophel (1681-1682) and Mac Flecknoe (1682) are the most remarkable of

Dryden's political satires. Among his other poetic works are noteworthy translations of Roman satirists and of the works of Virgil, and the Pindaric ode "Alexander's Feast," a tour de force of varied cadences, which was published in 1697.

The bulk of Dryden's work was in drama. By means of it, following the new mode of living of the professional literary man, he could derive his support from a large public rather than from private patrons.

In his heroic tragedies The Conquest of Granada (1670) and All for Love; or, The World Well Lost (1678), a rewriting of Shakespeare's Antony and Cleopatra in the new taste, Dryden showed a different and not always satisfying side of his talent and exemplified the dominant quality of all Restoration tragedy. In order to achieve splendor and surprise on the stage, he sacrificed reality of characterization and consistency in motivation for sensual display in exotic locales and extravagance in plot and situation, presented in a style verging on the bombastic.

The affinities of this kind of drama are with Beaumont and Fletcher rather than with the great Elizabethan age; and the indirect influence of Ben Johnson is apparent also, for these two men were Johnson's disciples. Probably the best example of this genre of tragedy was produced by Thomas Otway, whose Venice Preserved (1682) avoids the worst excesses to which this form is liable and also possesses considerable tenderness and sensibility. By this time, however, the vogue of heroic tragedy was coming to an end; the style already had been successfully parodied in The Rehearsal (1671), by George Villiers, 2nd duke of Buckingham, and his collaborators.

The comedy of the time is much more successful than the tragedy. It is derived directly from the comedies of Ben Johnson but tries for more refinement while displaying less strength. In a cool, satiric spirit, it criticizes middle-class ambition and other variations from the courtly social norm, of which the canons are aristocratic good taste and good sense, rarely conventional morality.

In the eyes of succeeding generations, the chief defects of Restoration comedy are its reduction of sentiment and emotion to silliness and its frequent amorality. Reaction against this type of comedy, known as the comedy of manners, already had developed by the time that its greatest practitioner, William Congreve, was displaying his subtle artistry in Love For Love (1695) and The Way of the World (1700).

Just as Dryden's poetry defined the tone of his time, so too did his easy, informal, clear prose style, notably in his Essay of Dramatic Poesie (1668) and in various prefaces to his plays and translations. Noteworthy prose of a rather different nature was produced by two other figures of the age, Samuel Pepys and John Bunyan. The appetite of the period for life at all levels, but particularly for the life of the senses, is suggested by the secret diary of Samuel Pepys, a high official of the Admiralty Office. This extraordinary work, valuable as it is as a document of contemporary taste, has much to say of the private, unheroic life and longings of people of all times.

A figure in stronger contrast to Pepys could hardly be imagined than John Bunyan, a Puritan preacher, completely alien to the aristocratic and professional world of letters. Bunyan wrote The Pilgrim's Progress from This World to That Which Is to Come (1st part published in 1678; 2nd part, 1684) and The Life and Death of Mr. Badman (1680), two rough-hewn, moving, allegorical narratives of the human journey at the level of the fundamental verities of life, death, and religion. The first of these is now a literary classic, but in spite of the penetrating characterization and vitality of both works, they initially attained popularity only among artisans, merchants, and the poor.

Age of Pope

In the age of Alexander Pope (dated from about the death of Dryden in 1700 to Pope's death in 1744), the classical spirit in English literature reached its highest point, and at the same time other forces became manifest. Dryden's poetry had achieved grandeur, amplitude, and sublimity within a particular definition of good taste and good sense and under the tutelage of the Roman and Greek classics. To the poetry of Pope this characterization applies even more stringently. More than any other English poet, he submitted himself to the requirement that the expressive force of poetic genius should issue forth only in a formulation as reasonable, lucid, balanced, compressed, final, and perfect as the power of human reason can make it.

Pope did not have Dryden's majesty. Perhaps, given his predilection for correctness of detail, he could not have had it. Also, the readers of succeeding times have concluded that the dictates of reason do not all converge on only one poetic formula, just as the heroic couplet, which Pope brought to final perfection, is not necessarily the most generally suitable of English poetic forms. Nevertheless, the ease, harmony, and grace of Pope's poetic line are still impressive, and his quality of precise but never labored expression of thought remains unequaled.

Pope's reputation rests in large part on his satires, but his didactic bent led him to formulate in verse An Essay on Criticism (1711) and An Essay on Man (1732-1734). The former attempts to show that poetry must be modeled on nature; but his conception of nature, a traditional one shared by all his contemporaries, differs from that of succeeding generations. For Pope, nature meant the rules that right reason has discovered to be immanent in all things, so that what the experience of reasonable minds through the ages has shown to be the greatest poetry-namely, that of classical antiquity-provides a perfect model for modern times. A similar conservatism reappears in An Essay on Man, which concludes with the much debated generalization that "Whatever is, is right."

Pope's brilliant satiric masterpiece, The Rape of the Lock (1712; revised edition 1714), makes an epic theme of a trifling drawing-room episode: the contention arising from a young lord's having covertly snipped a lock of hair from a young lady's head. His most sustained satire, The Dunciad (1728; final version 1743), follows Dryden's Mac Flecknoe in its elegantly pointed, often malicious but always high-spirited mockery of the literary dullards who were Pope's enemies.

Like Dryden, Pope made translations of classical works,

notably of the Iliad, which was a great popular and financial success. His edition of Shakespeare's works bears witness to a range of taste not usually ascribed to him. It is only natural that the 18th-century preoccupation with the power of reason and good sense should have produced a large number of works in the more sober medium of prose. Jonathan Swift, who was, like Pope, a Tory conservative for the latter half of his life and a satirist, wrote a number of mordantly satirical prose narratives in which a profound and despairing perception of human stupidities and evil are in contrast with the social criticism of his great contemporaries. Swift's Tale of a Tub (1704) reduces the quarrels among three important religious divisions of his day to an allegory of three disreputable brothers. His generous anger on behalf of the poor of Ireland produced "A Modest Proposal" (1729), in which, with horrifying mock seriousness, he proposed that the children of the poor should be raised for slaughter as food for the rich.

His best-known work, Gulliver's Travels (1726), purports to be a ship doctor's account of his voyages into strange places, but in reality it is a castigation of the human race. The accounts of Gulliver's first two voyages are often read as a children's book. The last part abandons, however, delicate fancy and unmasks the selfish and sick bestiality of humanity in the guise of the so-called Yahoos, who are the savage and improvident servants of a race of apparently reasonable and noble horses, called Houyhnhnms. This work, like all of Swift's, is written in a prose of unrivaled lucidity, energy, and polemical skill.

Similarly noteworthy for the quality of their prose are the Spectator papers (1711-1712; 1714), written mainly by Joseph Addison and Richard Steele. Published daily, these essays, like many others, corresponded to the newly felt need of the day for popular journalism, but their enlightened comment and their criticism of contemporary society separate them from the mass of similar publications.

The main intent of Addison and Steele may be defined in their own words: "To enliven morality with wit, and to temper wit with morality." In a series of informal, conversational essays describing the activities of various ideal representatives of social groups, such as the Tory country squire Sir Roger de Coverley and the Whig merchant Sir Andrew Freeport, Addison and Steele salvaged and united some of the best sides of the contemporary English character. The lightly borne, free-and-easy manners of the court and the older landed classes should, according to these papers, exist side by side with the industry, uprightness, and deeply felt morality of the newly rich city merchants.

The amorality associated with the one and the stubborn narrowness of the other should disappear. The emphasis on public decorum and individual rectitude and on sympathy with one's fellow beings in the Spectator papers is a measure of their distance from the cool indifference and frequent licentiousness of much Restoration literature, particularly comedy, although the purpose of both was to represent reason, moderation, and common sense.

A quite different kind of journalism is represented by the work of the middle-class adventurer, hack writer, and political agent Daniel Defoe. Separated from the life of the upper classes and their erudite writers, as Bunyan had been before him, he produced, among many pieces of commissioned writing, a series of purportedly true but actually fictitious memoirs and confessions. The first of these, and the greatest, is Robinson Crusoe (1719), which reports the life and adventures of a shipwrecked sailor.

Age of Johnson

The age of Samuel Johnson, from 1744 to about 1784, was a time of changing literary ideals. The developed classicism and literary conservatism associated with Johnson fought a rearguard action against the cult of sentiment and feeling associated in various ways with the harbingers of the coming age of romanticism.

Johnson composed poetry that continued the traditions and forms of Pope, but he is best known as a prose writer and as an extraordinarily gifted conversationalist and literary arbiter in the cultivated urban life of his time. His conservatism and sturdy common sense are what might be expected given his intellectual tradition, but his individual quality has little to do with literary tendencies. His curiously lovable and upright personality, along with his intellectual preeminence and idiosyncrasies, have been preserved in the most famous of English biographies, the Life of Samuel Johnson (1791), by James Boswell, a Scottish writer with an appetite for literary celebrities.

Johnson worked his way up from poverty by honest literary labors, among which was his Dictionary of the English Language (1755). A great success, it was the first such work prepared according to modern standards of lexicography. Like Addison and Steele, Johnson produced a series of journalistic essays, The Rambler (1750-1752), but because of their somewhat pedantic style and Latinate vocabulary, they lack the easy informality of the Spectator papers and serve to accentuate the opposition between his neoclassical formality and the succeeding romantic ideal of heart-to-heart communication.

Johnson's philosophical tale Rasselas (1759), of which the moral is that "human life is everywhere a state in which much is to be endured, and little to be enjoyed," is reminiscent of Swift (as well as of his contemporary the French writer Voltaire in his tale Candide) in its perception of the vanity of human wishes. For all his pessimism, however, the amazing detail, independence, and intellectual facility of Johnson's critical biographies of English poets since 1600 (Lives of the Poets, 1779-1781), written in his old age, show what critical discrimination and intellectual integrity can accomplish.

Johnson's friend Oliver Goldsmith was a curious mixture of the old and the new. His novel The Vicar of Wakefield (1766) begins with dry humor but passes quickly into tearful calamity. His poem The Deserted Village (1770) is in form reminiscent of Pope, but in the tenderness of its sympathy for the lower classes it foreshadows the romantic age. In such plays as She Stoops to Conquer (1773) Goldsmith, like the younger Richard Sheridan in his School for Scandal (1777), demonstrated an older tradition of satirical quality and artistic adroitness that was to be anathema to a younger generation.

The signs of this newer feeling, which resulted in romanticism, can be traced in the poetry of William Cowper and of Thomas Gray. The cultivation of a pensive and melancholy sensibility and the interruption of the rule of the heroic couplet, as in Gray's "Elegy Written in a Country Churchyard" (1751), hint at the period to come, as does Gray's interest in medieval, nonclassical literature. New interests are even more obvious in the highly original poetry of the self-educated artist and engraver William Blake. His work consists in part of simple, almost childlike lyrics (Songs of Innocence, 1789), as well as of powerful but lengthy and obscure declarations of a new mythological vision of life (The Book of Thel, 1789).

All Blake's poetry expresses a revolt against the ideal of reason (which he considered destructive to life) and advocates the life of feeling-but in a more vital and assertive sense than is the case with the other previously mentioned preromantics. Similarly robust and passionate are the lyrics of the Scottish poet Robert Burns, which are characterized by his use of regional Scottish vernacular.

The simplicity, forcefulness, and powerful emotion of the ancient ballads of the Scottish-English border region, as revealed in Reliques of Ancient English Poetry (1765), by Bishop Thomas Percy, were likewise influential in the development of romanticism. Among writers of the novel-a newly popular form in this period-an advocate of sentiment and simple, innocent feelings had already appeared in the person of Samuel Richardson. In his sentimental novel Clarissa (1747-1748), the plight of a young, innocent girl, destroyed by the man she loves, is represented through lengthy letters interchanged among the characters.

This device permits an unprecedented revelation of motives and feelings. Richardson's contemporary Henry Fielding evinced his connection with the earlier satirical spirit in his novel Joseph Andrews (1742), which parodies Richardson's other novel of virtue besieged, Pamela (1740). Fielding's greatest novel, Tom Jones (1749), reveals a robust and healthy spirit of good sense and comedy, in which well-intentioned vigor wins out over excessive hypocrisy. Fielding's contemporary, the Scottish-born Tobias Smollett, wrote a number of novels of picaresque adventure, the last and probably best of which is Humphry Clinker (1771). The Life and Opinions of Tristram Shandy, Gentleman (1759-1767), the masterpiece of another great British novelist of the century, Laurence Sterne, indulges in the new cult of sentiment, but by reason of its cast of eccentric characters and the skilled weaving of the most extraordinary behavior into the depiction of their personalities, this novel lies outside the usual historical categories.

Chapter 8

John Milton: Biography

Life of John Milton (1608-1674)

John Milton was born on December 9, 1608, in London, as the second child of John and Sara (neé Jeffrey). The family lived on Bread Street in Cheapside, near St. Paul's Cathedral. John Milton Sr. worked as a scrivener, a legal secretary whose duties included preparation and notarization of documents, as well as real estate transactions and money lending. Milton's father was also a composer of church music, and Milton himself experienced a lifelong delight in music. The family's financial prosperity afforded Milton to be taught classical languages, first by private tutors at home, followed by entrance to St. Paul's School at age twelve, in 1620.

In 1625, Milton was admitted to Christ's College, Cambridge. While Milton was a hardworking student, he was also argumentative to the extent that only a year later, in 1626, he got suspended after a dispute with his tutor, William Chappell. During his temporary return to London, Milton attended plays, and perhaps began his first forays into poetry. At his return to Cambridge, Milton was assigned a new tutor, Nathaniel Tovey. Life at Cambridge was still not easy on Milton; he felt he was disliked by many of his fellow students and he was dissatisfied with the curriculum. It was at Cambridge that he composed "On the Morning of Christ's Nativity" on December 25, 1629.

In 1632, Milton took his M.A. cum laude at Cambridge, after which he retired to the family homes in London and Horton, Buckinghamshire, for years of private study and literary composition. His poem, "On Shakespeare", was published in the same year in the Second Folio. From this period, hail also his "L'Allegro" and "Il Penseroso." Milton's Comus, a masque, was performed at Ludlow Castle in 1634, to be first published anonymously in 1637, music by the famed court composer Henry Lawes. In April 1637, Milton was nearing the end of his studies when his mother died and was buried at Horton. Only a few months later, in August, Milton's friend Edward King died as well, by drowning. In November, upon his memory, Milton composed the beautiful elegy, Lycidas. It was published in a memorial volume at Cambridge in 1638. As customary for young gentlemen of means, Milton set out for a tour of Europe in the spring of 1638. He met famed scholar Hugo Grotius in Paris, where he stayed briefly before continuing on to Italy. Milton arrived in Florence in the autumn, where he probably met with Galileo, who was then under house arrest by order of the Inquisition. In Rome, he was a guest of Cardinal Barberini, the Pope's nephew, and visited the Vatican Library.

In Naples, Milton met Giovanni Batista, biographer of Torquato Tasso. Milton wrote Mansus in his honor. Upon reaching Geneva to visit with Calvinist theologian Giovanni Diodati, Milton found out about the death of his childhood friend, Charles Diodati in London. Milton's tour of Europe was cut short with rumors of impending civil war in England, and he returned home in July 1639. Shortly after, Milton composed Epitaphium Damonis, a Latin poem to the memory of his dearest friend. Milton settled down in London, where he began schooling his two nephews, later also taking in children of the better families. The Civil War was brewing — King Charles I invaded Scotland in 1639, and the Long Parliament was convened in 1640. Milton began writing pamphlets on political and religious matters; Of Reformation, Animadversions, and Of Prelatical Episcopacy were published in 1641, The Reason for Church Government in February, 1642.

In the spring of 1642, Milton married Mary Powell, 17 years old to his 34, but the relationship was an unhappy one, and Mary left him to visit the family home briefly thereafter, and did not return. Matters were not improved when the Powells declared for the King in the Civil War, which broke out in August. This prompted Milton to write his so-called 'Divorce Tracts' speaking for divorce on the grounds of incompatibility. In 1643, Milton published the Doctrine and Discipline of Divorce, which had its second, longer edition in early 1644. In 1644, Milton also published The Judgement of Martin Bucer Concerning Divorce.

The 'Divorce Tracts' caused an uproar both in parliament and amidst the clergy, as well as with the general populace, which earned him the nickname "Milton the Divorcer." It is in reference to the attempted censorship of the same by the Stationers' Company, that Milton published his eloquent Areopagitica, an oration advocating freedom of the press, in late 1644. Milton had also had time to write a treatise Of Education, which prescribed a rigorous course of study for English youth. In 1645, Milton published Tetrachordon and Colasterion, and registered Poems of Mr. John Milton, Both English and Latin. Milton had made plans to remarry, when Mary Powell returned. The two seem to have reconciled, since their daughter Anne was born in 1646. The whole Powell clan moved in with the Miltons, because Royalists had been ousted from Oxford. The situation was not savory. The year 1647 saw the death of both Milton's father and his father-in-law. The Powells eventually moved out and the Miltons moved to the neighborhood of High Holborn, where their daughter Mary was born in 1648.

It is probable that Milton witnessed the public execution of Charles I on January 30, 1649. Tenure of Kings and Magistrates was published two weeks later. In March, the Cromwellian government appointed Milton Secretary for Foreign Tongues and ordered him to write an answer to Charles I's purported Eikon Basilike ("Royal Image"). After publishing Observations on the Articles of Peace, Milton published Eikonoklastes ("Image Breaker") in October, 1649. In 1650, the Council of State ordered Milton to write a response to Salmasius' Defensio Regia — the Continental outcry against the English action ("Defense of Kingship"). Defensio pro populo Anglicano was published in February, 1651. Milton's first son, John, was born in March and the Miltons moved to Westminster. The year 1652 was one of many personal losses for Milton. In February, Milton lost his sight. This prompted him to write the sonnet "When I Consider How My Light is Spent." In May, 1652, Mary gave birth to a daughter, Deborah, and died a few days later. In June, one year-old John died.

In 1654, Milton published Defensio Secunda, the response he had been ordered to write for Pierre du Moulin's Regii sanguinis clamor ("Clamor of the King's Blood"). Andrew Marvell had become his assistant, and he had aides to take dictation, to facilitate the carrying out of his duties as Secretary. In 1655, Defensio Pro Se ("Defense of Himself") was published. In 1656, Milton married Katherine Woodcock, but the happiness was short-lived. Milton's daughter Katherine was born in late 1657, but by early 1658, both mother and daughter had passed away. It is to the memory of Katherine Woodcock that Milton wrote the sonnet "Methought I saw my late espousèd saint." Lord Protector Oliver Cromwell died in October, 1658, and the days of the Commonwealth were coming to a close. In early 1659, Milton published A Treatise of Civil Power and Ready and Easy Way To Establish a Free Commonwealth. For his propaganda writings, Milton had to go into hiding, for fear of retribution from the followers of King Charles II. In June, 1659, both Defensio pro populo Anglicano and Eikonoklastes were publicly burned. In early autumn, Milton was arrested and thrown in prison, to be released by order of Parliament before Christmas. King Charles II was restored to the throne on May 30, 1660.

In 1663, Milton remarried again, to Elizabeth Minshull, a match his daughters opposed. He spent his time tutoring students and finishing his life's work, the epic, Paradise Lost. Among the greatest works ever to be written in English, the feat is all the more remarkable for Milton's blindness — he would compose verse upon verse at night in his head and then dictate them from memory to his aides in the morning. Paradise Lost finally saw publication in 1667, in ten books. It was reissued in 1668 with a new title-page and additional materials.

The book was met with instant success and amazement; even Dryden is reported to have said, "This man cuts us all out, and the ancients too." History of Britain was published in 1670; Paradise Regain'd and Samson Agonistes were published together in 1671. Of True Religion and Poems, &c. upon Several Occasions were published in 1673. In summer 1674, the second edition of Paradise Lost was published, in twelve books. Milton died peacefully of gout in November, 1674, and was buried in the church of St. Giles, Cripplegate. His funeral was attended by "his learned and great Friends in London, not without a friendly concourse of the Vulgar." A monument to Milton rests in Poets' Corner at Westminster Abbey.

Milton and History

Americans tend to forget that they weren't the first to have a revolution. The English had theirs more than 130 years before the Thirteen Colonies rebelled. The English revolution consisted of a bloody Civil War from 1642 to 1649, the beheading of King Charles I in January 1649, and ten years of Puritan republican rule; it ended finally with the restoration of the monarchy under King Charles II in 1660.

These events aren't merely the background to John Milton's life: they were his life. We usually think of the war as a conflict between the Cavaliers and the Roundheads. John Milton was a Roundhead. The Cavaliers, or Royalists, supported the king and tended toward Catholicism. They believed in an aristocracy that had the right to special privileges, both in politics and in religion. The Roundheads, or Puritans, believed in a wider distribution of political and economic power and the right of every man to enjoy direct access to God. Milton was so strongly committed to the Puritan cause that he accepted a government position under Oliver Cromwell, who ruled as Lord Protector from 1649 to 1658. Milton was a radical Christian individualist who objected strongly and vocally to all kinds of organized religions which, he believed, put barriers between man and God.

Milton was therefore a rebel because he identified himself with a revolutionary cause. Paradise Lost, his masterpiece, is about rebellion and its consequences. One way of looking at the poem is to see it as Milton's working out of his own position. Although many readers have thought that Milton is really Satan, he probably saw himself as Abdiel, the angel who refuses to go along with Satan. Milton was arrogant in his belief that he understood the truth and had a duty to explain it for everyone's good.

The revolution he lived through changed every aspect of English life. When he was born in 1608, Shakespeare was still alive and Queen Elizabeth was only five years dead. Her influence was still felt. She had been an absolute monarch who regarded Parliament as a necessary evil in order to get money for her projects. When Milton died in 1674, Charles II reigned as constitutional monarch without any real power except that granted to him by Parliament.

Milton's circumstances changed drastically during his life. His family was reasonably well-to-do. They lived in London, which was Milton's home for most of his life. His father was a scrivener, a sort of combined notary and banker, who was wealthy enough to afford private tutors for his son, then schooling at St. Paul's and Christ's College, Cambridge University. Perhaps just as important for Milton's development was the fact that his father was a musician and composer. One of the most attractive features of Milton's poetry is its marvelous musical qualities.

Since Milton had a small private income, he did not seek a profession when he left Cambridge, but stayed at home writing poetry and increasing his already amazing stock of knowledge. Some people have said that Milton was one of the most learned men England has ever known. He wrote poetry in Latin, Greek, and Italian, and read almost all the literature surviving from the Greek and Roman periods. He even read the Bible in Hebrew.

Just before the religious and political quarrels in England came to a head, Milton went abroad for fifteen months, meeting and talking with learned and famous men all over Europe. He met Galileo and looked through his telescope, a fact Milton mentions more than once in Paradise Lost.

When he returned, he put his learning and considerable rhetorical force at the service of the Puritan cause. He wrote a series of scorching political and religious pamphlets: he condemned bishops, not only the Catholic ones but those of the Protestant Church of England; defended the liberty of the press against censorship; even advocated divorce. Many of the controversies in which he engaged with heat and passion we find difficult to sympathize with now, but Milton championed them with vigor and made himself not only well known but also well hated.

The Civil War deeply affected his personal relations. His brother Christopher adhered to the Royalist side. Milton married into a Royalist family in 1642. He was swept off his feet by a fun-loving seventeen-year- old, Mary Powell, whose family was originally the source of Milton's private income (they had bought property from Milton's father). The Powells kept Mary away from Milton, in Oxford where King Charles I made his headquarters, and did not let her travel to London to live with her husband until 1645.

By that time Milton had been extremely vocal publicly on the subject of divorce (he even advocated polygamy at one time) and had had an affair with a Miss Davies. His was a lively household, for he looked after and educated his dead sister's three sons. (One of them became Milton's biographer and the source of most of what we know about Milton's life.) He took his duties as schoolmaster very seriously; the boys were beaten if they did not learn their Latin and Greek grammar. The civil disturbances flowed in and out of the house as Milton's pamphlets provoked angry opposition and his supporters cried for more.

Only six weeks after King Charles I's head rolled from his body (Milton's friend Marvell wrote a famous ode on the occasion), Milton became Latin secretary to Oliver Cromwell. It was his duty to compose all the government's diplomatic correspondence in Latin, a job probably concerned as much with public relations as with accurate translation. By this time Milton was blind, probably as a result of a cyst or tumor of the pituitary gland. For the rest of his life he depended on others to read to him and to write at his dictation. Because he was not a patient man-he had the arrogance of a person conscious of his talents-reading and writing for him was not easy. His daughters objected to the tyranny he showed in demanding their time and then complaining when they read incorrectly.

Mary died in 1652, leaving a blind man with three young daughters, the eldest mentally retarded. Milton married again in 1657, but his second wife, whom he called in a famous sonnet his "espoused saint," lived only fifteen months and died after giving birth to a daughter, who also died. Milton married a third time, to a woman who looked after him for the rest of his life and managed to bring order to a household full of quarreling daughters, relatives, and visitors to the famous writer. In 1658, Oliver Cromwell had died, leaving England in the incompetent hands of his son, Richard. The passions that had caused the Civil War had cooled, and the king's son was asked to return, but on the conditions which brought about the English constitutional monarchy.

The coming of Charles II meant the end of Milton's government job. For a time he was in danger of his life and had to be hidden by friends-one of his pamphlets had argued strongly in defense of Charles I's beheading. Milton retired from public life and devoted himself to the composition of Paradise Lost. By the time he had finished dictating it to whoever got up early in the morning, two other events had disturbed Milton's never very tranquil life. In 1665 he was forced by the Great Plague to leave London and live in a Buckinghamshire village. A year later, in the Great Fire in 1666, Milton lost the last piece of property he owned. He lived the last few years of his life in considerable poverty, quite unlike the comfort of his first pampered years in his father's house.

Paradise Lost (1667) is the culmination of his life's work. His early poems, the exquisite "L'Allegro," "Il Penseroso," "Lycidas," the masque Comus, and the sonnets would all secure him a place among the finest English poets. But it is Paradise Lost which makes it impossible for you to ignore Milton. He wrote Paradise Regained afterward, but it has nothing like the stature of Paradise Lost. (It is not, as you might think, about Christ's sacrifice, but about his three-day temptation in the desert by Satan.) Milton's final work, Samson Agonistes, is a Greek drama as impressive as Paradise Lost in everything except size.

Milton died in 1674, just after the second edition of Paradise Lost appeared. The poem was for that time a modest best seller. It sold 1,300 copies in the first eighteen months and earned Milton a total of ten pounds. By the end of the seventeenth century, the book had gone through six editions, including one published in 1678 with large engraved illustrations. It has never lost its status as a classic, and it has never stopped being a source of controversy. People love or hate Paradise Lost, for as many reasons as it has readers. The poem has retained its interest because it deals with subjects that will always concern us-good, evil, freedom, responsibility. And because, like any great work of literature, it's exciting to read.

Chapter 9

Milton's Youthful Works and Poetic Ambitions

Pastoral elegy: Read over Lycidas quickly don't sweat the details, but note that it is a pastoral elegy written in 1637 in memory of a college classmate, Edward King. As one of Milton's earliest works, it puts him squarely following in the footsteps of Virgil, who, as we recall from our discussion of Spenser, went from writing pastoral poetry in his youth to the epic in his maturity. Review pastoral works read earlier this quarter; know what poets (vernacular and classical) were models for Milton in this regard.

Note that the memorial volume in which Lycidas was published included twenty poems in Latin, three in Greek and only thirteen in English, clearly demonstrating the humanist training of these university students who (as Ascham and others advocated) learned to imitate classical poets in part by writing their own Latin and Greek verse. Note classical elements that denote the nobility of poetry (e.g. references to laurels, the Muses, and Orpheus).

Note also that the three explicit climaxes in Lycidas combine humanist and Christian concerns: first Phoebus Apollo, the God of poetry, answers a question concerning the reward of poetry then St. Peter, guardian of the gate to heaven, answers a question about spiritual shepherds and finally, Lycidas becomes a synthesis of both Classical and Christian "pastoral" imagery: he is in heaven with the lamb of God, an explicitly Christian God who is at once the Good Shepherd and the giver of poetic fame. Milton also wrote 24 sonnets between 1630-1658 (i.e. between the ages of 22 and 50). His knowledge of and respect for the vernacular origins of the sonnet form are demonstrated not only by the fact that he wrote five sonnets in Italian but also in that he followed Petrarchan rather than Shakespearean (English) form; note also his use of the "tailed sonnet" form (sonneto caudato) in "On the Late Massacre in Piedmont". Another formal innovation is his tendency to avoid end-stopped lines, a technique borrowed from another Italian poet, Giovanni Della Casa.

This technique is analogous to the Metaphysical poets' desire to emulate the cadences of natural speech because it focusses attention on sentences rather than lines of verse ("On the Late Massacre in Piedmont" also offers a good example of this tendency).

Read over the assigned sonnets quickly. Unlike Lycidas (or Donne's Holy Sonnets), most of Milton's sonnets are not explicitly Christian in content; they also diverge from earlier sonnet tradition by their lack of emphasis on erotic love (and by the fact that they do not together constitute a sonnet cycle). Rather, Milton's sonnets betray his interest in the political and religious controversies that dominate his attention during and after the period of Puritan Rule (see esp. the poem dedicated to Cromwell, the military dictator of the Puritan Commonwealth and Protectorate,.

Two notable exceptions are "When I Consider How My Light is Spent", which offers a first poetic reaction to Milton's blindness (a theme he will return to in Paradise Lost), and "Methought I Saw My Late Espousèd Saint", which records Milton's grief at the death of one of his wives from complications of childbirth.

Note that the "night" to which he refers in the poem's final line can be understood not only as his despair at his loss but as a reference to his physical condition. Since 1652, when he became completely blind, Milton can "see" only in dreams — or in his poetry.

Polemical Tracts and Pamphlets.

The introduction to "Voices of the War" mentions the

wide range of "tracts" and "pamphlets" that were written during the twenty years of Puritan rule. This proliferation of literally hundreds of published polemical texts came to be known as the "Pamphlet Wars." Milton was an active participant in these debates, represented for our purposes by the "Plans and Projects" section of The Reason of Church Government Urged Against Prelaty.

In this text (dating from 1642), note Milton's concern with the intersection between religion and politics (comparable to that found in his sonnet "On the New Forcers of Conscience Under the Long Parliament,". Pay particular attention to statements that reveal Milton's literary ambitions and to his comments on his own education. Milton's participation in the public debate of the "pamphlet wars" era also included e.g. arguments in favor of divorce for incompatibility and his Areopagitica (written in 1644), a defense of a free press.

The title of Areopagitica is a classical allusion that implies a connection between the ancient Greek tribunal and the English parliament (as well as between the Greek orator Isocrates and Milton himself). Milton's classical education is also felt in the structure of the tract, which follows the rules of classical rhetoric. While Areopagitica is not an assigned reading, be aware that Milton's final argument for freedom of the press introduces the theme of Free Will which he will develop in Paradise Lost: since God made man capable of free will, men should be allowed to choose between ideas.

In ancient Greece and Rome, poets had always requested "the muse" to fire them with creative genius when they began long narrative poems, called epics, about godlike heroes and villains. In Greek mythology, there were nine muses, all sisters, who were believed to inspire poets, historians, flutists, dancers, singers, astronomers, philosophers, and other thinkers and artists.

If one wanted to write a great poem, play a musical instrument with bravado, or develop a grand scientific or philosophical theory, he would ask for help from a muse. When a writer asked for help, he was said to be "invoking the muse." The muse of epic poetry was named Calliope.

However, in Book 7, Milton identifies Urania–the muse of astronomy–as the goddess to whom he addresses his plea for inspiration. In Milton's time, writers no longer believed in muses, of course. Nevertheless, since they symbolized inspiration, writers continued to invoke them. So it was that when Milton began Paradise Lost, he addressed the muse in the telling of his tale, writing, "I thence invoke thy aid to my adventurous Song."

Chapter 10

Life of Milton

The Life of Milton has been already written in so many forms and with such minute enquiry that I might perhaps more properly have contented myself with the addition of a few notes to Mr. Fenton's elegant Abridgement, but that a new narrative was thought necessary to the uniformity of this edition.

JOHN MILTON was by birth a gentleman, descended from the proprietors of Milton near Thame in Oxfordshire, one of whom forfeited his estate in the times of York and Lancaster. Which side he took I know not; his descendant inherited no veneration for the White Rose.

His grandfather John was keeper of the forest of Shotover, a zealous papist who disinherited his son, because he had forsaken the religion of his ancestors.

His father, John, who was the son disinherited, had recourse for his support to the profession of a scrivener. He was a man eminent for his skill in musick, many of his compositions being still to be found; and his reputation in his profession was such that he grew rich, and retired to an estate. He had probably more than common literature, as his son addresses him in one of his most elaborate Latin poems. He married a gentlewoman of the name of Caston, a Welsh family, by whom he had two sons, John the poet, and Christopher who studied the law, and adhered, as the law taught him, to the King's party, for which he was awhile persecuted; but having, by his brother's interest, obtained permission to live in quiet, he supported himself so honourably by chamber-practice, that soon after the accession of King James, he was knighted and made a Judge; but his constitution being too weak for business, he retired before any disreputable compliances became necessary.

He had likewise a daughter Anne, whom he married with a considerable fortune to Edward Philips, who came from Shrewsbury, and rose in the Crown-office to be secondary; by him she had two sons, John and Edward, who were educated by the poet, and from whom is derived the only authentick account of his domestick manners.

John, the poet, was born in his father's house, at the Spread-Eagle in Bread-street Dec. 9, 1608, between six and seven in the morning. His father appears to have been very solicitous about his education; for he was instructed at first by private tuition under the care of Thomas Young, who was afterwards chaplain to the English merchants at Hamburgh, and of whom we have reason to think well, since his scholar considered him as worthy of an epistolary Elegy.

He was then sent to St. Paul's School, under the care of Mr. Gill, and removed, in the beginning of his sixteenth year, to Christ's College in Cambridge, where he entered a sizar, Feb. 12, 1624.

He was at this time eminently skilled in the Latin tongue; and he himself by annexing the dates to his first compositions, a boast of which the learned Politian had given him an example, seems to commend the earliness of his own proficiency to the notice of posterity; but the products of his vernal fertility have been surpassed by many, and particularly by his contemporary Cowley. Of the powers of the mind it is difficult to form an estimate; many have excelled Milton in their first essays who never rose to works like *Paradise Lost*.

At fifteen, a date which he uses till he is sixteen, he translated or versified two Psalms, 114 and 136, which he thought worthy of the publick eye, but they raise no great expectations; they would in any numerous school have obtained praise, but not excited wonder.

Many of his elegies appear to have been written in his eighteenth year, by which it appears that he had then read the Roman authors with very nice discernment. I once heard Mr.

Hampton, the translator of Polybius, remark, what I think is true, that Milton was the first Englishman who, after the revival of letters, wrote Latin verses with classick elegance. If any exceptions can be made they are very few; Haddon and Ascham, the pride of Elizabeth's reign, however they may have succeeded in prose, no sooner attempt verses than they provoke derision. If we produced anything worthy of notice before the elegies of Milton it was perhaps Alabaster's *Roxana*.

Of these exercises which the rules of the University required, some were published by him in his maturer years. They had been undoubtedly applauded, for they were such as few can perform: yet there is reason to suspect that he was regarded in his college with no great fondness. That he obtained no fellowship is certain; but the unkindness with which he was treated was not merely negative: I am ashamed to relate what I fear is true, that Milton was one of the last students in either university that suffered the public indignity of corporal correction.

It was, in the violence of controversial hostility, objected to him that he was expelled; this he steadily denies, and it was apparently not true; but it seems plain from his own verses to Diodati that he had incurred *Rustication,* a temporary dismission into the country, with perhaps the loss of a term:

"Me tenet urbs refluâ quam Thamesis alluit undâ,
Meque nec invitum patria dulcis habet.
Jam nec arundiferum mihi cura revisere Camum,
Nec dudum vetiti me laris angit amor. —
Nec duri libet usque minas perferre magistri
Cæteraque ingenio non subeunda meo.
Si sit hoc exilium patrios adiisse penates,
Et vacuum curis otia grata sequi,
Non ego vel profugi nomen sortemve recuso,
Lætus et exilii conditione fruor."

I cannot find any meaning but this, which even kindness and reverence can give to the term *vetiti laris,* "a habitation from which he is excluded," or how *exile* can be otherwise interpreted. He declares yet more, that he is weary of enduring "the threats of a rigorous master, and something else, which a temper like his cannot undergo." What was more than threat was probably punishment. This poem, which mentions his *exile*, proves likewise that it was not perpetual, for it concludes with a resolution of returning some time to Cambridge. And it may be conjectured from the willingness with which he has perpetuated the memory of his exile, that its cause was such as gave him no shame.

He took both the usual degrees, that of Batchelor in 1628, and that of Master in 1632; but he left the university with no kindness for its institution, alienated either by the injudicious severity of his governors, or his own captious perverseness. The cause cannot now be known, but the effect appears in his writings. His scheme of education, inscribed to Hartlib, supersedes all academical instruction; being intended to comprise the whole time which men usually spend in literature, from their entrance upon grammar, "till they proceed, as it is called, masters of arts." And in his Discourse *On the likeliest Way to remove Hirelings out of the Church*, he ingeniously proposes that "the profits of the lands forfeited by the act for superstitious uses should be applied to such academies all over the land, where languages and arts may be taught together; so that youth may be at once brought up to a competency of learning and an honest trade, by which means such of them as had the gift, being enabled to support themselves (without tithes) by the latter, may, by the help of the former, become worthy preachers."

One of his objections to academical education as it was then conducted is that men designed for orders in the Church were permitted to act plays, "writhing and unboning their clergy limbs to all the antick and dishonest gestures of Trincalos, buffoons and bawds, prostituting the shame of that ministry which they had or were near having to the eyes of courtiers and court-ladies, their grooms and mademoiselles."

This is sufficiently peevish in a man who, when he mentions his exile from the college, relates with great luxuriance the compensation which the pleasures of the theatre afford him. Plays were therefore only criminal when they were acted by academicks.

He went to the university with a design of entering into the church, but in time altered his mind; for he declared that whoever became a clergyman must "subscribe slave and take an oath withal, which, unless he took with a conscience that could retch, he must straight perjure himself. He thought it better to prefer a blameless silence before the office of speaking, bought and begun with servitude and forswearing."

These expressions are I find applied to the subscription of the Articles, but it seems more probable that they relate to canonical obedience. I know not any of the Articles, which seem to thwart his opinions; but the thoughts of obedience, whether canonical or civil, raised his indignation.

His unwillingness to engage in the ministry, perhaps not yet advanced to a settled resolution of declining it, appears in a letter to one of his friends who had reproved his suspended and dilatory life, which he seems to have imputed to an insatiable curiosity and fantastic luxury of various knowledge. To this he writes a cool and plausible answer, in which he endeavors to persuade him that the delay proceeds not from the delights of desultory study, but from the desire of obtaining more fitness for his task; and that he goes on "not taking thought of being late, so it give advantage to be more fit."

When he left the university he returned to his father, then residing at Horton in Buckinghamshire, with whom he lived five years; in which time he is said to have read all the Greek and Latin writers. With what limitations this universality is to be understood who shall inform us?

It might be supposed that he who read so much should have done nothing else; but Milton found time to write the Masque of *Comus*, which was presented at Ludlow, then the residence of the Lord President of Wales, in 1634, and had the honour of being acted by the Earl of Bridgewater's sons and daughter. The fiction is derived from Homer's *Circe*; but we never can refuse to any modern the liberty of borrowing from Homer:

"— a quo ceu fonte perenni
Vatum Pieriis ora rigantur aquis."

His next production was *Lycidas*, an elegy written in 1637

on the death of Mr. King, the son of Sir John King, secretary for Ireland in the time of Elizabeth, James, and Charles. King was much a favourite at Cambridge, and many of the wits joined to do honour to his memory. Milton's acquaintance with the Italian writers may be discovered by a mixture of longer and shorter verses, according to the rules of Tuscan poetry, and his malignity to the Church by some lines which are interpreted as threatening its extermination.

He is supposed about this time to have written his *Arcades*; for while he lived at Horton he used sometimes to steal from his studies a few days, which he spent at Harefield, the house of the countess dowager of Derby, where the *Arcades* made part of a dramatick entertainment.

He began now to grow weary of the country, and had some purpose of taking chambers in the Inns of Court, when the death of his mother set him at liberty to travel, for which he obtained his father's consent and Sir Henry Wotton's directions, with the celebrated precept of prudence, *i pensieri stretti, ed il viso sciolto,* "thoughts close, and looks loose."

In 1638 he left England, and went first to Paris, where, by the favour of Lord Scudamore, he had the opportunity of visiting Grotius, then residing at the French court as ambassador from Christina of Sweden. From Paris he hasted into Italy, of which he had with particular diligence studied the language and literature; and, though he seems to have intended a very quick perambulation of the country, staid two months at Florence; where he found his way into the academies, and produced his compositions with such applause as appears to have exalted him in his own opinion, and confirmed him in the hope, that "by labour and intense study, which," says he, "I take to be my portion in this life, joined with a strong propensity of nature," he might "leave something so written to after-times, as they should not willingly let it die."

It appears in all his writings that he had the usual concomitant of great abilities, a lofty and steady confidence in himself, perhaps not without some contempt of others; for scarcely any man ever wrote so much and praised so few. Of his praise he was very frugal, as he set its value high; and considered his mention of a name as a security against the waste of time and a certain preservative from oblivion.

At Florence he could not indeed complain that his merit wanted distinction. Carlo Dati presented him with an encomiastick inscription, in the tumid lapidary style; and Francini wrote him an ode, of which the first stanza is only empty noise, the rest are perhaps too diffuse on common topicks, but the last is natural and beautiful.

From Florence he went to Sienna, and from Sienna to Rome, where he was again received with kindness by the Learned and the Great. Holstenius, the keeper of the Vatican Library, who had resided three years at Oxford, introduced him to Cardinal Barberini; and he at a musical entertainment waited for him at the door, and led him by the hand into the assembly. Here Selvaggi praised him in a distich and Salsilli in a tetrastick; neither of them of much value. The Italians were gainers by this literary commerce: for the encomiums with which Milton repaid Salsilli, though not secure against a stern grammarian, turn the balance indisputably in Milton's favour.

Of these Italian testimonies, poor as they are, he was proud enough to publish them before his poems; though he says, he cannot be suspected but to have known that they were said *non tam de se, quam supra se.*

At Rome, as at Florence, he staid only two months; a time indeed sufficient if he desired only to ramble with an explainer of its antiquities or to view palaces and count pictures, but certainly too short for the contemplation of learning, policy, or manners.

From Rome he passed on to Naples, in company of a hermit; a companion from whom little could be expected, yet to him Milton owed his introduction to Manso, marquis of Villa, who had been before the patron of Tasso. Manso was enough delighted with his accomplishments to honour him with a sorry distich, in which he commends him for every thing but his religion; and Milton in return addressed him in a Latin poem, which must have raised an high opinion of English elegance and literature.

His purpose was now to have visited Sicily and Greece,

but hearing of the differences between the king and parliament, he thought it proper to hasten home rather than pass his life in foreign amusements while his countrymen were contending for their rights. He therefore came back to Rome, though the merchants informed him of plots laid against him by the Jesuits, for the liberty of his conversations on religion. He had sense enough to judge that there was no danger, and therefore kept on his way, and acted as before, neither obtruding nor shunning controversy.

He had perhaps given some offence by visiting Galileo, then a prisoner in the Inquisition for philosophical heresy; and at Naples he was told by Manso that, by his declarations on religious questions, he had excluded himself from some distinctions which he should otherwise have paid him. But such conduct, though it did not please, was yet sufficiently safe; and Milton staid two months more at Rome, and went on to Florence without molestation.

From Florence he visited Lucca. He afterwards went to Venice, and having sent away a collection of musick and other books travelled to Geneva, which he probably considered as the metropolis of orthodoxy. Here he reposed as in a congenial element, and became acquainted with John Diodati and Frederick Spanheim, two learned professors of Divinity. From Geneva he passed through France, and came home after an absence of a year and three months.

At his return he heard of the death of his friend Charles Diodati; a man whom it is reasonable to suppose of great merit, since he was thought by Milton worthy of a poem, intituled *Epitaphium Damonis*, written with the common but childish imitation of pastoral life.

He now hired a lodging at the house of one Russel, a taylor in St. Bride's Churchyard, and undertook the education of John and Edward Philips, his sister's sons. Finding his rooms too little he took a house and garden in Aldersgate street, which was not then so much out of the world as it is now, and chose his dwelling at the upper end of a passage that he might avoid the noise of the street. Here he received more boys, to be boarded and instructed.

Let not our veneration for Milton forbid us to look with some degree of merriment on great promises and small performance, on the man who hastens home because his countrymen are contending for their liberty, and, when he reaches the scene of action, vapours away his patriotism in a private boarding-school. This is the period of his life from which all his biographers seem inclined to shrink. They are unwilling that Milton should be degraded to a schoolmaster; but, since it cannot be denied that he taught boys, one finds out that he taught for nothing, and another that his motive was only zeal for the propagation of learning and virtue; and all tell what they do not know to be true, only to excuse an act which no wise man will consider as in itself disgraceful. His father was alive, his allowance was not ample, and he supplied its deficiencies by an honest and useful employment.

It is told that in the art of education he performed wonders, and a formidable list is given of the authors, Greek and Latin, that were read in Aldersgate-street by youth between ten and fifteen or sixteen years of age. Those who tell or receive these stories should consider that nobody can be taught faster than he can learn. The speed of the horseman must be limited by the power of his horse. Every man that has ever undertaken to instruct others can tell what slow advances he has been able to make, and how much patience it requires to recall vagrant inattention, to stimulate sluggish indifference, and to rectify absurd misapprehension.

The purpose of Milton, as it seems, was to teach something more solid than the common literature of schools, by reading those authors that treat of physical subjects; such as the Georgick, and astronomical treatises of the ancients. This was a scheme of improvement which seems to have busied many literary projectors of that age. Cowley, who had more means than Milton of knowing what was wanting to the embellishments of life, formed the same plan of education in his imaginary College.

But the truth is that the knowledge of external nature, and the sciences which that knowledge requires or includes, are not the great or the frequent business of the human mind.

Whether we provide for action or conversation, whether we wish to be useful or pleasing, the first requisite is the religious and moral knowledge of right and wrong; the next is an acquaintance with the history of mankind, and with those examples which may be said to embody truth and prove by events the reasonableness of opinions.

Prudence and Justice are virtues and excellences of all times and of all places; we are perpetually moralists, but we are geometricians only by chance. Our intercourse with intellectual nature is necessary; our speculations upon matter are voluntary and at leisure. Physiological learning is of such rare emergence that one man may know another half his life without being able to estimate his skill in hydrostaticks or astronomy, but his moral and prudential character immediately appears.

Those authors, therefore, are to be read at schools that supply most axioms of prudence, most principles of moral truth, and most materials for conversation; and these purposes are best served by poets, orators, and historians.

Let me not be censured for this digression as pedantick or paradoxical, for if I have Milton against me I have Socrates on my side. It was his labour to turn philosophy from the study of nature to speculations upon life, but the innovators whom I oppose are turning off attention from life to nature. They seem to think that we are placed here to watch the growth of plants, or the motions of the stars. Socrates was rather of opinion that what we had to learn was, how to do good and avoid evil.

Hotti toi en megaroisi kakon t' agathon te tetuktai.

Of institutions we may judge by their effects. From this wonder-working academy I do not know that there ever proceeded any man very eminent for knowledge; its only genuine product, I believe, is a small *History of Poetry*, written in Latin by his nephew Philips, of which perhaps none of my readers has ever heard.

That in his school, as in every thing else which he undertook, he laboured with great diligence, there is no reason for doubting. One part of his method deserves general imitation: he was careful to instruct his scholars in religion.

Every Sunday was spent upon theology, of which he dictated a short system, gathered from the writers that were then fashionable in the Dutch universities.

He set his pupils an example of hard study and spare diet; only now and then he allowed himself to pass a day of festivity and indulgence with some gay gentlemen of Gray's Inn.

He now began to engage in the controversies of the times, and lent his breath to blow the flames of contention. In 1641 he published a treatise of *Reformation*, in two books, against the established Church; being willing to help the Puritans, who were, he says, "inferior to the Prelates in learning."

Hall, bishop of Norwich, had published an *Humble Remonstrance* in defense of Episcopacy, to which in 1641 six ministers, of whose names the first letters made the celebrated word *Smectymnuus*, gave their Answer. Of this answer a Confutation was attempted by the learned Usher; and to the Confutation Milton published a Reply, intituled *Of Prelatical Episcopacy, and whether it may be deduced from the Apostolical Times, by virtue of those testimonies which are alledged to that purpose in some late treatises, one whereof goes under the name of James, Lord Bishop of Armagh.*

I have transcribed this title to shew, by his contemptuous mention of Usher, that he had now adopted the puritanical savageness of manners. His next work was *The Reason of Church Government urged against Prelacy*, by Mr. John Milton, 1642. In this book he discovers, not with ostentatious exultation, but with calm confidence, his high opinion of his own powers; and promises to undertake something, he yet knows not what, that may be of use and honour to his country. "This," says he, "is not to be obtained but by devout prayer to that Eternal Spirit that can enrich with all utterance and knowledge, and sends out his Seraphim with the hallowed fire of his altar to touch and purify the lips of whom he pleases. To this must be added industrious and select reading, steady observation, and insight into all seemly and generous arts and affairs; till which in some measure be compast, I refuse not to sustain this expectation. From a promise like this, at once fervid, pious, and rational, might be expected the *Paradise Lost*.

He published the same year two more pamphlets upon the same question. To one of his antagonists, who affirms that he was "vomited out of the university," he answers in general terms: "The Fellows of the College wherein I spent some years, at my parting, after I had taken two degrees, as the manner is, signified many times how much better it would content them that I should stay. — As for the common approbation or dislike of that place as now it is, that I should esteem or disesteem myself the more for that, too simple is the answerer, if he think to obtain with me. Of small practice were the physician who could not judge, by what she and her sister have of long time vomited, that the worser stuff she strongly keeps in her stomach, but the better she is ever kecking at, and is queasy: she vomits now out of sickness; but before it be well with her she must vomit by strong physick. The university in the time of her better health, and my younger judgement, I never greatly admired, but now much less."

This is surely the language of a man who thinks that he has been injured. He proceeds to describe the course of his conduct, and the train of his thoughts; and, because he has been suspected of incontinence, gives an account of his own purity: "That if I be justly charged," says he, "with this crime, it may come upon me, with tenfold shame." The style of his piece is rough, and such perhaps was that of his antagonist. This roughness he justifies, by great examples, in a long digression. Sometimes he tries to be humorous:

"Lest I should take him for some chaplain in hand, some squire of the body to his prelate, one who serves not at the altar only, but at the Court-cupboard, he will bestow on us a pretty model of himself; and sets me out half a dozen ptisical mottos, wherever he had them, hopping short in the measure of convulsion fits; in which labour the agony of his wit having scaped narrowly, instead of well-sized periods, he greets us with a quantity of thumb-ring posies." — And thus ends this section, or rather dissection, of himself. Such is the controversial merriment of Milton; his gloomy seriousness is yet more offensive. Such is his malignity *that hell grows darker at his frown.*

His father, after Reading was taken by Essex, came to reside in his house; and his school increased. At Whitsuntide, in his thirty-fifth year, he married Mary, the daughter of Mr. Powel, a justice of the Peace in Oxfordshire. He brought her to town with him, and expected all the advantages of a conjugal life. The lady, however, seems not much to have delighted in the pleasures of spare diet and hard study; for, as Philips relates, "having for a month led a philosophical life, after having been used at home to a great house, and much company and joviality, her friends, possibly by her own desire, made earnest suit to have her company the remaining part of the summer; which was granted, upon a promise of her return at Michaelmas."

Milton was too busy to much miss his wife; he pursued his studies, and now and then visited the Lady Margaret Leigh, whom he has mentioned in one of his sonnets. At last Michaelmas arrived; but the lady had no inclination to return to the sullen gloom of her husband's habitation, and therefore very willingly forgot her promise. He sent her a letter, but had no answer; he sent more with the same success. It could be alleged that letters miscarry; he therefore dispatched a messenger, being by this time too angry to go himself. His messenger was sent back with some contempt. The family of the lady were Cavaliers.

In a man whose opinion of his own merit was like Milton's, less provocation than this might have raised violent resentment. Milton soon determined to repudiate her for disobedience; and, being one of those who could easily find arguments to justify inclination, published (in 1644) *The Doctrine and Discipline of Divorce,* which was followed by *The Judgement of Martin Bucer, concerning Divorce*; and the next year his Tetrachordon, *Expositions upon the four chief Places of Scripture which treat of Marriage.*

This innovation was opposed, as might be expected, by the clergy, who, then holding their famous assembly at Westminster, procured that the author should be called before the Lords; "but that House," says Wood, "whether approving the doctrine, or not favouring his accusers, did soon dismiss him."

There seems not to have been much written against him, nor any thing by any writer of eminence. The antagonist that appeared is styled by him, "a Serving man turned Solicitor." Howel in his letters mentions the new doctrine with contempt; and it was, I suppose, though more worthy of derision than of confutation. He complains of this neglect in two sonnets, of which the first is contemptible, and the second not excellent.

From this time it is observed that he became an enemy to the Presbyterians, whom he had favoured before. He that changes his party by his humour is not more virtuous than he that changes it by his interest; he loves himself rather than truth. His wife and her relations now found that Milton was not an unresisting sufferer of injuries; and perceiving that he had begun to put his doctrine in practice, by courting a young woman of great accomplishments, the daughter of one Doctor Davis, who was however not ready to comply, they resolved to endeavour a reunion.

He went sometimes to the house of one Blackborough, his relation, in the lane of St. Martin's-le-Grand, and at one of his usual visits was surprised to see his wife come from another room, and implore forgiveness on her knees. He resisted her intreaties for a while; "but partly," says Philips, "his own generous nature, more inclinable to reconciliation than to perseverance in anger or revenge, and partly the strong intercession of friends on both sides, soon brought him to an act of oblivion and a firm league of peace." It were injurious to omit, that Milton afterwards received her father and her brothers in his own house, when they were distressed, with other Royalists.

He published about the same time his *Areopagitica, a Speech of Mr. John Milton for the liberty of unlicensed Printing*. The danger of such unbounded liberty and the danger of bounding it have produced a problem in the science of Government, which human understanding seems hitherto unable to solve. If nothing may be published but what civil authority shall have previously approved, power must always be the standard of truth; if every dreamer of innovations may propagate his projects, there can be no settlement; if every murmurer at government may diffuse discontent, there can be no peace; and if every sceptick in theology may teach his follies, there can be no religion.

The remedy against these evils is to punish the authors; for it is yet allowed that every society may punish, though not prevent, the publication of opinions, which that society shall think pernicious: but this punishment, though it may crush the author, promotes the book; and it seems not more reasonable to leave the right of printing unrestrained, because writers may be afterwards censured, than it would be to sleep with doors unbolted, because by our laws we can hang a thief.

But whatever were his engagements, civil or domestick, poetry was never long out of his thoughts. About this time (1645) a collection of his Latin and English poems appeared, in which the *Allegro* and *Penseroso*, with some others, were first published. He had taken a larger house in Barbican for the reception of scholars, but the numerous relations of his wife, to whom he generously granted refuge for a while, occupied his rooms. In time, however, they went away; "and the house again," says Philips, "now looked like a house of the Muses only, though the accession of scholars was not great. Possibly his having proceeded so far in the education of youth may have been the occasion of his adversaries calling him pedagogue and school-master; whereas it is well known he never set up for a public school to teach all the young fry of a parish, but only was willing to impart his learning and knowledge to relations and the sons of gentlemen who were his intimate friends, and that neither his writings nor his way of teaching ever savored in the least of pedantry."

Thus laboriously does his nephew extenuate what cannot be denied, and what might be confessed without disgrace. Milton was not a man who could become mean by a mean employment. This, however, his warmest friends seem not to have found; they therefore shift and palliate. He did not sell literature to all comers at an open shop; he was a chamber-milliner, and measured his commodities only to his friends.

Philips, evidently impatient of viewing him in this state of degradation, tells us that it was not long continued; and, to raise his character again, has a mind to invest him with military splendour: "He is much mistaken," he says, "if there was not about this time a design of making him an adjutant-general in Sir William Waller's army. But the new modelling of the army proved an obstruction to the design." An event cannot be set at a much greater distance than by having been only *designed, about some time,* if a man *be not much mistaken.* Milton shall be a pedagogue no longer; for, if Philips be not much mistaken, somebody at some time designed him for a soldier.

About the time that the army was new-modelled (1645) he removed to a smaller house in Holbourn, which opened backward into Lincoln's-Inn-Fields. He is not known to have published any thing afterwards till the King's death, when, finding his murderers condemned by the Presbyterians, he wrote a treatise to justify it, and "to compose the minds of the people." He made some *Remarks on the Articles of Peace between Ormond and the Irish Rebels.* While he contented himself to write, he perhaps did only what his conscience dictated; and if he did not very vigilantly watch the influence of his own passions, and the gradual prevalence of opinions, first willingly admitted and then habitually indulged, if objections by being overlooked were forgotten, and desire superinduced conviction, he yet shared only the common weakness of mankind, and might be no less sincere than his opponents.

But as faction seldom leaves a man honest, however it might find him, Milton is suspected of having interpolated the book called *Icon Basilike,* which the Council of State, to whom he was now made Latin secretary, employed him to censure, by inserting a prayer taken from Sidney's *Arcadia,* and imputing it to the King; whom he charges, in his *Iconoclastes,* with the use of this prayer as with a heavy crime, in the indecent language with which prosperity had emboldened the advocates for rebellion to insult all that is venerable or great: "Who would have imagined so little fear in him of the true all-seeing Deity. . . as, immediately before his death, to pop into the hands of the grave bishop that attended him, as a special relique of his saintly exercises, a prayer stolen word for word from the mouth of a heathen woman praying to a heathen god?"

The papers which the King gave to Dr. Juxon on the scaffold the regicides took away, so that they were at least the publishers of this prayer; and Dr. Birch, who had examined the question with great care, was inclined to think them the forgers. The use of it by adaptation was innocent; and they who could so noisily censure it, with a little extension of their malice could contrive what they wanted to accuse.

King Charles the Second, being now sheltered in Holland, employed Salmasius, professor of Polite Learning at Leyden, to write a defence of his father and of monarchy; and, to excite his industry, gave him, as was reported, a hundred Jacobuses. Salmasius was a man of skill in languages, knowledge of antiquity, and sagacity of emendatory criticism, almost exceeding all hope of human attainment; and having by excessive praises been confirmed in great confidence of himself, though he probably had not much considered the principles of society or the rights of government, undertook the employment without distrust of his own qualifications; and, as his expedition in writing was wonderful, in 1649 published *Defensio Regis*.

To this Milton was required to write a sufficient answer, which he performed (1651) in such a manner that Hobbes declared himself unable to decide whose language was best, or whose arguments were worst. In my opinion, Milton's periods are smoother, neater, and more pointed; but he delights himself with teasing his adversary as much as with confuting him. He makes a foolish allusion of Salmasius, whose doctrine he considers as servile and unmanly, to the stream of Salmacis, which whoever entered left half his virility behind him. Salmasius was a Frenchman, and was unhappily married to a scold. "Tu es Gallus," says Milton, "et, ut aiunt, nimium gallinaceus." But his supreme pleasure is to tax his adversary, so renowned for criticism, with vitious Latin. He opens his book with telling that he has used *Persona*, which, according to Milton, signifies only a *Mask*, in a sense not known to the Romans, by applying it as we apply *Person*.

But as Nemesis is always on the watch, it is memorable that he has enforced the charge of a solecism by an expression in itself grossly solecistical, when, for one of those supposed blunders, he says, as Ker, and I think some one before him, has remarked, "propino te grammatistis tuis *vapulandum.*" From *vapulo,* which has a passive sense, *vapulandus* can never be derived. No man forgets his original trade: the rights of nations and of kings sink into questions of grammar, if grammarians discuss them.

Milton when he undertook this answer was weak of body and dim of sight; but his will was forward, and what was wanting of health was supplied by zeal. He was rewarded with a thousand pounds, and his book was much read; for paradox, recommended by spirit and elegance, easily gains attention: and he who told every man that he was equal to his King could hardly want an audience.

That the performance of Salmasius was not dispersed with equal rapidity or read with equal eagerness, is very credible. He taught only the stale doctrine of authority and the unpleasing duty of submission; and he had been so long not only the monarch but the tyrant of literature that almost all mankind were delighted to find him defied and insulted by a new name, not yet considered as any one's rival.

If Christina, as is said, commended the *Defence of the people,* her purpose must be to torment Salmasius, who was then at her Court; for neither her civil station nor her natural character could dispose her to favour the doctrine, who was by birth a queen and by temper despotick.

That Salmasius was, from the appearance of Milton's book, treated with neglect, there is not much proof; but to a man so long accustomed to admiration, a little praise of his antagonist would be sufficiently offensive, and might incline him to leave Sweden; from which, however, he was dismissed, not with any mark of contempt, but with a train of attendance scarce less than regal. He prepared a reply, which, left as it was imperfect, was published by his son in the year of the Restoration. In the beginning, being probably most in pain for his Latinity, he endeavors to defend his use of the word *persona*; but, if I remember right, he misses a better authority than any that he has found, that of Juvenal in his fourth satire;

"— Quid agis cum dira & foedior omni
Crimine Persona est?"

As Salmasius reproached Milton with losing his eyes in the quarrel, Milton delighted himself with the belief that he had shortened Salmasius's life; and both perhaps with more malignity than reason. Salmasius died at the Spa, Sept. 3, 1653; and, as controvertists are commonly said to be killed by their last dispute, Milton was flattered with the credit of destroying him.

Cromwell had now dismissed the parliament by the authority of which he had destroyed monarchy, and commenced monarch himself under the title of protector, but with kingly and more than kingly power. That his authority was lawful, never was pretended; he himself founded his right only in necessity: but Milton, having now tasted the honey of publick employment, would not return to hunger and philosophy, but, continuing to exercise his office under a manifest usurpation, betrayed to his power that liberty which he had defended. Nothing can be more just than that rebellion should end in slavery: that he, who had justified the murder of his king, for some acts which to him seemed unlawful, should now sell his services and his flatteries to a tyrant, of whom it was evident that he could do nothing lawful.

He had now been blind for some years; but his vigour of intellect was such that he was not disabled to discharge his office of Latin secretary, or continue his controversies: his mind was too eager to be diverted, and too strong to be subdued.

About this time his first wife died in childbed, having left him three daughters. As he probably did not much love her he did not long continue the appearance of lamenting her, but after a short time married Catherine, the daughter of one captain Woodcock of Hackney; a woman doubtless educated in opinions like his own. She died within a year of childbirth, or some distemper that followed it; and her husband has honoured her memory with a poor sonnet.

The first Reply to Milton's *Defensio Populi* was published in 1651, called *Apologia pro Rege et Populo Anglicano, contra Johannis Polypragmatici (alias Miltoni) defensionem destructivam*

Regis et Populi. Of this the author was not known; but Milton and his nephew Philips, under whose name he published an answer so much corrected by him that it might be called his own, imputed it to Bramhal, and, knowing him no friend to regicides, thought themselves at liberty to treat him as if they had known what they only suspected.

Next year appeared *Regii Sanguinis clamor ad Coelum*. Of this the author was Peter du Moulin, who was afterwards prebendary of Canterbury; but Morus, or More, a French minister, having the care of its publication, was treated as the writer by Milton in his *Defensio Secunda*, and overwhelmed by such violence of invective that he began to shrink under the tempest, and gave his persecutors the means of knowing the true author. Du Moulin was now in great danger, but Milton's pride operated against his malignity; and both he and his friends were more willing that Du Moulin should escape than that he should be convicted of mistake.

In this second Defence he shews that his eloquence is not merely satirical; the rudeness of his invective is equalled by the grossness of his flattery.

"Deserimur, Cromuelle; tu solus superes, ad te summa nostrarum rerum rediit, in te solo consistit, insuperabili tuæ virtuti cedimus cuncti, nemine vel obloquente, nisi qui æquales inæqualis ipse honores sibi quærit, aut digniori concessos invidet, aut non intelligit nihil esse in societate hominum magis vel Deo gratum, vel rationi consentaneum, esse in civitate nihil æquius, nihil utilius, quam potiri rerum dignissimum. Eum te agnoscunt omnes, Cromuelle, ea tu civis maximus et gloriosissimus, dux publici consilii, fortissimorum exercituum imperator, pater patriæ gessisti. Sic tu spontanea bonorum omnium et animitus missa voce salutaris."

Cæsar when he assumed the perpetual dictatorship had not more servile or more elegant flattery. A translation may shew its servility, but its elegance is less attainable. Having exposed the unskilfulness or selfishness of the former government

"We were left," says Milton, "to ourselves; the whole national interest fell into your hands, and subsists only in your abilities. To your virtue, overpowering and resistless, every man gives way, except some who without equal qualifications aspire to equal honours, who envy the distinctions of merit greater than their own, or who have yet to learn that in the coalition of human society nothing is more pleasing to God or more agreeable to reason than that the highest mind should have the sovereign power. Such, Sir, are you by general confession; such are the things atchieved by you, the greatest and most glorious of our countrymen, the director of our publick councils, the leader of unconquered armies, the father of your country: for by that title does every good man hail you, with sincere and voluntary praise."

Next year, having defended all that wanted defence, he found leisure to defend himself: he undertook his own vindication against More, whom he declares in his title to be justly called the author of the *Regii Sanguinis clamor*. In this there is no want of vehemence nor eloquence, nor does he forget his wonted wit, "Morus es? an Momus? an uterque idem est?" He then remembers that *Morus* is Latin for a Mulberry-tree, and hints at the known transformation:

"Poma alba ferebat
Quæ post nigra tulit Morus."

With this piece ended his controversies; and he from this time gave himself up to his private studies and his civil employment. As secretary to the Protector he is supposed to have written the Declaration of the reasons for a war with Spain. His agency was considered as of great importance; for when a treaty with Sweden was artfully suspended, the delay was publickly imputed to Mr. Milton's indisposition; and the Swedish agent was provoked to express his wonder, that only one man in England could write Latin, and that man blind.

Being now forty-seven years old, and seeing himself disencumbered from external interruptions, he seems to have recollected his former purposes, and to have resumed three great works which he had planned for his future employment: an epick poem, the history of his country, and a dictionary of the Latin tongue. To collect a dictionary seems a work of all others least practicable in a state of blindness, because it depends upon perpetual and minute inspection and collation. Nor would Milton probably have begun it after he had lost his eyes, but, having had it always before him, he continued it, says Philips, "almost to his dying-day; but the papers were so discomposed and deficient, that they could not be fitted for the press." The compilers of the Latin dictionary printed at Cambridge had the use of those collections in three folios; but what was their fate afterwards is not known.

"The Persons.

Michael.
Chorus of Angels.
Heavenly Love.
Lucifer.
Adam, } with the
Eve, } Serpent.
Conscience.
Death.
Labour, }
Sickness, }
Discontent, }
Ignorance, Mutes.
with }
others; }
Faith.
Hope.
Charity.

The Persons.

Moses.
Divine Justice, Wisdom,
Heavenly Love.
The Evening Star,
Hesperus.
Chorus of Angels.
Lucifer.
Adam.
Eve.
Conscience.
Labour, }
Sickness, }
Discontent, } Mutes.
Ignorance, }
Fear, }
Death; }
Faith.
Hope.
Charity.

PARADISE LOST

The Persons

"Moses *prologizei,* recounting how he assumed his true body: that it corrupts not, because it is with God in the mount; declares the like of Enoch and Elijah; besides the purity of the place, that certain pure winds, dews, and clouds preserve it from corruption; whence exhorts to the sight of God; tells they cannot see Adam in the state of innocence, by reason of their sin.

Justice, } debating what should become of man, if
Mercy, he fall.
Wisdom,
Chorus of Angels singing a hymn of the Creation.

ACT II.

Heavenly Love.
Evening Star.
Chorus sing the marriage-song and describe Paradise.

ACT III.

Lucifer, contriving Adam's ruin.
Chorus fears for Adam, and relates Lucifer's rebellion and fall.

ACT IV.

Adam, } fallen. Eve,
Conscience cites them to God's examination. Chorus bewails, and tells the good Adam has lost.

ACT V.

Adam and "	Eve driven out of Paradise. "presented by an angel with
Labour, Grief Hatred, Envy, War, Famine, Pestilence, Sickness, Dis-content, Ignorance, Fear, Death	Mutes

To whom he gave their names. Likewise Winter, Heat, Tempest, &c.

Faith, Hope, Charity	comfort him and instruct him

To compile a history from various authors, when they can

only be consulted by other eyes, is not easy nor possible, but with more skilful and attentive help than can be commonly obtained; and it was probably the difficulty of consulting and comparing that stopped Milton's narrative at the Conquest; a period at which affairs were not yet very intricate nor authors very numerous. For the subject of his epick poem, after much deliberation, "long chusing, and beginning late," he fixed upon *Paradise Lost*; a design so comprehensive that it could be justified only by success. He had once designed to celebrate King Arthur, as he hints in his verses to Mansus; but "Arthur was reserved," says Fenton, "to another destiny."

It appears by some sketches of poetical projects left in manuscript, and to be seen in a library at Cambridge, that he had digested his thoughts on this subject into one of those wild dramas which were anciently called Mysteries; and Philips had seen what he terms part of a tragedy, beginning with the first ten lines of Satan's address to the Sun. These Mysteries consist of allegorical persons, such as *Justice, Mercy, Faith*. Of the tragedy or mystery of *Paradise Lost* there are two plans:

Chorus briefly concludes."

Such was his first design, which could have produced only an allegory or mystery. The following sketch seems to have attained more maturity."Adam unparadised:

"The angel Gabriel, either descending or entering; shewing, since this globe was created, his frequency as much on earth as in heaven; describes Paradise. Next, the Chorus, shewing the reason of his coming — to keep his watch in Paradise, after Lucifer's rebellion, by command from God; and withal expressing his desire to see and know more concerning this excellent new creature, man. The angel Gabriel, as by his name signifying a prince of power, tracing Paradise with a more free office, passes by the station of the Chorus, and, desired by them, relates what he knew of man; as the creation of Eve, with their love and marriage. After this, Lucifer appears; after his overthrow, bemoans himself, seeks revenge on man.

The Chorus prepare resistance at his first approach. At last, after discourse of enmity on either side, he departs:

whereat the Chorus sings of the battle and victory in heaven, against him and his accomplices: as before, after the first act, was sung a hymn of the creation. Here again may appear Lucifer, relating and insulting in what he had done to the destruction of man. Man next, and Eve having by this time been seduced by the Serpent, appears confusedly covered with leaves. Conscience, in a shape, accuses him; Justice cites him to the place whither Jehovah called for him. In the mean while the Chorus entertains the stage, and is informed by some angel the manner of the Fall.

Here the Chorus bewails Adam's fall; Adam then and Eve return; accuse one another; but especially Adam lays the blame to his wife; is stubborn in his offence. Justice appears, reasons with him, convinces him. The Chorus admonisheth Adam, and bids him beware Lucifer's example of impenitence. The angel is sent to banish them out of Paradise; but before causes to pass before his eyes, in shapes, a mask of all the evils of this life and world. He is humbled, relents, despairs: at last appears Mercy, comforts him, promises the Messiah; then calls in Faith, Hope, and Charity; instructs him; he repents, gives God the glory, submits to his penalty. The Chorus briefly concludes. Compare this with the former draught."

These are very imperfect rudiments of *Paradise Lost*, but it is pleasant to see great works in their seminal state pregnant with latent possibilities of excellence; nor could there be any more delightful entertainment than to trace their gradual growth and expansion, and to observe how they are sometimes suddenly advanced by accidental hints, and sometimes slowly improved by steady meditation.

Invention is almost the only literary labour which blindness cannot obstruct, and therefore he naturally solaced his solitude by the indulgence of his fancy and the melody of his numbers. He had done what he knew to be necessarily previous to poetical excellence: he had made himself acquainted with "seemly arts and affairs," his comprehension was extended by various knowledge, and his memory stored with intellectual treasures. He was skilful in many languages, and had by reading and composition attained the full mastery of his own. He would have wanted little help from books, had he retained the power of perusing them.

But while his greater designs were advancing, having now, like many other authors, caught the love of publication, he amused himself as he could with little productions. He sent to the press (1658) a manuscript of Raleigh, called *The Cabinet Council*, and next year gratified his malevolence to the clergy by a *Treatise of Civil Power in Ecclesiastical Cases*, and *The Means of removing Hirelings out of the Church*.

Oliver was now dead; Richard was constrained to resign: the system of extemporary government, which had been held together only by force, naturally fell into fragments when that force was taken away; and Milton saw himself and his cause in equal danger. But he had still hope of doing something. He wrote letters, which Toland has published, to such men as he thought friends to the new commonwealth; and even in the year of the Restoration he "bated no jot of heart or hope," but was fantastical enough to think that the nation, agitated as it was, might be settled by a pamphlet, called *A ready and easy way to establish a Free Commonwealth*, which was, however, enough considered to be both seriously and ludicrously answered.

The obstinate enthusiasm of the commonwealthmen was very remarkable. When the king was apparently returning, Harrington, with a few associates as fanatical as himself, used to meet, with all the gravity of political importance, to settle an equal government by rotation; and Milton, kicking when he could strike no longer, was foolish enough to publish, a few weeks before the Restoration, *Notes* upon a sermon preached by one Griffiths, intituled *The Fear of God and the King*. To these notes an answer was written by L'Estrange, in a pamphlet petulantly called *No blind Guides*.

But whatever Milton could write or men of greater activity could do the king was now about to be restored with the irresistible approbation of the people. He was therefore no longer secretary, and was consequently obliged to quit the house which he held by his office; and, proportioning his sense of danger to his opinion of the importance of his writings, thought it convenient to seek some shelter, and hid himself for a time in Bartholomew-Close by West Smithfield.

I cannot but remark a kind of respect, perhaps unconsciously, paid to this great man by his biographers: every house in which he resided is historically mentioned, as if it were an injury to neglect naming any place that he honoured by his presence.

The King, with lenity of which the world has had perhaps no other example, declined to be the judge or avenger of his own or his father's wrongs, and promised to admit into the Act of Oblivion all, except those whom the parliament should except; and the parliament doomed none to capital punishment but the wretches who had immediately co-operated in the murder of the King. Milton was certainly not one of them; he had only justified what they had done.

This justification was indeed sufficiently offensive; and (June 16) an order was issued to seize Milton's *Defence,* and Goodwin's *Obstructors of Justice,* another book of the same tendency, and burn them by the common hangman. The attorney-general was ordered to prosecute the authors; but Milton was not seized, nor perhaps very diligently pursued.

Not long after (August 19) the flutter of innumerable bosoms was stilled by an act, which the King, that his mercy might want no recommendation of elegance, rather called an *act of oblivion* than of grace. Goodwin was named, with nineteen more, as incapacitated for any publick trust; but of Milton there was no exception.

Of this tenderness shewn to Milton the curiosity of mankind has not forborne to enquire the reason. Burnet thinks he was forgotten; but this is another instance which may confirm Dalrymple's observation, who says, "that whenever Burnet's narrations are examined, he appears to be mistaken."

Forgotten he was not, for his prosecution was ordered; it must be therefore by design that he was included in the general oblivion. He is said to have had friends in the House, such as Marvel, Morrice, and Sir Thomas Clarges; and undoubtedly a man like him must have had influence. A very particular story of his escape is told by Richardson in his Memoirs, which he received from Pope, as delivered by Betterton, who might have heard it from Davenant. In the war between the King and Parliament, Davenant was made prisoner and condemned to die, but was spared at the request of Milton.

When the turn of success brought Milton into the like danger, Davenant repaid the benefit by appearing in his favour. Here is a reciprocation of generosity and gratitude so pleasing that the tale makes its own way to credit. But if help were wanted, I know not where to find it. The danger of Davenant is certain from his own relation; but of his escape there is no account. Betterton's narration can be traced no higher; it is not known that he had it from Davenant. We are told that the benefit exchanged was life for life, but it seems not certain that Milton's life ever was in danger.

Goodwin, who had committed the same kind of crime, escaped with incapacitation; and as exclusion from publick trust is a punishment which the power of government can commonly inflict without the help of a particular law, it required no great interest to exempt Milton from a censure little more than verbal. Something may be reasonably ascribed to veneration and compassion — to veneration of his abilities, and compassion for his distresses, which made it fit to forgive his malice for his learning. He was now poor and blind; and who would pursue with violence an illustrious enemy, depressed by fortune, and disarmed by nature?

The publication of the act of oblivion put him in the same condition with his fellow-subjects. He was however, upon some pretence not now known, in the custody of the serjeant in December; and when he was released, upon his refusal of the fees demanded, he and the serjeant were called before the House. He was now safe within the shade of oblivion, and knew himself to be as much out of the power of a griping officer as any other man. How the question was determined is not known. Milton would hardly have contended, but that he knew himself to have right on his side.

He then removed to Jewin-street, near Aldersgate-street; and being blind, and by no means wealthy, wanted a domestick companion and attendant, and therefore, by the recommendation of Dr. Paget, married Elizabeth Minshul, of a gentleman's family in Cheshire, probably without a fortune. All his wives were virgins, for he has declared that he thought it gross and indelicate to be a second husband: upon what other principles his choice was made cannot now be known, but marriage afforded not much of his happiness. The first wife left him in disgust, and was brought back only by terror; the second, indeed, seems to have been more a favourite, but her life was short; the third, as Philips relates, oppressed his children in his life-time, and cheated them at his death.

Soon after his marriage, according to an obscure story, he was offered the continuance of his employment, and, being pressed by his wife to accept it, answered, "You, like other women, want to ride in your coach; my wish is to live and die an honest man." If he considered the Latin secretary as exercising any of the powers of government, he that had shared authority either with the Parliament or Cromwell might have forborne to talk very loudly of his honesty; and if he thought the office purely ministerial, he certainly might have honestly retained it under the king. But this tale has too little evidence to deserve a disquisition; large offers and sturdy rejections are among the most common topicks of falsehood.

He had so much either of prudence or gratitude that he forbore to disturb the new settlement with any of his political or ecclesiastical opinions, and from this time devoted himself to poetry and literature. Of his zeal for learning in all its parts he gave a proof by publishing the next year (1661) *Accidence commenced Grammar*; a little book which has nothing remarkable, but that its author, who had been lately defending the supreme powers of his country and was then writing *Paradise Lost,* could descend from his elevation to rescue children from the perplexity of grammatical confusion, and the trouble of lessons unnecessarily repeated.

About this time Elwood the quaker, being recommended to him as one who would read Latin to him, for the advantage of his conversation, attended him every afternoon, except on Sundays. Milton, who, in his letter to Hartlib, had declared that "to read Latin with an English mouth is as ill a hearing as

Law French," required that Elwood should learn and practise the Italian pronunciation, which, he said, was necessary, if he would talk with foreigners. This seems to have been a task troublesome without use. There is little reason for preferring the Italian pronunciation to our own, except that it is more general; and to teach it to an Englishman is only to make him a foreigner at home. He who travels, if he speaks Latin, may so soon learn the sounds which every native gives it, that he need make no provision before his journey; and if strangers visit us, it is their business to practise such conformity to our modes as they expect from us in their own countries. Elwood complied with the directions, and improved himself by his attendance; for he relates that Milton, having a curious ear, knew by his voice when he read what he did not understand, and would stop him and "open the most difficult passages."

In a short time he took a house in the Artillery Walk, leading to Bunhill fields; the mention of which concludes the register of Milton's removals and habitations. He lived longer in this place than in any other.

He was now busied by *Paradise Lost*. Whence he drew the original design has been variously conjectured by men who cannot bear to think themselves ignorant of that which, at last, neither diligence nor sagacity can discover. Some find the hint in an Italian tragedy. Voltaire tells a wild and unauthorised story of a farce seen by Milton in Italy, which opened thus: "Let the Rainbow be the Fiddlestick of the Fiddle of Heaven." It has been already shewn that the first conception was a tragedy or mystery, not of a narrative but a dramatick work, which he is supposed to have begun to reduce to its present form about the time (1655) when he finished his dispute with the defenders of the King.

He long before had promised to adorn his native country by some great performance, while he had yet perhaps no settled design, and was stimulated only by such expectations as naturally arose from the survey of his attainments and the consciousness of his powers. What he should undertake it was difficult to determine. He was "long chusing, and began late."

While he was obliged to divide his time between his

private studies and affairs of state, his poetical labour must have been often interrupted; and perhaps he did little more in that busy time than construct the narrative, adjust the episodes, proportion the parts, accumulate images and sentiments, and treasure in his memory or preserve in writing such hints as books or meditation would supply. Nothing particular is known of his intellectual operations while he was a statesman, for, having every help and accommodation at hand, he had no need of uncommon expedients.

Being driven from all publick stations he is yet too great not to be traced by curiosity to his retirement, where he has been found by Mr. Richardson, the fondest of his admirers, sitting "before his door in a grey coat of coarse cloth, in warm sultry weather, to enjoy the fresh air; and so, as well as in his own room, receiving the visits of people of distinguished parts as well as quality. His visitors of high quality must now be imagined to be few; but men of parts might reasonably court the conversation of a man so generally illustrious, that foreigners are reported by Wood to have visited the house in Bread-street where he was born. According to another account he was seen in a small house, "neatly enough dressed in black cloaths, sitting in a room hung with rusty green; pale but not cadaverous, with chalkstones in his hands. He said, that if it were not for the gout, his blindness would be tolerable."

In the intervals of his pain, being made unable to use the common exercises, he used to swing in a chair, and sometimes played upon an organ.

He was now confessedly and visibly employed upon his poem, of which the progress might be noted by those with whom he was familiar; for he was obliged, when he had composed as many lines as his memory would conveniently retain, to employ some friend in writing them, having, at least for part of the time, no regular attendant. This gave opportunity to observations and reports.

Mr. Philips observes that there was a very remarkable circumstance in the composure of *Paradise Lost*, "which I have a particular reason," says he, "to remember; for whereas I had the perusal of it from the very beginning for some years, as I went from time to time to visit him, in parcels of ten, twenty, or thirty verses at a time (which, being written by whatever hand came next, might possibly want correction as to the orthography and pointing), having, as the summer came on, not been shewed any for a considerable while, and desiring the reason thereof, was answered that his vein never happily flowed but from the Autumnal Equinox to the Vernal; and that whatever he attempted at other times was never to his satisfaction, though he courted his fancy never so much: so that, in all the years he was about this poem, he may be said to have spent half his time therein."

Upon this relation Toland remarks, that in his opinion Philips has mistaken the time of the year; for Milton, in his Elegies, declares that with the advance of the Spring he feels the increase of his poetical force, "redeunt in carmina vires." To this it is answered, that Philips could hardly mistake time so well marked; and it may be added that Milton might find different times of the year favourable to different parts of life. Mr. Richardson conceives it impossible that "such a work should be suspended for six months, or for one. It may go on faster or slower, but it must go on." By what necessity it must continually go on, or why it might not be laid aside and resumed, it is not easy to discover.

This dependance of the soul upon the seasons, those temporary and periodical ebbs and flows of intellect, may, I suppose, justly be derided as the fumes of vain imagination. "Sapiens dominabitur astris." The author that thinks himself weather-bound will find, with a little help from hellebore, that he is only idle or exhausted; but while this notion has possession of the head, it produces the inability which it supposes. Our powers owe much of their energy to our hopes; "possunt quia posse videntur." When success seems attainable, diligence is enforced; but when it is admitted that the faculties are suppressed by a cross wind or a cloudy sky the day is given up without resistance; for who can contend with the course of Nature? From such prepossessions Milton seems not to have been free. There prevailed in his time an opinion that the world was in its decay, and that we have had the misfortune to be produced in the decrepitude of Nature. It was suspected that the whole creation languished, that neither trees nor animals had the height or bulk of their predecessors, and that every thing was daily sinking by gradual diminution. Milton appears to suspect that souls partake of the general degeneracy, and is not without some fear that his book is to be written in "an age too late" for heroick poesy.

Another opinion wanders about the world, and sometimes finds reception among wise men — an opinion that restrains the operations of the mind to particular regions, and supposes that a luckless mortal may be born in a degree of latitude too high or too low for wisdom or for wit. From this fancy, wild as it is, he had not wholly cleared his head, when he feared lest the "climate" of his country might be "too cold" for flights of imagination. Into a mind already occupied by such fancies, another not more reasonable might easily find its way. He that could fear lest his genius had fallen upon too old a world or too chill a climate, might consistently magnify to himself the influence of the seasons, and believe his faculties to be vigorous only half the year. His submission to the seasons was at least more reasonable than his dread of decaying Nature or a frigid zone, for general causes must operate uniformly in a general abatement of mental power; if less could be performed by the writer, less likewise would content the judges of his work. Among this lagging race of frosty grovellers he might still have risen into eminence by producing something which "they should not willingly let die."

However inferior to the heroes who were born in better ages, he might still be great among his contemporaries, with the hope of growing every day greater in the dwindle of posterity: he might still be the giant of the pygmies, the one-eyed monarch of the blind.

Of his artifices of study or particular hours of composition we have little account, and there was perhaps little to be told. Richardson, who seems to have been very diiigent in his enquiries, but discovers always a wish to find Milton discriminated from other men, relates, that

"he would sometimes lie awake whole nights, but not a

verse could he make; and on a sudden his poetical faculty would rush upon him with an *impetus* or *oestrum*, and his daughter was immediately called to secure what came. At other times he would dictate perhaps forty lines in a breath, and then reduce them to half the number."

These bursts of lights and involutions of darkness, these transient and involuntary excursions and retrocessions of invention, having some appearance of deviation from the common train of Nature, are eagerly caught by the lovers of a wonder. Yet something of this inequality happens to every man in every mode of exertion, manual or mental.

The mechanick cannot handle his hammer and his file at all times with equal dexterity; there are hours, he knows not why, when "his hand is out." By Mr. Richardson's relation casually conveyed much regard cannot be claimed. That in his intellectual hour Milton called for his daughter "to secure what came," may be questioned, for unluckily it happens to be known that his daughters were never taught to write; nor would he have been obliged, as is universally confessed, to have employed any casual visiter in disburthening his memory, if his daughter could have performed the office.

The story of reducing his exuberance has been told of other authors, and, though doubtless true of every fertile and copious mind, seems to have been gratuitously transferred to Milton. What he has told us, and we cannot now know more, is that he composed much of his poem in the night and morning, I suppose before his mind was disturbed with common business; and that he poured out with great fluency his "unpremeditated verse." Versification, free, like his, from the distresses of rhyme, must by a work so long be made prompt and habitual; and, when his thoughts were once adjusted, the words would come at his command.

At what particular times of his life the parts of his work were written cannot often be known. The beginning of the third book shews that he had lost his sight; and the Introduction to the seventh that the return of the King had clouded him with discountenance, and that he was offended by the licentious festivity of the Restoration. There are no other internal notes of time. Milton, being now cleared from all effects of his disloyalty, had nothing required from him but the common duty of living in quiet, to be rewarded with the common right of protection; but this, which, when he sculked from the approach of his King, was perhaps more than he hoped, seems not to have satisfied him, for no sooner is he safe than he finds himself in danger, "fallen on evil days and evil tongues, and with darkness and with danger compass'd round." This darkness, had his eyes been better employed, had undoubtedly deserved compassion; but to add the mention of danger was ungrateful and unjust. He was fallen indeed on "evil days"; the time was come in which regicides could no longer boast their wickedness. But of "evil tongues" for Milton to complain required impudence at least equal to his other powers — Milton, whose warmest advocates must allow that he never spared any asperity of reproach or brutality of insolence.

But the charge itself seems to be false, for it would be hard to recollect any reproach cast upon him, either serious or ludicrous, through the whole remaining part of his life. He pursued his studies or his amusements without persecution, molestation, or insult. Such is the reverence paid to great abilities, however misused: they who contemplated in Milton the scholar and the wit were contented to forget the reviler of his King. When the plague (1665) raged in London, Milton took refuge at Chalfont in Bucks, where Elwood, who had taken the house for him, first saw a complete copy of *Paradise Lost*, and, having perused it, said to him, "Thou hast said a great deal upon *Paradise Lost*, what hast thou to say upon *Paradise Found*?"

Next year, when the danger of infection had ceased, he returned to Bunhill-fields, and designed the publication of his poem. A license was necessary, and he could expect no great kindness from a chaplain of the archbishop of Canterbury. He seems, however, to have been treated with tenderness; for though objections were made to particular passages, and among them to the simile of the sun eclipsed in the first book, yet the license was granted; and he sold his copy, April 27, 1667, to Samuel Simmons, for an immediate payment of five pounds, with a stipulation to receive five pounds more when thirteen hundred should be sold of the first edition, and again, five pounds after the sale of the same number of the second edition, and another five pounds after the same sale of the third. None of the three editions were to be extended beyond fifteen hundred copies. The first edition was ten books, in a small quarto. The titles were varied from year to year; and an advertisement and the arguments of the book were omitted in some copies, and inserted in others.

The sale gave him in two years a right to his second payment, for which the receipt was signed April 26, 1669. The second edition was not given till 1674; it was printed in small octavo, and the number of books was increased to twelve, by a division of the seventh and twelfth, and some other small improvements were made. The third edition was published in 1678, and the widow, to whom the copy was then to devolve, sold all her claims to Simmons for eight pounds, according to her receipt given Dec. 21, 1680. Simmons had already agreed to transfer the whole right to Brabazon Aylmer for twenty-five pounds; and Aylmer sold to Jacob Tonson half, August 17, 1683, and half, March 24, 1690, at a price considerably enlarged. In the history of *Paradise Lost* a deduction thus minute will rather gratify than fatigue.

The slow sale and tardy reputation of this poem have been always mentioned as evidences of neglected merit and of the uncertainty of literary fame, and enquiries have been made and conjectures offered about the causes of its long obscurity and late reception. But has the case been truly stated? Have not lamentation and wonder been lavished on an evil that was never felt? That in the reigns of Charles and James the *Paradise Lost* received no publick acclamations is readily confessed. Wit and literature were on the side of the Court; and who that solicited favour or fashion would venture to praise the defender of the regicides? All that he himself could think his due, from "evil tongues" in "evil days," was that reverential silence which was generously preserved. But it cannot be inferred that his poem was not read or not, however unwillingly, admired.

The sale, if it be considered, will justify the publick. Those who have no power to judge of past times but by their own, should always doubt their conclusions. The call for books was not in Milton's age what it is in the present. To read was not then a general amusement; neither traders nor often gentlemen thought themselves disgraced by ignorance. The women had not then aspired to literature, nor was every house supplied with a closet of knowledge. Those, indeed, who professed learning were not less learned than at any other time; but of that middle race of students who read for pleasure or accomplishment and who buy the numerous products of modern typography, the number was then comparatively small. To prove the paucity of readers, it may be sufficient to remark that the nation had been satisfied, from 1623 to 1664, that is, forty-one years, with only two editions of the works of Shakespeare, which probably did not together make one thousand copies.

The sale of thirteen hundred copies in two years, in opposition to so much recent enmity and to a style of versification new to all and disgusting to many, was an uncommon example of the prevalence of genius. The demand did not immediately increase; for many more readers than were supplied at first the nation did not afford. Only three thousand were sold in eleven years; for it forced its way without assistance: its admirers did not dare to publish their opinion, and the opportunities now given of attracting notice by advertisements were then very few. The means of proclaiming the publication of new books have been produced by that general literature which now pervades the nation through all its ranks.

But the reputation and price of the copy still advanced, till the Revolution put an end to the secrecy of love, and *Paradise Lost* broke into open view with sufficient security of kind reception.

Fancy can hardly forbear to conjecture with what temper Milton surveyed the silent progress of his work, and marked his reputation stealing its way in a kind of subterraneous current through fear and silence. I cannot but conceive him calm and confident, little disappointed, not at all dejected, relying on his own merit with steady consciousness, and waiting without impatience the vicissitudes of opinion and the impartiality of a future generation.

In the mean time he continued his studies, and supplied the want of sight by a very odd expedient, of which Philips gives the following account:

Mr. Philips tells us,

"that though our author had daily about him one or other to read, some persons of man's estate, who, of their own accord, greedily catched at the opportunity of being his readers, that they might as well reap the benefit of what they read to him as oblige him by the benefit of their reading, and others of younger years were sent by their parents to the same end; yet excusing only the eldest daughter, by reason of her bodily infirmity and difficult utterance of speech (which, to say truth, I doubt was the principal cause of excusing her), the other two were condemned to the performance of reading and exactly pronouncing of all the languages of whatever book he should at one time or other think fit to peruse, viz. the Hebrew (and I think the Syriac), the Greek, the Latin, the Italian, Spanish, and French. All which sorts of books to be confined to read, without understanding one word, must needs be a trial of patience almost beyond endurance. Yet it was endured by both for a long time, though the irksomeness of this employment could not be always concealed, but broke out more and more into expressions of uneasiness; so that at length they were all, even the eldest also, sent out to learn some curious and ingenious sorts of manufacture, that are proper for women to learn; particularly embroideries in gold or silver."

In the scene of misery which this mode of intellectual labour sets before our eyes, it is hard to determine whether the daughters or the father are most to be lamented. A language not understood can never be so read as to give pleasure, and very seldom so as to convey meaning. If few men would have had resolution to write books with such embarrassments, few likewise would have wanted ability to find some better expedient.

Three years after his *Paradise Lost* (1667), he published his *History of England*, comprising the whole fable of Geoffry of Monmouth, and continued to the Norman invasion. Why he should have given the first part, which he seems not to believe, and which is universally rejected, it is difficult to conjecture. The style is harsh; but it has something of rough vigour, which perhaps may often strike though it cannot please.

On this history the licenser again fixed his claws, and before he would transmit it to the press tore out several parts. Some censures of the Saxon monks were taken away, lest they should be applied to the modern clergy; and a character of the Long Parliament and Assembly of Divines was excluded, of which the author gave a copy to the Earl of Anglesea, and which, being afterwards published, has been since inserted in its proper place.

The same year were printed *Paradise Regained* and *Sampson Agonistes*, a tragedy written in imitation of the Ancients and never designed by the author for the stage. As these poems were published by another bookseller it has been asked, whether Simmons was discouraged from receiving them by the slow sale of the former? Why a writer changed his bookseller a hundred years ago I am far from hoping to discover. Certainly he who in two years sells thirteen hundred copies of a volume in quarto, bought for two payments of five pounds each, has no reason to repent his purchase.

When Milton shewed *Paradise Regained* to Elwood, "This," said he, "is owing to you; for you put it in my head by the question you put to me at Chalfont, which otherwise I had not thought of."

His last poetical offspring was his favourite. He could not, as Elwood relates, endure to hear *Paradise Lost* preferred to *Paradise Regained*. Many causes may vitiate a writer's judgement of his own works. On that which has cost him much labour he sets a high value, because he is unwilling to think that he has been diligent in vain: what has been produced without toilsome efforts is considered with delight as a proof of vigorous faculties and fertile invention; and the last work, whatever it be, has necessarily most of the grace of novelty.

Milton, however it happened, had this prejudice, and had it to himself.

To that multiplicity of attainments and extent of comprehension that entitle this great author to our veneration may be added a kind of humble dignity, which did not disdain the meanest services to literature. The epick poet, the controvertist, the politician, having already descended to accommodate children with a book of rudiments, now in the last years of his life composed a book of Logick, for the initiation of students in philosophy, and published (1672) *Artis Logicæ plenior Institutio ad Petri Rami methodum concinnata*, that is, "A new Scheme of Logick, according to the Method of Ramus." I know not whether even in this book he did not intend an act of hostility against the Universities; for Ramus was one of the first oppugners of the old philosophy, who disturbed with innovations the quiet of the schools.

His polemical disposition, again revived. He had now been safe so long that he forgot his fears, and published a treatise *Of true Religion, Heresy, Schism, Toleration, and the best Means to prevent the Growth of Popery*.

But this little tract is modestly written, with respectful mention of the Church of England and an appeal to the thirty-nine articles. His principle of toleration is agreement in the sufficiency of the Scriptures, and he extends it to all who, whatever their opinions are, profess to derive them from the sacred books. The papists appeal to other testimonies, and are therefore in his opinion not to be permitted the liberty of either publick or private worship; for though they plead conscience, "we have no warrant," he says, "to regard conscience which is not grounded in Scripture."

Those who are not convinced by his reasons may be perhaps delighted with his wit: the term "Roman catholick" is, he says, "one of the Pope's bulls; it is particular universal, or catholick schismatick."

He has, however, something better. As the best preservative against Popery he recommends the diligent perusal of the Scriptures; a duty, from which he warns the busy part of mankind not to think themselves excused.

He now reprinted his juvenile poems with some additions. In the last year of his life he sent to the press, seeming to take delight in publication, a collection of Familiar Epistles in Latin; to which, being too few to make a volume, he added some academical exercises, which perhaps he perused with pleasure, as they recalled to his memory the days of youth; but for which nothing but veneration for his name could now procure a reader.

When he had attained his sixty-sixth year the gout, with which he had been long tormented, prevailed over the enfeebled powers of nature. He died by a quiet and silent expiration, about the tenth of November 1674, at his house in Bunhill-fields, and was buried next his father in the chancel of St. Giles at Cripplegate. His funeral was very splendidly and numerously attended.

Upon his grave there is supposed to have been no memorial; but in our time a monument has been erected in Westminster-Abbey *To the Author of Paradise Lost*, by Mr. Benson, who has in the inscription bestowed more words upon himself than upon Milton.

When the inscription for the monument of Philips, in which he was said to be *soli Miltono secundus*, was exhibited to Dr. Sprat, then dean of Westminster, he refused to admit it; the name of Milton was, in his opinion, too detestable to be read on the wall of a building dedicated to devotion. Atterbury, who succeeded him, being author of the inscription, permitted its reception. "And such has been the change of publick opinion," said Dr. Gregory, from whom I heard this account, "that I have seen erected in the church a statue of that man, whose name I once knew considered as a pollution of its walls."

Milton has the reputation of having been in his youth eminently beautiful, so as to have been called the Lady of his college. His hair, which was of a light brown, parted at the foretop, and hung down upon his shoulders, according to the picture which he has given of Adam. He was, however, not of the heroick stature, but rather below the middle size, according to Mr. Richardson, who mentions him as having narrowly escaped from being "short and thick." He was vigorous and active, and delighted in the exercise of the sword, in which he is related to have been eminently skilful. His weapon was, I believe, not the rapier, but the backsword, of which he recommends the use in his book on Education.

His eyes are said never to have been bright; but, if he was a dexterous fencer, they must have been once quick.

His domestick habits, so far as they are known, were those of a severe student. He drank little strong drink of any kind, and fed without excess in quantity, and in his earlier years without delicacy of choice. In his youth he studied late at night; but afterwards changed his hours, and rested in bed from nine to four in the summer, and five in winter.

The course of his day was best known after he was blind. When he first rose he heard a chapter in the Hebrew Bible, and then studied till twelve; then took some exercise for an hour; then dined; then played on the organ, and sung, or heard another sing; then studied to six; then entertained his visiters till eight; then supped, and, after a pipe of tobacco and a glass of water, went to bed.

So is his life described; but this even tenour appears attainable only in Colleges. He that lives in the world will sometimes have the succession of his practice broken and confused. Visiters, of whom Milton is represented to have had great numbers, will come and stay unseasonably; business, of which every man has some, must be done when others will do it. When he did not care to rise early he had something read to him by his bedside; perhaps at this time his daughters were employed. He composed much in the morning and dictated in the day, sitting obliquely in an elbow-chair with his leg thrown over the arm.

Fortune appears not to have had much of his care. In the civil wars he lent his personal estate to the parliament, but when, after the contest was decided, he solicited repayment, he met not only with neglect, but "sharp rebuke"; and, having tired both himself and his friends, was given up to poverty and hopeless indignation, till he shewed how able he was to do greater service. He was then made Latin secretary, with two hundred pounds a year, and had a thousand pounds for his *Defence of the People*. His widow, who after his death retired to Namptwich in Cheshire, and died about 1729, is said to have reported that he lost two thousand pounds by entrusting it to a scrivener; and that, in the general depredation upon the Church, he had grasped an estate of about sixty pounds a year belonging to Westminster-Abbey, which, like other sharers of the plunder of rebellion, he was afterwards obliged to return. Two thousand pounds, which he had placed in the Excise-office, were also lost. There is yet no reason to believe that he was ever reduced to indigence: his wants being few were competently supplied. He sold his library before his death, and left his family fifteen hundred pounds; on which his widow laid hold, and only gave one hundred to each of his daughters.

His literature was unquestionably great. He read all the languages which are considered either as learned or polite: Hebrew, with its two dialects, Greek, Latin, Italian, French, and Spanish. In Latin his skill was such as places him in the first rank of writers and criticks; and he appears to have cultivated Italian with uncommon diligence. The books in which his daughter, who used to read to him, represented him as most delighting, after Homer, which he could almost repeat, were Ovid's *Metamorphoses* and Euripides. His Euripides is, by Mr. Cradock's kindness, now in my hands: the margin is sometimes noted, but I have found nothing remarkable.

Of the English poets he set most value upon Spenser, Shakespeare, and Cowley. Spenser was apparently his favourite; Shakespeare he may easily be supposed to like, with every other skilful reader, but I should not have expected that Cowley, whose ideas of excellence were different from his own, would have had much of his approbation. His character of Dryden, who sometimes visited him, was that he was a good rhymist, but no poet.

His theological opinions are said to have been first Calvinistical, and afterwards, perhaps when he began to hate the Presbyterians, to have tended towards Arminianism. In the mixed questions of theology and government he never thinks that he can recede far enough from popery or prelacy;

but what Baudius says of Erasmus seems applicable to him: "magis habuit quod fugeret, quam quod sequeretur." He had determined rather what to condemn than what to approve. He has not associated himself with any denomination of Protestants: we know rather what he was not, than what he was. He was not of the church of Rome; he was not of the church of England.

To be of no church is dangerous. Religion, of which the rewards are distant and which is animated only by Faith and Hope, will glide by degrees out of the mind unless it be invigorated and reimpressed by external ordinances, by stated calls to worship, and the salutary influence of example. Milton, who appears to have had full conviction of the truth of Christianity, and to have regarded the Holy Scriptures with the profoundest veneration, to have been untainted by any heretical peculiarity of opinion, and to have lived in a confirmed belief of the immediate and occasional agency of Providence, yet grew old without any visible worship. In the distribution of his hours, there was no hour of prayer, either solitary or with his household; omitting publick prayers, he omitted all.

Of this omission the reason has been sought, upon a supposition which ought never to be made, that men live with their own approbation, and justify their conduct to themselves. Prayer certainly was not thought superfluous by him, who represents our first parents as praying acceptably in the state of innocence, and efficaciously after their fall. That he lived without prayer can hardly be affirmed; his studies and meditations were an habitual prayer. The neglect of it in his family was probably a fault for which he condemned himself, and which he intended to correct, but that death, as too often happens, intercepted his reformation.

His political notions were those of an acrimonious and surly republican, for which it is not known that he gave any better reason than that "a popular government was the most frugal; for the trappings of a monarchy would set up an ordinary commonwealth." It is surely very shallow policy, that supposes money to be the chief good; and even this without considering that the support and expence of a Court is for the most part only a particular kind of traffick, by which money is circulated without any national impoverishment.

Milton's republicanism was, I am afraid, founded in an envious hatred of greatness, and a sullen desire of independence; in petulance impatient of controul, and pride disdainful of superiority. He hated monarchs in the state and prelates in the church; for he hated all whom he was required to obey. It is to be suspected that his predominant desire was to destroy rather than establish, and that he felt not so much the love of liberty as repugnance to authority.

It has been observed that they who most loudly clamour for liberty do not most liberally grant it. What we know of Milton's character in domestick relations is, that he was severe and arbitrary. His family consisted of women; and there appears in his books something like a Turkish contempt of females, as subordinate and inferior beings. That his own daughters might not break the ranks, he suffered them to be depressed by a mean and penurious education. He thought woman made only for obedience, and man only for rebellion.

Of his family some account may be expected. His sister, first married to Mr. Philips, afterwards married Mr. Agar, a friend of her first husband, who succeeded him in the Crown-office. She had by her first husband Edward and John, the two nephews whom Milton educated; and by her second two daughters.

His brother, Sir Christopher, had two daughters, Mary and Catherine, and a son Thomas, who succeeded Agar in the Crown-office, and left a daughter living in 1749 in Grosvenorstreet.

Milton had children only by his first wife: Anne, Mary, and Deborah. Anne, though deformed, married a master-builder, and died of her first child. Mary died single. Deborah married Abraham Clark, a weaver in Spitalfields, and lived seventy-six years, to August 1727. This is the daughter of whom publick mention has been made. She could repeat the first lines of Homer, the *Metamorphoses*, and some of Euripides, by having often read them. Yet here incredulity is ready to make a stand. Many repetitions are necessary to fix in the memory lines not understood; and why should Milton wish or want to hear them so often! These lines were at the beginning of the poems. Of a book written in a language not understood the beginning raises no more attention than the end, and as those that understand it know commonly the beginning best, its rehearsal will seldom be necessary. It is not likely that Milton required any passage to be so much repeated as that his daughter could learn it, nor likely that he desired the initial lines to be read at all; nor that the daughter, weary of the drudgery of pronouncing unideal sounds, would voluntarily commit them to memory.

To this gentlewoman Addison made a present, and promised some establishment; but died soon after. Queen Caroline sent her fifty guineas. She had seven sons and three daughters; but none of them had any children, except her son Caleb and her daughter Elizabeth. Caleb went to Fort St. George in the East Indies, and had two sons, of whom nothing is now known. Elizabeth married Thomas Foster, a weaver in Spitalfields, and had seven children, who all died. She kept a petty grocer's or chandler's shop, first at Holloway, and afterwards in Cock-lane near Shoreditch Church. She knew little of her grandfather, and that little was not good. She told of his harshness to his daughters, and his refusal to have them taught to write; and, in opposition to other accounts, represented him as delicate, though temperate in his diet.

In 1750, April 5, *Comus* was played for her benefit. She had so little acquaintance with diversion or gaiety, that she did not know what was intended when a benefit was offered her. The profits of the night were only one hundred and thirty pounds, though Dr. Newton brought a large contribution; and twenty pounds were given by Tonson, a man who is to be praised as often as he is named. Of this sum one hundred pounds was placed in the stocks, after some debate between her and her husband in whose name it should be entered; and the rest augmented their little stock, with which they removed to Islington. This was the greatest benefaction that *Paradise Lost* ever procured the author's descendents; and to this he who has now attempted to relate his Life, had the honour of contributing a Prologue.

IN the examination of Milton's poetical works I shall pay so much regard to time as to begin with his juvenile productions. For his earlier pieces he seems to have had a degree of fondness not very laudable: what he has once written he resolves to preserve, and gives to the publick an unfinished poem, which he broke off because he was "nothing satisfied with what he had done," supposing his readers less nice than himself. These preludes to his future labours are in Italian, Latin, and English. Of the Italian I cannot pretend to speak as a critick, but I have heard them commended by a man well qualified to decide their merit. The Latin pieces are lusciously elegant; but the delight which they afford is rather by the exquisite imitation of the ancient writers, by the purity of the diction, and the harmony of the numbers, than by any power of invention or vigour of sentiment. They are not all of equal value; the elegies excell the odes, and some of the exercises on Gunpowder Treason might have been spared. The English poems, though they make no promises of *Paradise Lost,* have this evidence of genius, that they have a cast original and unborrowed. But their peculiarity is not excellence: if they differ from verses of others, they differ for the worse; for they are too often distinguished by repulsive harshness; the combinations of words are new, but they are not pleasing; the rhymes and epithets seem to be laboriously sought and violently applied.

That in the early parts of his life he wrote with much care appears from his manuscripts, happily preserved at Cambridge, in which many of his smaller works are found as they were first written, with the subsequent corrections. Such reliques shew how excellence is acquired: what we hope ever to do with ease we may learn first to do with diligence.

Those who admire the beauties of this great poet sometimes force their own judgement into false approbation of his little pieces, and prevail upon themselves to think that admirable which is only singular. All that short compositions can commonly attain is neatness and elegance. Milton never learned the art of doing little things with grace; he overlooked the milder excellence of suavity and softness: he was a "Lion" that had no skill "in dandling the Kid."

One of the poems on which much praise has been bestowed is *Lycidas*; of which the diction is harsh, the rhymes uncertain, and the numbers unpleasing. What beauty there is we must therefore seek in the sentiments and images. It is not to be considered as the effusion of real passion; for passion runs not after remote allusions and obscure opinions. Passion plucks no berries from the myrtle and ivy, nor calls upon Arethuse and Mincius, nor tells of "rough satyrs and fauns with cloven heel." "Where there is leisure for fiction there is little grief."

In this poem there is no nature, for there is no truth; there is no art, for there is nothing new. Its form is that of a pastoral, easy, vulgar, and therefore disgusting: whatever images it can supply are long ago exhausted; and its inherent improbability always forces dissatisfaction on the mind. When Cowley tells of Hervey that they studied together, it is easy to suppose how much he must miss the companion of his labours and the partner of his discoveries; but what image of tenderness can be excited by these lines!

"We drove a field, and both together heard
What time the grey fly winds her sultry horn,
Battening our flocks with the fresh dews of night."

We know that they never drove a field, and that they had no flocks to batten; and though it be allowed that the representation may be allegorical, the true meaning is so uncertain and remote that it is never sought because it cannot be known when it is found.

Among the flocks and copses and flowers appear the heathen deities, Jove and Phoebus, Neptune and Æolus, with a long train of mythological imagery, such as a College easily supplies. Nothing can less display knowledge or less exercise invention than to tell how a shepherd has lost his companion and must now feed his flocks alone, without any judge of his skill in piping; and how one god asks another god what is become of Lycidas, and how neither god can tell. He who thus grieves will excite no sympathy; he who thus praises will confer no honour. This poem has yet a grosser fault. With these trifling fictions are mingled the most awful and sacred truths, such as ought never to be polluted with such irreverent combinations. The shepherd likewise is now a feeder of sheep, and afterwards an ecclesiastical pastor, a superintendent of a Christian flock. Such equivocations are always unskilful; but here they are indecent, and at least approach to impiety, of which, however, I believe the writer not to have been conscious.

Such is the power of reputation justly acquired that its blaze drives away the eye from nice examination. Surely no man could have fancied that he read *Lycidas* with pleasure had he not known its author.

Of the two pieces, *L'Allegro* and *Il Penseroso*, I believe opinion is uniform; every man that reads them, reads them with pleasure. The author's design is not, what Theobald has remarked, merely to shew how objects derived their colours from the mind, by representing the operation of the same things upon the gay and the melancholy temper, or upon the same man as he is differently disposed; but rather how, among the successive variety of appearances, every disposition of mind takes hold on those by which it may be gratified.

The *chearful* man hears the lark in the morning; the *pensive* man hears the nightingale in the evening. The *chearful* man sees the cock strut, and hears the horn and hounds echo in the wood; then walks "not unseen" to observe the glory of the rising sun or listen to the singing milk-maid, and view the labours of the plowman and the mower; then casts his eyes about him over scenes of smiling plenty, and looks up to the distant tower, the residence of some fair inhabitant: thus he pursues rural gaiety through a day of labour or of play, and delights himself at night with the fanciful narratives of superstitious ignorance.

The *pensive* man at one time walks "unseen" to muse at midnight, and at another hears the sullen curfew. If the weather drives him home he sits in a room lighted only by "glowing embers"; or by a lonely lamp outwatches the North

Star to discover the habitation of separate souls, and varies the shades of meditation by contemplating the magnificent or pathetick scenes of tragick and epick poetry. When the morning comes, a morning gloomy with rain and wind, he walks into the dark trackless woods, falls asleep by some murmuring water, and with melancholy enthusiasm expects some dream of prognostication or some musick played by aerial performers.

Both Mirth and Melancholy are solitary, silent inhabitants of the breast that neither receive nor transmit communication; no mention is therefore made of a philosophical friend or a pleasant companion. The seriousness does not arise from any participation of calamity, nor the gaiety from the pleasures of the bottle.

The man of *chearfulness* having exhausted the country tries what "towered cities" will afford, and mingles with scenes of splendor, gay assemblies, and nuptial festivities; but he mingles a mere spectator as, when the learned comedies of Jonson or the wild dramas of Shakespeare are exhibited, he attends the theatre.

The *pensive* man never loses himself in crowds, but walks the cloister or frequents the cathedral. Milton probably had not yet forsaken the Church.

Both his characters delight in musick; but he seems to think that chearful notes would have obtained from Pluto a compleat dismission of Eurydice, of whom solemn sounds only procured a conditional release.

For the old age of Chearfulness he makes no provision; but Melancholy he conducts with great dignity to the close of life. His Chearfulness is without levity, and his Pensiveness without asperity.

Through these two poems the images are properly selected and nicely distinguished, but the colours of the diction seem not sufficiently discriminated. I know not whether the characters are kept sufficiently apart. No mirth can, indeed, be found in his melancholy; but I am afraid that I always meet some melancholy in his mirth. They are two noble efforts of imagination.

The greatest of his juvenile performances is the *Mask of Comus,* in which may very plainly be discovered the dawn or twilight of *Paradise Lost*. Milton appears to have formed very early that system of diction and mode of verse which his maturer judgement approved, and from which he never endeavoured nor desired to deviate.

Nor does *Comus* afford only a specimen of his language: it exhibits likewise his power of description and his vigour of sentiment, employed in the praise and defence of virtue. A work more truly poetical is rarely found; allusions, images, and descriptive epithets embellish almost every period with lavish decoration. As a series of lines, therefore, it may be considered as worthy of all the admiration with which the votaries have received it.

As a drama it is deficient. The action is not probable. A Masque, in those parts where supernatural intervention is admitted, must indeed be given up to all the freaks of imagination; but so far as the action is merely human it ought to be reasonable, which can hardly be said of the conduct of the two brothers, who, when their sister sinks with fatigue in a pathless wilderness, wander both away in search of berries too far to find their way back, and leave a helpless Lady to all the sadness and danger of solitude. This however is a defect over-balanced by its convenience.

What deserves more reprehension is that the prologue spoken in the wild wood by the attendant Spirit is addressed to the audience; a mode of communication so contrary to the nature of dramatick representation that no precedents can support it.

The discourse of the Spirit is too long, an objection that may be made to almost all the following speeches; they have not the spriteliness of a dialogue animated by reciprocal contention, but seem rather declamations deliberately composed and formally repeated on a moral question. The auditor therefore listens as to a lecture, without passion, without anxiety.

The song of Comus has airiness and jolity; but, what may recommend Milton's morals as well as his poetry, the invitations to pleasure are so general that they excite no distinct images of corrupt enjoyment, and take no dangerous hold on the fancy.

The following soliloquies of Comus and the Lady are elegant, but tedious. The song must owe much to the voice, if it ever can delight. At last the Brothers enter, with too much tranquillity; and when they have feared lest their sister should be in danger, and hoped that she is not in danger, the Elder makes a speech in praise of chastity, and the Younger finds how fine it is to be a philosopher.

Then descends the Spirit in form of a shepherd; and the Brother, instead of being in haste to ask his help, praises his singing, and enquires his business in that place. It is remarkable that at this interview the Brother is taken with a short fit of rhyming. The Spirit relates that the Lady is in the power of Comus, the Brother moralises again, and the Spirit makes a long narration, of no use because it is false, and therefore unsuitable to a good Being.

In all these parts the language is poetical and the sentiments are generous, but there is something wanting to allure attention.

The dispute between the Lady and Comus is the most animated and affecting scene of the drama, and wants nothing but a brisker reciprocation of objections and replies, to invite attention and detain it.

The songs are vigorous and full of imagery; but they are harsh in their diction, and not very musical in their numbers.

Throughout the whole the figures are too bold and the language too luxuriant for dialogue: it is a drama in the epick style, inelegantly splendid, and tediously instructive.

The *Sonnets* were written in different parts of Milton's life upon different occasions. They deserve not any particular criticism; for of the best it can only be said that they are not bad, and perhaps only the eighth and the twenty-first are truly entitled to this slender commendation. The fabrick of a sonnet, however adapted to the Italian language, has never succeeded in ours, which, having greater variety of termination, requires the rhymes to be often changed. Those little pieces may be dispatched without much anxiety; a greater work calls for greater care. I am now to examine *Paradise Lost,* a poem which, considered with respect to design, may claim the first place, and with respect to performance the second, among the productions of the human mind.

By the general consent of criticks the first praise of genius is due to the writer of an epick poem, as it requires an assemblage of all the powers which are singly sufficient for other compositions. Poetry is the art of uniting pleasure with truth, by calling imagination to the help of reason. Epick poetry undertakes to teach the most important truths by the most pleasing precepts, and therefore relates some great event in the most affecting manner. History must supply the writer with the rudiments of narration, which he must improve and exalt by a nobler art, must animate by dramatick energy, and diversify by retrospection and anticipation; morality must teach him the exact bounds and different shades of vice and virtue; from policy and the practice of life he has to learn the discriminations of character and the tendency of the passions, either single or combined; and physiology must supply him with illustrations and images. To put these materials to poetical use is required an imagination capable of painting nature and realizing fiction. Nor is he yet a poet till he has attained the whole extension of his language, distinguished all the delicacies of phrase, and all the colours of words, and learned to adjust their different sounds to all the varieties of metrical modulation.

Bossu is of opinion that the poet's first work is to find a *moral,* which his fable is afterwards to illustrate and establish. This seems to have been the process only of Milton: the moral of other poems is incidental and consequent; in Milton's only it is essential and intrinsick. His purpose was the most useful and the most arduous: "to vindicate the ways of God to man"; to shew the reasonableness of religion, and the necessity of obedience to the Divine Law.

To convey this moral there must be a *fable,* a narration artfully constructed so as to excite curiosity and surprise expectation. In this part of his work Milton must be confessed to have equalled every other poet. He has involved in his account of the Fall of Man the events which preceded, and those that were to follow it: he has interwoven the whole system of theology with such propriety that every part appears to be necessary, and scarcely any recital is wished shorter for the sake of quickening the progress of the main action.

The subject of an epic poem is naturally an event of great importance. That of Milton is not the destruction of a city, the conduct of a colony, or the foundation of an empire. His subject is the fate of worlds, the revolutions of heaven and of earth; rebellion against the Supreme King raised by the highest order of created beings; the overthrow of their host and the punishment of their crime; the creation of a new race of reasonable creatures; their original happiness and innocence, their forfeiture of immortality, and their restoration to hope and peace.

Great events can be hastened or retarded only by persons of elevated dignity. Before the greatness displayed in Milton's poem all other greatness shrinks away. The weakest of his agents are the highest and noblest of human beings, the original parents of mankind; with whose actions the elements consented; on whose rectitude or deviation of will depended the state of terrestrial nature and the condition of all the future inhabitants of the globe.

Of the other agents in the poem the chief are such as it is irreverence to name on slight occasions. The rest were lower powers;

"of which the least could wield
Those elements, and arm him with the force
Of all their regions";

powers which only the control of Omnipotence restrains from laying creation waste, and filling the vast expanse of space with ruin and confusion. To display the motives and actions of beings thus superiour, so far as human reason can examine them or human imagination represent them, is the task which this mighty poet has undertaken and performed.

In the examination of epick poems much speculation is commonly employed upon the *characters*. The characters in the

Paradise Lost which admit of examination are those of angels and of man; of angels good and evil, of man in his innocent and sinful state.

Among the angels the virtue of Raphael is mild and placid, of easy condescension and free communication; that of Michael is regal and lofty, and, as may seem, attentive to the dignity of his own nature. Abdiel and Gabriel appear occasionally, and act as every incident requires; the solitary fidelity of Abdiel is very amiably painted.

Of the evil angels the characters are more diversified. To Satan, as Addison observes, such sentiments are given as suit "the most exalted and most depraved being." Milton has been censured by Clarke for the impiety which sometimes breaks from Satan's mouth. For there are thoughts, as he justly remarks, which no observation of character can justify, because no good man would willingly permit them to pass, however transiently, through his own mind. To make Satan speak as a rebel, without any such expressions as might taint the reader's imagination, was indeed one of the great difficulties in Milton's undertaking, and I cannot but think that he has extricated himself with great happiness. There is in Satan's speeches little that can give pain to a pious ear. The language of rebellion cannot be the same with that of obedience. The malignity of Satan foams in haughtiness and obstinacy; but his expressions are commonly general, and no otherwise offensive than as they are wicked.

The other chiefs of the celestial rebellion are very judiciously discriminated in the first and second books; and the ferocious character of Moloch appears, both in the battle and the council, with exact consistency.

To Adam and to Eve are given during their innocence such sentiments as innocence can generate and utter. Their love is pure benevolence and mutual veneration; their repasts are without luxury and their diligence without toil. Their addresses to their Maker have little more than the voice of admiration and gratitude. Fruition left them nothing to ask, and Innocence left them nothing to fear.

But with guilt enter distrust and discord, mutual

accusation, and stubborn self-defence; they regard each other with alienated minds, and dread their Creator as the avenger of their transgression. At last they seek shelter in his mercy, soften to repentance, and melt in supplication. Both before and after the Fall the superiority of Adam is diligently sustained.

Of the *probable* and the *marvellous*, two parts of a vulgar epick poem which immerge the critick in deep consideration, the *Paradise Lost* requires little to be said. It contains the history of a miracle, of Creation and Redemption; it displays the power and the mercy of the Supreme Being: the probable therefore is marvellous, and the marvellous is probable. The substance of the narrative is truth; and as truth allows no choice, it is, like necessity, superior to rule. To the accidental or adventitious parts, as to every thing human, some slight exceptions may be made. But the main fabrick is immovably supported.

It is justly remarked by Addison that this poem has, by the nature of its subject, the advantage above all others, that it is universally and perpetually interesting. All mankind will, through all ages, bear the same relation to Adam and to Eve, and must partake of that good and evil which extend to themselves.

Of the *machinery*, so called from *Theos apo mêchanês*, by which is meant the occasional interposition of supernatural power, another fertile topic of critical remarks, here is no room to speak, because every thing is done under the immediate and visible direction of Heaven; but the rule is so far observed that no part of the action could have been accomplished by any other means.

Of *episodes* I think there are only two, contained in Raphael's relation of the war in heaven and Michael's prophetick account of the changes to happen in this world. Both are closely connected with the great action; one was necessary to Adam as a warning, the other as a consolation.

To the completeness or *integrity* of the design nothing can be objected; it has distinctly and clearly what Aristotle requires, a beginning, a middle, and an end. There is perhaps no poem of the same length from which so little can be taken without apparent mutilation. Here are no funeral games, nor is there any long description of a shield. The short digressions at the beginning of the third, seventh, and ninth books might doubtless be spared; but superfluities so beautiful who would take away? or who does not wish that the author of the *Iliad* had gratified succeeding ages with a little knowledge of himself? Perhaps no passages are more frequently or more attentively read than those extrinsick paragraphs; and, since the end of poetry is pleasure, that cannot be unpoetical with which all are pleased.

The questions, whether the action of the poem be strictly *one*, whether the poem can be properly termed *heroick*, and who is the hero, are raised by such readers as draw their principles of judgement rather from books than from reason. Milton, though he intituled *Paradise Lost* only a "poem," yet calls it himself "heroick song." Dryden, petulantly and indecently, denies the heroism of Adam because he was overcome; but there is no reason why the hero should not be unfortunate except established practice, since success and virtue do not go necessarily together. Cato is the hero of Lucan, but Lucan's authority will not be suffered by Quintilian to decide. However, if success be necessary, Adam's deceiver was at last crushed; Adam was restored to his Maker's favour, and therefore may securely resume his human rank. After the scheme and fabrick of the poem must be considered its component parts, the sentiments, and the diction.

The *sentiments*, as expressive of manners or appropriated to characters, are for the greater part unexceptionably just.

Splendid passages containing lessons of morality or precepts of prudence occur seldom. Such is the original formation of this poem that as it admits no human manners till the Fall, it can give little assistance to human conduct. Its end is to raise the thoughts above sublunary cares or pleasures. Yet the praise of that fortitude, with which Abdiel maintained his singularity of virtue against the scorn of multitudes, may be accommodated to all times; and Raphael's reproof of Adam's curiosity after the planetary motions, with the answer returned by Adam, may be confidently opposed to any rule of life which any poet has delivered.

The thoughts which are occasionally called forth in the progress are such as could only be produced by an imagination in the highest degree fervid and active, to which materials were supplied by incessant study and unlimited curiosity. The heat of Milton's mind might be said to sublimate his learning, to throw off into his work the spirit of science, unmingled with its grosser parts.

He had considered creation in its whole extent, and his descriptions are therefore learned. He had accustomed his imagination to unrestrained indulgence, and his conceptions therefore were extensive. The characteristick quality of his poem is sublimity. He sometimes descends to the elegant, but his element is the great. He can occasionally invest himself with grace; but his natural port is gigantick loftiness. He can please when pleasure is required; but it is his peculiar power to astonish.

He seems to have been well acquainted with his own genius, and to know what it was that Nature had bestowed upon him more bountifully than upon others; the power of displaying the vast, illuminating the splendid, enforcing the awful, darkening the gloomy, and aggravating the dreadful: he therefore chose a subject on which too much could not be said, on which he might tire his fancy without the censure of extravagance.

The appearances of nature and the occurrences of life did not satiate his appetite of greatness. To paint things as they are requires a minute attention, and employs the memory rather than the fancy. Milton's delight was to sport in the wide regions of possibility; reality was a scene too narrow for his mind. He sent his faculties out upon discovery, into worlds where only imagination can travel, and delighted to form new modes of existence, and furnish sentiment and action to superior beings, to trace the counsels of hell, or accompany the choirs of heaven.

But he could not be always in other worlds: he must sometimes revisit earth, and tell of things visible and known. When he cannot raise wonder by the sublimity of his mind he gives delight by its fertility.

Whatever be his subject he never fails to fill the imagination. But his images and descriptions of the scenes or operations of Nature do not seem to be always copied from original form, nor to have the freshness, raciness, and energy of immediate observation. He saw Nature, as Dryden expresses it, "through the spectacles of books"; and on most occasions calls learning to his assistance. The garden of Eden brings to his mind the vale of Enna, where Proserpine was gathering flowers. Satan makes his way through fighting elements, like Argo between the Cyanean rocks, or Ulysses between the two *Sicilian* whirlpools, when he shunned Charybdis "on the larboard." The mythological allusions have been justly censured, as not being always used with notice of their vanity; but they contribute variety to the narration, and produce an alternate exercise of the memory and the fancy.

His similes are less numerous and more various than those of his predecessors. But he does not confine himself within the limits of rigorous comparison: his great excellence is amplitude, and he expands the adventitious image beyond the dimensions which the occasion required. Thus, comparing the shield of Satan to the orb of the Moon, he crowds the imagination with the discovery of the telescope and all the wonders which the telescope discovers.

Of his moral sentiments it is hardly praise to affirm that they excel those of all other poets; for this superiority he was indebted to his acquaintance with the sacred writings. The ancient epick poets, wanting the light of Revelation, were very unskilful teachers of virtue: their principal characters may be great, but they are not amiable. The reader may rise from their works with a greater degree of active or passive fortitude, and sometimes of prudence; but he will be able to carry away few precepts of justice, and none of mercy.

From the Italian writers it appears that the advantages of even Christian knowledge may be possessed in vain. Ariosto's pravity is generally known; and, though the *Deliverance of Jerusalem* may be considered as a sacred subject, the poet has been very sparing of moral instruction.

In Milton every line breathes sanctity of thought and

purity of manners, except when the train of the narration requires the introduction of the rebellious spirits; and even they are compelled to acknowledge their subjection to God in such a manner as excites reverence and confirms piety.

Of human beings there are but two; but those two are the parents of mankind, venerable before their fall for dignity and innocence, and amiable after it for repentance and submission. In their first state their affection is tender without weakness, and their piety sublime without presumption. When they have sinned they shew how discord begins in mutual frailty, and how it ought to cease in mutual forbearance; how confidence of the divine favour is forfeited by sin, and how hope of pardon may be obtained by penitence and prayer. A state of innocence we can only conceive, if indeed in our present misery it be possible to conceive it; but the sentiments and worship proper to a fallen and offending being we have all to learn, as we have all to practise.

The poet whatever be done is always great. Our progenitors in their first state conversed with angels; even when folly and sin had degraded them they had not in their humiliation "the port of mean suitors;" and they rise again to reverential regard when we find that their prayers were heard.

As human passions did not enter the world before the Fall, there is in the *Paradise Lost* little opportunity for the pathetick; but what little there is has not been lost. That passion which is peculiar to rational nature, the anguish arising from the consciousness of transgression and the horrours attending the sense of the Divine Displeasure, are very justly described and forcibly impressed. But the passions are moved only on one occasion; sublimity is the general and prevailing quality in this poem — sublimity variously modified, sometimes descriptive, sometimes argumentative.

The defects and faults of *Paradise Lost*, for faults and defects every work of man must have, it is the business of impartial criticism to discover. As in displaying the excellence of Milton I have not made long quotations, because of selecting beauties there had been no end, I shall in the same general manner mention that which seems to deserve censure; for what

Englishman can take delight in transcribing passages, which, if they lessen the reputation of Milton, diminish in some degree the honour of our country?

The generality of my scheme does not admit the frequent notice of verbal inaccuracies which Bentley, perhaps better skilled in grammar than in poetry, has often found, though he sometimes made them, and which he imputed to the obtrusions of a reviser whom the author's blindness obliged him to employ. A supposition rash and groundless, if he thought it true; and vile and pernicious, if, as is said, he in private allowed it to be false.

The plan of *Paradise Lost* has this inconvenience, that it comprises neither human actions nor human manners. The man and woman who act and suffer are in a state which no other man or woman can ever know. The reader finds no transaction in which he can be engaged, beholds no condition in which he can by any effort of imagination place himself; he has, therefore, little natural curiosity or sympathy.

We all, indeed, feel the effects of Adam's disobedience; we all sin like Adam, and like him must all bewail our offences; we have restless and insidious enemies in the fallen angels, and in the blessed spirits we have guardians and friends; in the Redemption of mankind we hope to be included: in the description of heaven and hell we are surely interested, as we are all to reside hereafter either in the regions of horrour or of bliss. But these truths are too important to be new: they have been taught to our infancy; they have mingled with our solitary thoughts and familiar conversation, and are habitually interwoven with the whole texture of life. Being therefore not new they raise no unaccustomed emotion in the mind: what we knew before we cannot learn; what is not unexpected, cannot surprise.

Of the ideas suggested by these awful scenes, from some we recede with reverence, except when stated hours require their association; and from others we shrink with horrour, or admit them only as salutary inflictions, as counterpoises to our interests and passions. Such images rather obstruct the career of fancy than incite it.

Pleasure and terrour are indeed the genuine sources of poetry; but poetical pleasure must be such as human imagination can at least conceive, and poetical terrour such as human strength and fortitude may combat. The good and evil of Eternity are too ponderous for the wings of wit; the mind sinks under them in passive helplessness, content with calm belief and humble adoration.

Known truths however may take a different appearance, and be conveyed to the mind by a new train of intermediate images. This Milton has undertaken, and performed with pregnancy and vigour of mind peculiar to himself. Whoever considers the few radical positions which the Scriptures afforded him will wonder by what energetick operations he expanded them to such extent and ramified them to so much variety, restrained as he was by religious reverence from licentiousness of fiction.

Here is a full display of the united force of study and genius; of a great accumulation of materials, with judgement to digest and fancy to combine them: Milton was able to select from nature or from story, from ancient fable or from modern science, whatever could illustrate or adorn his thoughts. An accumulation of knowledge impregnated his mind, fermented by study and exalted by imagination.

It has been therefore said without an indecent hyperbole by one of his encomiasts, that in reading *Paradise Lost* we read a book of universal knowledge.

But original deficience cannot be supplied. The want of human interest is always felt. *Paradise Lost* is one of the books which the reader admires and lays down, and forgets to take up again. None ever wished it longer than it is. Its perusal is a duty rather than a pleasure. We read Milton for instruction, retire harassed and overburdened, and look elsewhere for recreation; we desert our master, and seek for companions.

Another inconvenience of Milton's design is that it requires the description of what cannot be described, the agency of spirits. He saw that immateriality supplied no images, and that he could not show angels acting but by instruments of action; he therefore invested them with form and matter. This being necessary was therefore defensible; and he should have secured the consistency of his system by keeping immateriality out of sight, and enticing his reader to drop it from his thoughts. But he has unhappily perplexed his poetry with his philosophy. His infernal and celestial powers are sometimes pure spirit and sometimes animated body. When Satan walks with his lance upon the "burning marle" he has a body; when in his passage between hell and the new world he is in danger of sinking in the vacuity and is supported by a gust of rising vapours he has a body; when he animates the toad he seems to be mere spirit that can penetrate matter at pleasure; when he "starts up in his own shape," he has at least a determined form; and when he is brought before Gabriel he has "a spear and a shield," which he had the power of hiding in the toad, though the arms of the contending angels are evidently material.

The vulgar inhabitants of Pandæmonium, being "incorporeal spirits," are "at large though without number" in a limited space, yet in the battle when they were overwhelmed by mountains their armour hurt them, "crushed in upon their substance, now grown gross by sinning." This likewise happened to the uncorrupted angels, who were overthrown "the sooner for their arms, for unarmed they might easily as spirits have evaded by contraction or remove." Even as spirits they are hardly spiritual, for "contraction" and "remove" are images of matter; but if they could have escaped without their armour, they might have escaped from it and left only the empty cover to be battered. Uriel, when he rides on a sun-beam, is material; Satan is material when he is afraid of the prowess of Adam.

The confusion of spirit and matter which pervades the whole narration of the war of heaven fills it with incongruity; and the book in which it is related is, I believe, the favourite of children, and gradually neglected as knowledge is increased.

After the operation of immaterial agents which cannot be explained may be considered that of allegorical persons, which have no real existence. To exalt causes into agents, to invest abstract ideas with form, and animate them with activity has always been the right of poetry. But such airy beings are for the most part suffered only to do their natural office, and retire. Thus Fame tells a tale and Victory hovers over a general or perches on a standard; but Fame and Victory can do no more. To give them any real employment or ascribe to them any material agency is to make them allegorical no longer, but to shock the mind by ascribing effects to non-entity. In the *Prometheus* of Æschylus we see Violence and Strength, and in the *Alcestis* of Euripides we see Death, brought upon the stage, all as active persons of the drama; but no precedents can justify absurdity.

Milton's allegory of Sin and Death is undoubtedly faulty. Sin is indeed the mother of Death, and may be allowed to be the portress of hell; but when they stop the journey of Satan, a journey described as real, and when Death offers him battle, the allegory is broken. That Sin and Death should have shewn the way to hell might have been allowed; but they cannot facilitate the passage by building a bridge, because the difficulty of Satan's passage is described as real and sensible, and the bridge ought to be only figurative. The hell assigned to the rebellious spirits is described as not less local than the residence of man. It is placed in some distant part of space, separated from the regions of harmony and order by a chaotick waste and an unoccupied vacuity; but Sin and Death worked up a "mole of aggregated soil," cemented with asphaltus; a work too bulky for ideal architects.

This unskilful allegory appears to me one of the greatest faults of the poem; and to this there was no temptation, but the author's opinion of its beauty.

To the conduct of the narrative some objections may be made. Satan is with great expectation brought before Gabriel in Paradise, and is suffered to go away unmolested. The creation of man is represented as the consequence of the vacuity left in heaven by the expulsion of the rebels; yet Satan mentions it as a report "rife in heaven" before his departure.

To find sentiments for the state of innocence was very difficult; and something of anticipation perhaps is now and then discovered. Adam's discourse of dreams seems not to be the speculation of a new-created being. I know not whether his answer to the angel's reproof for curiosity does not want something of propriety: it is the speech of a man acquainted with many other men. Some philosophical notions, especially when the philosophy is false, might have been better omitted. The angel in a comparison speaks of "timorous deer," before deer were yet timorous, and before Adam could understand the comparison.

Dryden remarks that Milton has some flats among his elevations. This is only to say that all the parts are not equal. In every work one part must be for the sake of others; a palace must have passages, a poem must have transitions. It is no more to be required that wit should always be blazing than that the sun should always stand at noon. In a great work there is a vicissitude of luminous and opaque parts, as there is in the world a succession of day and night. Milton, when he has expatiated in the sky, may be allowed sometimes to revisit earth; for what other author ever soared so high or sustained his flight so long?

Milton, being well versed in the Italian poets, appears to have borrowed often from them; and, as every man catches something from his companions, his desire of imitating Ariosto's levity has disgraced his work with the "Paradise of Fools"; a fiction not in itself ill-imagined, but too ludicrous for its place.

His play on words, in which he delights too often; his equivocations, which Bentley endeavours to defend by the example of the ancients; his unnecessary and ungraceful use of terms of art, it is not necessary to mention, because they are easily remarked and generally censured, and at last bear so little proportion to the whole that they scarcely deserve the attention of a critick.

Such are the faults of that wonderful performance *Paradise Lost*; which he who can put in balance with its beauties must be considered not as nice but as dull, as less to be censured for want of candour than pitied for want of sensibility.

Of *Paradise Regained* the general judgement seems now to

be right, that it is in many parts elegant, and every-where instructive. It was not to be supposed that the writer of *Paradise Lost* could ever write without great effusions of fancy and exalted precepts of wisdom. The basis of *Paradise Regained* is narrow; a dialogue without action can never please like an union of the narrative and dramatick powers. Had this poem been written, not by Milton but by some imitator, it would have claimed and received universal praise.

If *Paradise Regained* has been too much depreciated, *Sampson Agonistes* has in requital been too much admired. It could only be by long prejudice and the bigotry of learning that Milton could prefer the ancient tragedies with their encumbrance of a chorus to the exhibitions of the French and English stages; and it is only by a blind confidence in the reputation of Milton that a drama can be praised in which the intermediate parts have neither cause nor consequence, neither hasten nor retard the catastrophe.

In this tragedy are however many particular beauties, many just sentiments and striking lines; but it wants that power of attracting attention which a well-connected plan produces.

Milton would not have excelled in dramatick writing; he knew human nature only in the gross, and had never studied the shades of character, nor the combinations of concurring or the perplexity of contending passions. He had read much and knew what books could teach; but had mingled little in the world, and was deficient in the knowledge which experience must confer.

Through all his greater works there prevails an uniform peculiarity of *Diction*, a mode and cast of expression which bears little resemblance to that of any former writer, and which is so far removed from common use that an unlearned reader when he first opens his book finds himself surprised by a new language.

This novelty has been, by those who can find nothing wrong in Milton, imputed to his laborious endeavours after words suitable to the grandeur of his ideas. "Our language," says Addison, "sunk under him." But the truth is, that both in prose and verse, he had formed his style by a perverse and pedantick principle. He was desirous to use English words with a foreign idiom.

This in all his prose is discovered and condemned, for there judgement operates freely, neither softened by the beauty nor awed by the dignity of his thoughts; but such is the power of his poetry that his call is obeyed without resistance, the reader feels himself in captivity to a higher and a nobler mind, and criticism sinks in admiration.

Milton's style was not modified by his subject: what is shown with greater extent in *Paradise Lost* may be found in *Comus*. One source of his peculiarity was his familiarity with the Tuscan poets: the disposition of his words is, I think, frequently Italian; perhaps sometimes combined with other tongues. Of him, at last, may be said what Jonson says of Spenser, that "he wrote no language," but has formed what Butler calls "a Babylonish Dialect," in itself harsh and barbarous, but made by exalted genius and extensive learning the vehicle of so much instruction and so much pleasure that, like other lovers, we find grace in its deformity.

Whatever be the faults of his diction he cannot want the praise of copiousness and variety; he was master of his language in its full extent, and has selected the melodious words with such diligence that from his book alone the Art of English Poetry might be learned.

After his diction something must be said of his versification. "The measure," he says, "is the English heroic verse without rhyme." Of this mode he had many examples among the Italians, and some in his own country. The Earl of Surrey is said to have translated one of Virgil's books without rhyme, and besides our tragedies a few short poems had appeared in blank verse; particularly one tending to reconcile the nation to Raleigh's wild attempt upon Guiana, and probably written by Raleigh himself. These petty performances cannot be supposed to have much influenced Milton, who more probably took his hint from Trisino's *Italia Liberata*; and, finding blank verse easier than rhyme, was desirous of persuading himself that it is better.

"Rhyme," he says, and says truly, "is no necessary adjunct of true poetry." But perhaps of poetry as a mental operation meter or music is no necessary adjunct; it is however by the music of meter that poetry has been discriminated in all languages, and in languages melodiously constructed with a due proportion of long and short syllables meter is sufficient. But one language cannot communicate its rules to another; where meter is scanty and imperfect some help is necessary. The music of the English heroic line strikes the ear so faintly that it is easily lost, unless all the syllables of every line co-operate together; this co-operation can be only obtained by the preservation of every verse unmingled with another as a distinct system of sounds, and this distinctness is obtained and preserved by the artifice of rhyme.

The variety of pauses, so much boasted by the lovers of blank verse, changes the measures of an English poet to the periods of a declaimer; and there are only a few skilful and happy readers of Milton who enable their audience to perceive where the lines end or begin. "Blank verse," said an ingenious critick, "seems to be verse only to the eye."

Poetry may subsist without rhyme, but English poetry will not often please; nor can rhyme ever be safely spared but where the subject is able to support itself. Blank verse makes some approach to that which is called the "lapidary style"; has neither the easiness of prose nor the melody of numbers, and therefore tires by long continuance. Of the Italian writers without rhyme, whom Milton alleges as precedents, not one is popular; what reason could urge in its defence has been confuted by the ear.

But whatever be the advantage of rhyme I cannot prevail on myself to wish that Milton had been a rhymer, for I cannot wish his work to be other than it is; yet like other heroes he is to be admired rather than imitated. He that thinks himself capable of astonishing may write blank verse, but those that hope only to please must condescend to rhyme.

The highest praise of genius is original invention. Milton cannot be said to have contrived the structure of an epick poem, and therefore owes reverence to that vigour and amplitude of mind to which all generations must be indebted for the art of poetical narration, for the texture of the fable, the variation of incidents, the interposition of dialogue, and all the stratagems that surprise and enchain attention. But of all the borrowers from Homer Milton is perhaps the least indebted. He was naturally a thinker for himself, confident of his own abilities and disdainful of help or hindrance; he did not refuse admission to the thoughts or images of his predecessors, but he did not seek them. From his contemporaries he neither courted nor received support; there is in his writings nothing by which the pride of other authors might be gratified or favour gained, no exchange of praise nor solicitation of support. His great works were performed under discountenance and in blindness, but difficulties vanished at his touch; he was born for whatever is arduous; and his work is not the greatest of heroick poems, only because it is not the first.

Chapter 11

Explanatory Notes

Already written: A number of biographies of Milton had appeared by the time Johnson's *Life* appeared in 1779, some as standalone biographies, others in editions of Milton's works. Among most notable are Wood's *Athenae Oxoniensis* (1691-92); *Letters of State Written by Milton, with Life* (1694), by Milton's nephew, Edward Phillips; John Toland's radical Whiggish *Life* (1698);

Jonathan Richardson (father and son), *Explanatory Notes, &c. on Paradise Lost* (1734); *Milton's Prose Works*, ed. Thomas Birch (1738); *Milton's Poems*, ed. Thomas Newton (1749-52).

The uniformity of this edition: Johnson's *Life of Milton* originally appeared as one contribution in a series of fifty-two biographical and critical prefaces to a multi-volume edition of *The Works of the English Poets*. Now known as *The Lives of the Poets*, these works were originally published in their own right as *Prefaces Biographical and Critical to the Works of the English Poets*, 10 vols. (London, 1779-81).

The white rose: The white rose was the symbol of the York family, who battled against the Lancasters (symbolized by the red rose) in the War of the Roses.

The king's party: John Milton was one of the most vociferous critics of Charles I throughout the Civil War of the 1640s and through the Interregnum. The poet's brother Christopher, however, remained loyal to the king.

Edward Philips: Edward Phillips, Milton's nephew, was Milton's first biographer.

Sizar: "In the University of Cambridge, and at Trinity College, Dublin, an undergraduate member admitted under this designation and receiving an allowance from the college to enable him to study" (OED).

The learned Politian: Angelo Poliziano (1454-94), Italian poet and scholar, and one of the important early figures in the Italian Renaissance.

One of Johnson's publishing plans when he first arrived in London in the 1730s was an edition of Politian's works.

Cowley: Abraham Cowley (1618-67), English poet. Johnson included a *Life of Cowley* in his *Lives of the Poets*, in which he famously describes the characteristics of "metaphysical" poetry.

Haddon and Ascham: Walter Haddon (1516-72) and Roger Ascham (1515-68), English scholars.

Alabaster's Roxana: William Alabaster (1567-1640), author of a Latin poem modeled on Seneca called *Alabaster*, written 1592, and published in 1632.

Rustication: A temporary suspension from a university.

Me tenet . . .: Milton's *Elegy* to his friend Diodati. In the late eighteenth century, William Cowper translated the lines thus: "I well content, where Thames with influent tide/ My native city laves, meantime reside,/ Nor zeal nor duty now my steps impel/ To ready Cam, and my forbidden cell./. . . / 'Tis time that I a pedant's threats disdain,/ And fly from wrongs my woul will ne'er sustain./ If peaceful days, in letter'd leisure spent/ Beneath my father's roof, be banishment,/ Then call me banish'd, I will ne'er refuse/ A name expressive of the lot I choose."

Hartlib: Samuel Hartlib (c. 1600-70), English educational theorist, born in Germany.

Permitted to act plays: Many Puritans vigorously attacked the theatre throughout the seventeenth century, and succeeded in closing all public theatres in Britain between 1642 and 1660.

Trincalos: Trincalo is a character in *Albumazar* by Thomas Tomkis (1614).

A quo ceu fonte . . .: From Ovid's *Amores*, 3.9.25: As translated by John Nichol, "from whose perennial lay / Flow the rich fonts of the Pierian wave / To wet the lips of bards."

non tam de se, quam supra se: Said "not so much *about* him as *over* him."

Tasso: Torquato Tasso (1544-95), Renaissance Italian poet, known for *Gerusalemme liberata*.

The differences between the king and parliament: Throughout the late 1630s and early '40s, tension was growing between Charles I and an increasingly Puritan Parliament, leading to a series of Civil Wars in the 1640s and the execution of Charles in 1649.

Galileo: Galileo Galilei (1564-1642), Italian astronomer. In 1632 he was imprisoned by the Church for espousing the heretical heliocentric theory of Copernicus. Milton alludes to Galileo as "the Tuscan artist" in *Paradise Lost* 1.288.

Hotti toi en megaroisi kakon t' agathon te tetuktai: "What evil and what good has happened in your house" (*Odyssey* 4.392).

Smectymnuus: Stephen Marshall, Edmund Calamy, Thomas Young, Matthew Newcomen, and William Spurstow — five ministers not six, as Johnson writes — combined their initials (counting *W* as *UU*) to produce the pen name *Smectymnuus*.

The learned Usher: James Usher (or Ussher) (1581-1656), Irish divine and Royalist.

That hell grows darker at his frown: From *Paradise Lost* 2.719.

The family of the lady were Cavaliers: "Cavalier" was a common name for royalists, i.e., defenders of the king against whom the Puritans struggled.

Presbyterians: The sect of Puritanism that took hold in Scotland, whose name comes from Greek *presbyter*, "elder." Presbyterians rejected priests for a council of elders, and though Milton began by supporting them, he later came to insist "New Presbyter is but old priest writ large."

Acollection of his Latin and English poems: The 1645 collection of *Poems* includes many of Milton's most famous shorter works.

Salmasius: Claude de Saumaise (1588-1653), French scholar, perhaps the most famous scholar in Europe during his lifetime. His *Defensio regio pro Carolo I* appeared in 1649.

Quid agis cum dira . . .: Slightly misquoted from Juvenal, *Satires* 4.14.

Cromwell: Oliver Cromwell (1599-1658), leader of the English Protectorate from the execution of Charles I in 1649 until his death. His son, Richard, took over in 1658, but in 1660 Charles II, son of the executed king, was restored to power.

Poma alba ferebat . . .: "Which once bore white fruit, but now is turned black by blood" (Ovid, *Metamorphoses* 4.51).

To collection a dictionary: Johnson himself compiled one of the most important English dictionaries in 1755.

long chusing, and beginning late: Quoted from *Paradise Lost* 9.26. Johnson quotes it again in paragraph 110.

Oliver: Oliver Cromwell, succeeded by his son Richard.

Harrington: James Harrington (1611-77), political theorist, best known for his description of a commonwealth, *Oceana* (1656).

Griffiths: Matthew Griffith (c. 1599-1665), Royalist preacher.

L'Estrange: Sir Roger L'Estrange (1616-1704), English polemical journalist and Royalist.

Act of Oblivion: Upon assuming the throne in 1660, Charles II, son of the executed Charles I, issued a blanket pardon for most of those who fought on the Parliamentarian side.

Marvell: Andrew Marvell (1621-78), English poet.

To read Latin with an English mouth: There have been different standards for the pronunciation of Latin in various countries. The English tended to pronounce the vowels as if they were English vowels.

He who travels, if he speaks Latin: Latin was nearly dead as a spoken language in Johnson's day, although he famously spoke to priests only in Latin the one time he visited France.

Mr. Richardson: Jonathan Richardson, and his son of the same name, make the point in their *Explanatory Notes, &c. on Paradise Lost* (1734).

Redeunt in carmina vires: From Milton's fifth *Elegy*: "Fallor? an et nobis redeunt in carmina vires,/ Ingeniumque mihi munere veris adest?" ("Am I deluded? Or are my powers of song returning, and is my inspiration with me again?").

Sapiens dominabitur astris: Anonymous proverb, "The wise man will rule the stars."

Possunt quia posse videntur: "They can because they are seen to be able" (Virgil, *Aeneid* 5.231).

An age too late: Quoting *Paradise Lost* 9.44: "Unless an age too late, or cold/ Climate, or years, damp my intended wing/ Depress'd."

Unpremeditated verse: From *Paradise Lost* 9.20-24: "If answerable style I can obtain/ Of my celestial patroness, who deigns/ Her nightly visitation unimplor'd,/ And dictates to me slumb'ring, or inspires/ Easy my unpremeditated verse."

The beginning of the third book: "Hail holy Light, offspring of Heav'n first-born,/ Or of th' Eternal Coeternal beam/ May I express the unblam'd? since God is Light,/ And never but in unapproached Light/ Dwelt from Eternity, dwelt then in thee,/ Bright effluence of bright essence increate.. . . Thee I revisit safe,/ And feel thy sovran vital Lamp; but thou/ Revisit'st not these eyes, that roll in vain/ To find thy piercing ray, and find no dawn" (*Paradise Lost* 1-24).

Fallen on evil days and evil tongues: "More safe I Sing with mortal voice, unchang'd/ To hoarse or mute, though fall'n on evil days,/ On evil days though fall'n, and evil tongues;/ In darkness, and with dangers compast round,/ And solitude" (*Paradise Lost* 7.24-28).

When the plague (1665) raged in London: Bubonic plague gripped London in 1665 and 1666, causing many to flee to the country. The most famous accounts of this plague are Samuel Pepys's *Diary* and Daniel Defoe's *Journal of the Plague Year*.

The Revolution: In 1688-89, the Catholic James II was driven from England in the so-called "Glorious Revolution," and was replaced by the Dutch Protestant William of Orange, who ruled with his wife, Mary.

Geoffry of Monmouth: Geoffrey of Monmouth (c. 1100-1154), Welsh chronicler and Bishop of St. Asaph. He is best known for his *Historia regum Britanniae, History of the Kings of England*, a collection of mostly legendary material. It contains many tales of Arthur and Camelot, is the source of Shakespeare's *King Lear* and *Cymbeline*.

Ramus: Petrus Ramus, or Pierre de la Ramée (1515-72), French philosopher, known for his work of philosophy, *Dialectic* (1544).

The thirty-nine articles: The official statement of faith of the Anglican Church.

Soli Miltono secundus: "Second only to Milton."

The picture which he has given of Adam: "Hyacinthin locks/ Round from his parted forelock manly hung/ Clustr'ing, but not beneath his shoulders broad" (*Paradise Lost* 4.301-3).

Spenser: Edmund Spenser (c. 1552-99), English poet, best known for his epic poem, *The Faerie Queene* (1590-96). John Dryden relates that "Milton has acknowledged to me that Spenser was his original."

Arminianism: The followers of Jacobus Arminius rejected Calvin's doctrine of absolute predestination.

An acrimonious and surly republican: Johnson's rejection of Milton's anti-monarchical politics is often quoted in discussions of Johnson's own political opinions.

They who most loudly clamour for liberty do not most liberally grant it: Compare Johnson's comment on cries for independence among American slaveholders: "How is it we hear the loudest yelps for liberty from the drivers of negroes?"

A "Lion" that had no skill "in dandling the Kid": "Sporting the lion ramp'd, and in his paw/ Dandl'd the kid" (*Paradise Lost*, 4.343-44). Compare Johnson's remark to Hannah More: "Milton, Madam, was a genius that could cut a Colossus from a rock, but could not carve heads upon cherry-stones."

A pastoral, easy, vulgar, and therefore disgusting: Johnson rejects the artificiality of the pastoral in a number of his critical essays.

We drove a field . . .: *Lycidas*, 27-29.

Sacred truths, such as ought never to be polluted with such irreverent combinations: Johnson often comments on poetry's inability to express religious truths. Here he complains that Christian morality is being reduced to the stock images of classical pastoral poetry.

The fabrick of a sonnet. . . has never succeeded in ours: Although surprising to modern sensibilities, Johnson's judgment of English sonnets was not idiosyncratic in his day. The sonnets of Sidney, Spenser, and Shakespeare were little read, and almost no poets of note produced English sonnets between Milton and Charlotte Smith in the 1790s. A similar complaint about the paucity of English rhymes appears in many discussions of the Spenserian stanza.

The first praise of genius is due to the writer of an epick poem: Aristotle placed tragedy above epic in his hierarchy of genres, though few eighteenth-century critics followed him in this; Johnson reports the conventional wisdom of his day.

Uniting pleasure with truth: Recalling Horace's observation that the function of poetry is to instruct and delight.

Bossu: René Le Bossu (1631-80), French critic, best known for his *Traité du poem epique* (1675).

To vindicate the ways of God to man: Johnson apparently confuses *Paradise Lost,* 1.26 ("And justify the ways of God to Men"), with Pope's *Essay on Man,* 1.16 ("But vindicate the ways of God to Man").

Fable: The common term for *plot,* with no suggestions of Aesopian fables.

As Addison observes: See *Spectator* 303: "His Sentiments are every way answerable to his Character, and suitable to a created Being of the most exalted and most depraved Nature."

Clarke: John Clarke, author of an *Essay upon Study,* little read today.

Theos apo mêchanês: Greek for "god from the machine"; cf. Latin *deus ex machina.* Aristotle warns in the *Poetics,* "Obviously the resolutions of plots should come from the plot itself, and not from a *deus ex machina* as in the *Medea* and the departure scene in the *Iliad.* The *deus ex machina* should be used on events outside the play, preceding events beyond human knowledge, or later events that require prediction and announcement" .

A beginning, a middle, and an end: See Aristotle's *Poetics:* "Tragedy is the imitation of an action that is complete, whole, and of magnitude (for you can have a whole that has no magnitude). A whole is that which has a beginning, a middle, and an end. A beginning is that which doesn't follow necessarily from something else, but after which something naturally happens. An end, on the other hand, is that which occurs naturally (whether necessarily or usually) after an event that came before, but it needn't be followed by anything. A middle is that which follows an earlier event and has further consequences. Well-constructed plots, should therefore neither begin nor end at an arbitrary point" . *Here are no funeral games, nor is there any long description of a shield*: References to the funeral games in *Iliad*, 23.257 and *Aeneid*, 5.104, and to the description of Achilles' shield in *Iliad*, 18.478.

The characteristick quality of his poem is sublimity: Compare Addison: "*Milton*'s chief Talent, and indeed his distinguishing Excellence, lies in the Sublimity of his Thoughts" (*Spectator* 279), and John Dennis: "Milton. . . carried away the Prize of Sublimity from both Ancients and Moderns." Dennis goes on to call sublimity "his distinguishing and Characteristick Quality,. . . which sets him above Mankind" (*Letters on Milton and Wycherley*, Letter I).

his element is the great: Compare Johnson's comment in conversation that Milton "was a genius who could cut a Colossus from a rock; but could not carve heads upon cherry-stones."

Ariosto's pravity is generally known: Ludovico Ariosto (1474-1533), often criticized in the eighteenth century for the structure of his epic-romance, *Orlando Furioso* (1516).

Deliverance of Jerusalem: Torquato Tasso's *Gerusalemme liberata*.

verbal inaccuracies which Bentley. . . has often found: Richard Bentley's edition of *Paradise Lost* appeared in 1732. In it he proposes thousands of textual corrections, arguing that Milton, being blind, "could only dictate his Verses to be writ by another. Whence it naturally follows, that any Errors in Spelling, Pointing, nay even in whole Words of a like or near Sound in Pronunciation, are not to be charg'd upon the Poet, but on the Amanuensis." He goes on to argue that an anonymous editor, "knowing *Milton*'s bad Circumstances,. . . thought he had a fit Opportunity to foist into the Book several of his own Verses." Of the thousands of changes Bentley proposed, virtually none are accepted today.

None ever wished it longer than it is: Compare Johnson's remark to Mrs. Thrale, "Was there ever yet any thing written by mere man that was wished longer by its readers, excepting Don Quixote, Robinson Crusoe, and the Pilgrim's Progress?"

Milton's allegory of Sin and Death is undoubtedly faulty: *Paradise Lost*, 2.648. Many eighteenth-century critics, including

Addison, agreed.

His play on words, in which he delights too often: Eighteenth-century critics were singularly unforgiving of puns and other wordplay. Compare Johnson's comments on Shakespeare: "A quibble [pun] is to *Shakespeare,* what luminous vapours are to the traveller; he follows it at all adventures, it is sure to lead him out of his way, and sure to engulf him in the mire. It has some malignant power over his mind, and its fascinations are irresistible. Whatever be the dignity or profundity of his disquisition, whether he be enlarging knowledge or exalting affection, whether he be amusing attention with incidents, or enchaining it in suspense, let but a quibble spring up before him, and he leaves his work unfinished. A quibble is the golden apple for which he will always turn aside from his career, or stoop from his elevation. A quibble poor and barren as it is, gave him such delight, that he was content to purchase it, by the sacrifice of reason, propriety and truth. A quibble was to him the fatal *Cleopatra* for which he lost the world, and was content to lose it."

Chapter 12

The Essential Elements of the Preface

It is the fate of those who toil at the lower employments of life, to be rather driven by the fear of evil, than attracted by the prospect of good; to be exposed to censure, without hope of praise; to be disgraced by miscarriage, or punished for neglect, where success would have been without applause, and diligence without reward.

Among these unhappy mortals is the writer of dictionaries; whom mankind have considered, not as the pupil, but the slave of science, the pionier of literature, doomed only to remove rubbish and clear obstructions from the paths through which Learning and Genius press forward to conquest and glory, without bestowing a smile on the humble drudge that facilitates their progress. Every other authour may aspire to praise; the lexicographer can only hope to escape reproach, and even this negative recompense has been yet granted to very few.

I have, notwithstanding this discouragement, attempted a dictionary of the English language, which, while it was employed in the cultivation of every species of literature, has itself been hitherto neglected; suffered to spread, under the direction of chance, into wild exuberance; resigned to the tyranny of time and fashion; and exposed to the corruptions of ignorance, and caprices of innovation.

When I took the first survey of my undertaking, I found our speech copious without order, and energetick without rules: wherever I turned my view, there was perplexity to be disentangled, and confusion to be regulated; choice was to be made out of boundless variety, without any established principle of selection; adulterations were to be detected, without a settled test of purity; and modes of expression to be rejected or received, without the suffrages of any writers of classical reputation or acknowledged authority.

Having therefore no assistance but from general grammar, I applied myself to the perusal of our writers; and noting whatever might be of use to ascertain or illustrate any word or phrase, accumulated in time the materials of a dictionary, which, by degrees, I reduced to method, establishing to myself, in the progress of the work, such rules as experience and analogy suggested to me; experience, which practice and observation were continually increasing; and analogy, which, though in some words obscure, was evident in others.

In adjusting the *orthography*, which has been to this time unsettled and fortuitous, I found it necessary to distinguish those irregularities that are inherent in our tongue, and perhaps coeval with it, from others which the ignorance or negligence of later writers has produced. Every language has its anomalies, which, though inconvenient, and in themselves once unnecessary, must be tolerated among the imperfections of human things, and which require only to be registered, that they may not be increased, and ascertained, that they may not be confounded: but every language has likewise its improprieties and absurdities, which it is the duty of the lexicographer to correct or proscribe.

As language was at its beginning merely oral, all words of necessary or common use were spoken before they were written; and while they were unfixed by any visible signs, must have been spoken with great diversity, as we now observe those who cannot read catch sounds imperfectly, and utter them negligently. When this wild and barbarous jargon was first reduced to an alphabet, every penman endeavoured to express, as he could, the sounds which he was accustomed to pronounce or to receive, and vitiated in writing such words as were already vitiated in speech. The powers of the letters, when they were applied to a new language, must have been vague and unsettled, and therefore different hands would exhibit the same sound by different combinations.

From this uncertain pronunciation arise in a great part the various dialects of the same country, which will always be observed to grow fewer, and less different, as books are multiplied; and from this arbitrary representation of sounds by letters, proceeds that diversity of spelling observable in the Saxon remains, and I suppose in the first books of every nation, which perplexes or destroys analogy, and produces anomalous formations, that, being once incorporated, can never be afterward dismissed or reformed.

Of this kind are the derivatives *length* from *long, strength* from *strong, darling* from *dear, breadth* from *broad,* from *dry, drought,* and from *high, height,* which Milton, in zeal for analogy, writes *highth; Quid te exempta juvat spinis de pluribus una* ("What good would it do to remove one out of many errors?"); to change all would be too much, and to change one is nothing. This uncertainty is most frequent in the vowels, which are so capriciously pronounced, and so differently modified, by accident or affectation, not only in every province, but in every mouth, that to them, as is well known to etymologists, little regard is to be shewn in the deduction of one language from another.

Such defects are not errours in orthography, but spots of barbarity impressed so deep in the English language, that criticism can never wash them away: these, therefore, must be permitted to remain untouched; but many words have likewise been altered by accident, or depraved by ignorance, as the pronunciation of the vulgar has been weakly followed; and some still continue to be variously written, as authours differ in their care or skill: of these it was proper to enquire the true orthography, which I have always considered as depending on their derivation, and have therefore referred them to their original languages: thus I write *enchant, enchantment, enchanter,* after the French and *incantation* after the Latin; thus *entire* is chosen rather than *intire,* because it passed to us not from the Latin *integer,* but from the French *entier*.

Of many words it is difficult to say whether they were immediately received from the Latin or the French, since at the time when we had dominions in France, we had Latin service in our churches. It is, however, my opinion, that the French generally supplied us; for we have few Latin words, among the terms of domestick use, which are not French; but many French, which are very remote from Latin.

Even in words of which the derivation is apparent, I have been often obliged to sacrifice uniformity to custom; thus I write, in compliance with a numberless majority, *convey* and *inveigh, deceit* and *receipt, fancy* and *phantom;* sometimes the derivative varies from the primitive, as *explain* and *explanation, repeat* and *repetition.*

Some combinations of letters having the same power are used indifferently without any discoverable reason of choice, as in *choak, choke; soap, sope; jewel, fuel,* and many others; which I have sometimes inserted twice, that those who search for them under either form, may not search in vain.

In this work, when it shall be found that much is omitted, let it not be forgotten that much likewise is performed; and though no book was ever spared out of tenderness to the author, and the world is little solicitous to know whence proceeded the faults of that which it condemns; yet it may gratify curiosity to inform it, that the *English Dictionary* was written with little assistance of the learned, and without any patronage of the great; not in the soft obscurities of retirement, or under the shelter of academic bowers, but amidst inconvenience and distraction, in sickness and in sorrow.

It may repress the triumph of malignant criticism to observe, that if our language is not here fully displayed, I have only failed in an attempt which no human powers have hitherto completed. If the lexicons of ancient tongues, now immutably fixed, and comprised in a few volumes, be yet, after the toil of successive ages, inadequate and delusive; if the aggregated knowledge, and co-operating diligence of the Italian academicians, did not secure them from the censure of Beni; if the embodied critics of France, when fifty years had been spent upon their work, were obliged to change its economy, and give their second edition another form, I may surely be contented without the praise of perfection, which, if I could obtain, in this gloom of solitude, what would it avail me? I have protracted my work till most of those whom I wished to please have sunk into the grave, and success and miscarriage are empty sounds: I therefore dismiss it with frigid tranquility, having little to fear or hope from censure or from praise.

The Last Days of the Great Essayist

The last days of the great essayist and dictionary-maker Dr Johnson were recorded in vivid detail by his biographer, James Boswell. Breathless and in pain, Johnson, aged 75, prepared himself for death willi admirable courage. He had been plagued all his life by a fear of the dark, by the insomniac's dread of not waking up; a dread made sharper by his fervent belief in Purgatory, Hell and the Day of judgment.

For Johnson, religion was no panacea and the prospect of death was appalling. And yet, with characteristic moral strength, he also contemplated his approaching demise with rational detachment. He asked his physician, Dr Brocklesby, to tell him plainly whether or not he would recover. When told that it would take a miracle, Johnson replied, 'Then, I will take no more physick, not even my opiates; for I have prayed that I may render up my soul to God unclouded.' At seven o'clock, in the deep, dank darkness of a December evening, he died, watched over by his manservant Francis Barber and by Mrs Desmoulins, the last remaining female member of his mismatched household. But, as a new exhibition at Dr Johnson's House in London reveals, by the morning of the second day, his body had been carried down the stairs of No. 8 Bolt Court and into a waiting cart. Anyone who had followed the cart would have seen that it was driven up the Strand and beyond Covent Garden to the yard of a house in Great Windmill Street. No plaque advertised the house's business, but this was William Hunter's school of anatomy, where student surgeons were instructed in the art of dissection.

On display in The Tyranny of Treatment: Samuel Johnson, His Friends and Georgian Medicine is the autopsy report. We discover that the body was Opened', in the presence of his surgeon William Cruikshank and other doctors who had witnessed Johnson's last illness. His lungs, apparently, 'did not collapse as they usually do when air is admitted; but remained distended as if they had lost the power of contraction'; a gallstone 'about the size of a pigeon's egg' was removed (no wonder Johnson suffered such pain in his last years); his left kidney was in good shape, but his right was 'almost entirely destroyed'; and while his left testicle was 'sound', his right was diseased. His brain was left untouched - perhaps in deference to Johnson's eminence as a thinker?

The report was written up as a casestudy under the heading 'Asthma', not 'Dr Samuel Johnson' (who it is now thought was killed by emphysema). It fails to record lhat several of Johnson's organs were removed from his body and ended up as exhibits. Where now, for example, is Johnson's left lung? At one time it was thought to have been sold by Cruikshank to a museum in St Petersburg - but the lung has since disappeared. Efforts to find it by the curators of the exhibition, Natasha McEnroe and Rachel Kennedy, have so far failed. Did it never reach Russia? Simon Chaplin, senior curator at the Royal College of Surgeons, believes that it may have ended up in the college's Hunterian collection of anatomical exhibits and been destroyed when the college was hit by German bombs during the Blitz.

Where now is his right kidney - also known to have been removed? How much of Johnson was in fact buried in Poet's Corner on Monday, 20 December, after a funeral service in which these words from Corinthians would have been read, 'How are the dead raised up? And with what body do they come?' Did Johnson sign anything granting his permission for his body to be carved up before burial in this way? The Tyranny of Treatment is surprising not so much for what it shows us about medical practice in the late 18th century, but for what it suggests about Georgian attitudes to death and disease - and our own.

The autopsy has the scientific precision of a modern-day post-mortem, and yet it was conducted almost in secret, as if by subterfuge. William Hunter had warned his students only a year earlier 'to take particular care' not to advertise the proceedings of his academy for fear of 'giving offence to the populace'. It was necessary, he said, 'to shut our doors against strangers, or such people as might chuse to visit us from an idle or malevolent curiosity'. At the time Hunter was professor of anatomy at the Royal Academy; his brother John was surgeon-extraordinary to the King. But their profession was still regarded by many with repugnance.

The increasing desire for more understanding of the human body meant that anatomy had been taught in England using the dissection of dead bodies since the 16th century, but it was strictly restricted by Act of Parliament: the only bodies that could be used for such a purpose were those of felons and murderers. At a time when religion still held sway, it was believed that the body needed to be buried whole; it clothed the soul.

Attitudes, however, were changing with the revival of Platonic philosophy and the development of new ideas about man's place in the universe stimulated by the Enlightenment. It became more possible to conceive of the soul as being separate from the body: the body was a tool; your real self was something else. Death was in any case regarded by the Georgians with much more detachment than we would find possible - or acceptable. When Georgiana, Duchess of Devonshire's two-year-old son Richard died of whooping cough in 1791, she wrote to her sister the next day: 'The poor little fellow has been opened & the disorder found to be exactly such as Ke. [the physician] had described'. She then goes on, only hours, minutes later, to give details of what the doctor found: 'thick glutinous phlegm adhering to the lower part of the wind pipe so firmly as not to be detached, which occasioned the hooping noise that always attends this fatal complaint'. Reading Johnson's autopsy report now, with its lack of any connection to the man who wrote Rasselas or compiled the Dictionary, is discomfiting. It provoked me to wonder just how much more rational and scientific are we than the Georgians? When last year Gunther von Hagen staged Body Worlds, his exhibition of dead humans, shot through with dyes to illustrate the internal workings of the body, he aroused a furious debate about the ethics of using human bodies in this way. How many of those reading this article will be carrying donororgan cards? How many of us will ever have seen the dead body of a relative or friend? Other exhibits in The Tyranny of Treatment also suggest this confusion between superstition and rationalism. Johnson wore all his life the gold medallion given to him by Queen Anne when as a child he was brought to London to be 'touched' as a cure for scrofula, a kind of tuberculosis. (Queen Anne was the last of the English monarchs to carry on the practice, based on the superstitious belief in the healing power that resided in monarchy.)

But most dramatic of all is the Death Mask. Immediately after the completion of the autopsy, the artist Sir Joshua Reynolds arranged for a plaster-of-Paris cast to be made of his friend's head (another reason why the brain was left untouched?) from which copies were made for other members of Johnson's circle. Eyeless, with none of the spirit or expression of the Reynolds portraits, it yet dominates the Garret Room where Johnson and his assistants compiled the Dictionary.

It's haunting: an image of a dead man, a man stripped bare. Somehow it does bring you closer to what must have been the extraordinary power of Johnson's personality. And yet, would you want to keep such a memorial of your best friend on your sideboard?

Johnson and his friends accepted death as part of life; the ultimate resolution. We, however, in spite of our rational secularism, tend now to hurry away our dead, or else to indulge in outbursts of absurd sentimentalism. Few among us would be able to contemplate our end with such composure as Johnson, both devout and rational.

Studied Barbarity: Johnson, Spenser, and Literary Progress

Neat "meta-narratives" of literary history are a favorite

target of recent critics, justly suspicious of teleological accounts of literary development. One of the most significant of these meta-narratives is the Renaissance, the progression from Medieval barbarism toward modern enlightenment, but this notion of an emergence from rudeness to refinement has come under fire from recent critics. The nineteenth century has so far provided much of the ammunition for this reversionary assault, and it is only natural that Schiller, Burckhardt, Pater, Hegel, and Marx should be central in the project. But Augustan critics were formulating their own ideas about the Renaissance, and we can gain a great deal of insight by looking at their approach to, say, Shakespeare or Milton. We can perhaps gain even more by looking at the problem cases. The third member of the English Renaissance poetic triumvirate, Edmund Spenser, was manifestly one of these problems, and he fit uneasily in the eighteenth century's progressive version of the Renaissance.

Spenser was much on the mind of Samuel Johnson, one of the most active and important of those developing our notion of the Renaissance — not in any extended treatment, but in scattered comments from the 1730s through the '80s. Spenser's position in Johnson's thought has received little attention, but tugging on these Spenserian loose ends reveals a thread woven across the entire fabric of Johnson's criticism. Focusing on Johnson and his age may help us better understand the meta-narrative called the Renaissance, and focusing on the rise of the Renaissance may in turn help us better understand Johnson and his age.

The word "Renaissance" was not englished until around 1840, but the lack of the term did not prevent Johnson's contemporaries from recognizing the phenomenon. Johnson himself refers, for instance, to "the Revival of Learning in Europe," and dates "the golden age of our language" from "the accession of Elizabeth."

The metaphors used for this period show the importance of progression: "refinement," for instance, a metaphor from metallurgy, suggests that modern purity came from burning away the imperfections of the past; "cultivation" suggests our arable land once lay fallow. Impressing readers with the darkness of the Dark Ages was *de rigueur* for early eighteenth-century writers such as Addison, for whom the Middle Ages were a time of "Darkness and Superstition." Critics whose interest in Medieval authors extended beyond mere antiquarianism valued only their anticipation of what was to come. Winstanley, for instance, finds Gower "the first refiner of our *English* Tongue," and praises Chaucer's "earnest desire to enrich and beautifie our *English* Tongue, which in those days was very rude and barren." Writers who were not part of this march from rudeness to refinement were ill regarded. Skelton, for example, is "now accounted only a Rhymer," and "Whoso reads him, will find he hath a miserable, loose, rambling Style;... yet were good Poets so scarce in his Age, that he had the good fortune to be chosen Poet Laureat."

Like Skelton, Spenser sat uncomfortably in a tradition that valued forward-looking authors, and he was therefore a problem for the eighteenth century. Spenser, somewhere between Medieval rudeness and modern civilization, perversely refused to let go of what appeared to be vulgar errors, and could not be reconciled with progressive Augustan critical bromides. This peculiar failure of Spenser's judgment led to scathing attacks, of which Addison's dismissal is typical: "But now the mystic tale, that pleas'd of yore,/ Can charm an understanding age no more."

The lapses in Spenser's taste can be arranged under three heads: design, allegory, and language. Most upsetting is his disregard for the Aristotelian unity of action. The romance design, with its Ariostan *entrelacement* and multiple heroes, was no more appreciated by early eighteenth-century critics than by those of the Renaissance. Allegory, another holdover from the Dark Ages, was also scorned: as Addison complains, "The long-spun allegories fulsome grow,/ While the dull moral lies too plain below." And Spenser's metrical "imperfections" and his archaic diction were considered more perverse than charming before mid-century.

This paradox frustrated eighteenth-century critics, who found that his poetical power, for all its faults, could be neither denied nor resisted. Spenser, educated in the classics in an enlightened age, rejected many aesthetic principles the eighteenth century held not only dear but self-evident. Johnson's censure of Spenser's "studied barbarity" is one expression of this frustration; Hughes's account is another: "It may seem strange indeed, since *Spenser* appears to have been well acquainted with the best Writers of Antiquity, that he has not imitated them."

Even Spenser's defenders had to admit he was incompatible with the Renaissance-as-progression paradigm, and this contributed to the changes in critical sensibility over the course of the century. Hughes was among the first to formulate an aesthetics different from the classical inheritance, an early stage in the development of a new Romantic sensibility. He begins with an architectural metaphor picked up from Rymer, who confesses "I have thought our Poetry of the last Age was as rude as our Architecture." What was censure in Rymer is praise in Hughes:

> Indeed the whole Frame of it wou'd appear monstrous, if it were to be examin'd by the Rules of Epick Poetry.... But... the Author never design'd it by these Rules.... To compare it therefore with the Models of Antiquity, wou'd be like drawing a Parallel between the *Roman* and the *Gothick* Architecture.... Tho the former is more majestick in the whole, the latter may be very surprizing and agreeable in its Parts.

This Gothic aesthetic grew, with the help of others like Warton and Hurd, over the course of the century. Spenser provided, along with Percy's ballads, a rallying-cry for a generation of Romantic critics engaged in rewriting the eighteenth century's version of literary history.

Samuel Johnson not only witnessed this change; he was a major participant in it. But he was also an important representative of the earlier sensibility, who in many ways agrees with the progressive paradigm for the Renaissance. He contrasts the na‹vet, of earlier ages with Elizabethan enlightenment: in the Preface to the *Dictionary*, for instance, he writes, "Every language has a time of rudeness antecedent to perfection." Likewise the Preface to Shakespeare: "Nations, like individuals, have their infancy.... The study of those who then aspired to plebeian learning was laid out upon adventures, giants, dragons, and enchantments." The best Renaissance writers slew these dragons, and "*Sidney*'s work" is therefore "the boundary, beyond which I make few excursions. From the authors which rose in the time of *Elizabeth*, a speech might be formed adequate to all the purposes of use and elegance."

Spenser is a major figure in this age of awakening, and Johnson's interest — even fascination — with Spenser was lifelong. In *Idler*, for instance, Johnson "consider[s] the whole succession [of poets] from Spenser to Pope, as superiour to any names which the continent can boast." Spenser appears nearly three thousand times in the *Dictionary*, and gives Johnson his designation for "the writers before the restoration, whose works I regard as *the wells of English undefiled*."

But for all his fondness of Spenser, Johnson saw the same problems as his contemporaries, and they produced in him the same tensions. He refused, however, to let *a priori* notions of periodization direct his reading. His comment on the object of critical inquiry is well known: "It is... the task of criticism to establish principles; to improve opinion into knowledge." This task includes rendering the past intelligible by building historical narratives. But though the rules and schemata have their place, the empiricist critic must also

> distinguish those means of pleasing which depend upon known causes and rational deduction, from the nameless and inexplicable elegancies... which may well be termed the enchantresses of the soul. Criticism reduces those regions of literature under the dominion of science, which have hitherto known only the anarchy of ignorance, the caprices of fancy, and the tyranny of prescription.

Johnson wants, where possible, to explain away the "enchantresses of the soul" by annexing their territory into the realm of literary history, but he recognizes — perhaps uncomfortably — that some authors cannot, and should not, be subdued. Guarding against "the tyranny of prescription," therefore, is as important as reducing literature to rules.

Of the three categories considered above—design, allegory, and language—Johnson says nothing about Spenser's design, but we can speculate on his opinion. Though he was instrumental in removing the unities of time and place from English criticism, he preserved one Neoclassical unity — "nothing is essential to the fable, but unity of action" — and here Spenser is manifestly deficient. But up rises Johnson's empiricism: "Since the end of poetry is pleasure, that cannot be unpoetical with which all are pleased," and this critical honesty accounts for his fondness for Medieval romances.

This honesty accounts for many of his departures from the taste of his age. Though allegory was widely condemned, Spenser the allegorist was dear to Johnson. Boswell notes that he "praised John Bunyan highly," and that Johnson said "There is reason to think that he had read Spenser." His own allegorical writings owe much to Spenser; the personified Truth and Falsehood of *Rambler*, for instance, and "the 'Gulph of Intemperance,' a dreadful whirlpool, interspersed with rocks" in *Rambler* echo specific passages in *The Faerie Queene*. His *Vision of Theodore* is especially reminiscent of Spenser's allegory, while the title of his never-completed *"Palace of Sloth, — a vision"* has an unmistakable Spenserian ring.

Language is a more considerable problem than design or allegory. No party-line ancient or modern, Johnson considers language neither degenerative nor progressive, but he does see in it a kind of development or trajectory: "Every language has a time of rudeness antecedent to perfection, as well as of false refinement and declension." This is not historical relativism but its opposite; it suggests a trans-historical linguistic ideal, an ideal to which ages succeed or fail in attaining. The Renaissance marks the beginning of this linguistic perfection.

Johnson's concern for this ideal made him uneasy at seeing "the imitation of Spenser... likely to gain upon the age," and Spenser's unmusical stanza and versification were especially loathsome: the imitators

> seem to conclude, that when they have disfigured their lines with a few obsolete syllables, they have accomplished

their design.... Perhaps... the stile of Spenser might by long labour be justly copied; but life is surely given us for higher purposes than to gather what our ancestors have wisely thrown away.

Johnson here is able to "conside[r] the metrical art simply as a science," a positivist science in which the clear failures of the past should be abandoned, and in which modern poets can advance by degrees beyond their precursors.

Johnson also faults Spenser's diction, which he, like Ben Jonson, found to be "no language." *The Shepheardes Calender* draws Johnson's scorn for its "obsolete terms and rustick words, which they very learnedly call Dorick"; this "studied barbarity" calls forth Johnson's most devastating sarcasm: "Surely at the same time that a shepherd learns theology," he writes acidly, "he may gain some acquaintance with his native language." Johnson's dismissal of Spenser's archaism shows the critical tension Johnson felt at discovering major failings in a major poet, a poet who could not be rescued from "the nameless and inexplicable elegancies which appeal wholly to the fancy." It shows, in short, the limits of systematic criticism.

That Spenser could draw both the highest approbation and the most stinging sarcasm leads us to seek Johnson's particular notion of the Renaissance, one that admits Spenserian allegory but not Spenser's language. A candidate for the kind of progress he saw in the Renaissance appears throughout his works; one especially clear statement comes in his praise of Homer:

His positions are general, and his representations natural, with very little dependence on local or temporary customs, on those changeable scenes of artificial life, which, by mingling original with accidental notions, and crowding the mind with images, which time effaces, produce ambiguity in diction, and obscurity in books. To this open display of unadulterated nature it must be ascribed, that Homer has fewer passages of doubtful meaning than any other poet either in the learned or in modern languages.

Here is one of Johnson's favorite pairs of polar opposites, generality *versus* "accident," and I suggest Johnson saw the

Renaissance as Europe's passage from one pole to the other. Faux Medieval diction is a recollection of the "remote allusions and obscure opinions" of a justly forgotten age. These are Johnson's targets in his attacks on Spenser's obfuscatory archaism, which leads only to "obscurity in books," and which time justly "effaces."

Generality and "unadulterated nature," on the other hand, are dissociated from "changeable scenes of artificial life" with their "accidental notions" — the very business of allegory, which works by moving from the specific to the general. Allegory educates us in generality, teaching us not to depend on the "local and temporary customs" of the Middle Ages. The "revival of learning" amounts to the revival of general nature, the nature that appears in Shakespeare at his most "universal."

The Renaissance is therefore Europe's maturity, its accession to general nature, its abandonment of the peculiarities of archaism. But even the most mature literature has room for the generality of allegory, the bridge between the details consigned to antiquarians and the universal nature valuable to every reader, just as the Renaissance is the bridge between darkness and light. Spenser more than any other poet is the wedge that splits allegory from archaism, and forces Johnson's empirical criticism to come to terms with Renaissance poetic progress.

Life of Milton by Samuel Johnson

Such was the simple and unpretending advertisement that announced the Lives of the English Poets; a work that gave to the British nation a new style of biography. Johnson's decided taste for this species of writing, and his familiarity with the works of those whose lives he has recorded, peculiarly fitted him for the task; but it has been denounced by some as dogmatically, and even morose; minute critics have detected inaccuracies; the admirers of particular authors have complained of an insufficiency of praise to the objects of their fond and exclusive regard; and the political zealot has affected to decry the staunch and unbending champion of regal and ecclesiastical rights. Those, again, of high and imaginative minds, who "lift themselves up to look to the sky of poetry, and far removed from the dull-making cataract of Nilus, listen to the planet-like music of poetry;" these accuse Johnson of a heavy and insensible soul, because he avowed that nature's "world was brazen, and that the poets only delivered a golden."

But in spite of the censures of political opponents, private friends, and angry critics, it will be acknowledged, by the impartial, and by every lover of virtue and of truth, that Johnson's honest heart, penetrating mind, and powerful intellect, has given to the world memoirs fraught with what is infinitely more valuable than mere verbal criticism, or imaginative speculation; he has presented, in his Lives of the English Poets, the fruits of his long and careful examination of men and manners, and repeated in his age, with the authoritative voice of experience, the same dignified lessons of morality, with which he had instructed his readers in his earlier years. And if these lives contained few merits of their own, they confessedly amended the criticism of the nation, and opened the path to a more enlarged and liberal style of biography than had, before their publication, appeared.

The bold manner in which Johnson delivered what he believed to be the truth, naturally provoked hostile attack, and we are not prepared to say, that, in many instances, the strictures passed upon him might not be just. We will call the attention of our readers to some few of the charges brought against the work now before us, and then leave it to their candid and unbiased judgment to decide, whether the deficiencies pointed out are but as dust in the balance, when brought to weigh against the sterling excellence with which this last and greatest production of our Moralist abounds.

He has been accused of indulging a spirit of political animosity, of an illiberal and captious method of criticism, of frequent inaccuracies, and of a general haughtiness of manner, indicative of a feeling of superiority over the subjects of his memorial.

In the life of Milton his political prejudices are most apparent. It is not our duty, neither our inclination, in this place, to discuss the accuracy of Johnson's political wisdom. We cannot, however, but respect the integrity with which he clung to the instructions of his youth, amidst poverty, and all those inconveniencies, which usually drive men to a discontent with things as they are.

Those who censure him without qualification or reserve, are as bad, or worse, on the opposite side.

They accuse him of narrow-minded prejudice, and of bigoted attachment to powers that be with a rancour little befitting the liberality of which they make such vaunting professions. Johnson had a really benevolent heart, but despised and detested the affectation of a sentimental and universal philanthropy, which neglects the practical charities of home and kindred, in its wild and excursive flights after distant and romantic objects.

He was no tyrant, even in theory, but he dreaded, and, therefore, sought to expose, the lurking designs of those who opposed constituted authorities, because they hated subjection; and who, when they gained power themselves, proved the well-grounded nature of the fears entertained respecting their sincerity. Johnson was a firm English character, and his surly expressions were often philanthropy in disguise. They have little studied his real disposition, who impute his occasional austerity of manner to misanthropy at heart. The man who is smooth to all alike, is frequently the friend of none, and those who entertain no aversions, have, perhaps, few of the warmer emotions of friendship.

In dwelling thus long on a part of Johnson's character, on which we have elsewhere avowed that we could not speak with perfect pleasure, we are not attempting to vindicate him in all his violent reproaches of those whom he politically disliked. We would, however, wish to deprecate unmitigated condemnation, and also to ask, whether the conduct of those whom he denounced, was not, in its turn, so harsh and arbitrary, as almost to justify the utmost severity of censure. Were they not men who would "scarcely believe in the substance of their liberty, if they did not see it cast a shadow of slavery over others."

With respect to Johnson's powers as a critic, we confess that he had but little natural taste for poetry, as such; for that poetry of emotion which produces in its cultivators and admirers an intensity of excitement, to which language can scarcely afford an utterance, to which art can give no body, and which spreads a dream and a glory around us. All this Johnson felt not, and, therefore, understood not; for he wanted that deep feeling which is the only sure and unerring test of poetic excellence. He sought the didactic in poetry, and wished for reasoning in numbers.

Hence his undivided admiration of Pope and the French school, who cultivated exclusively the poetry of idea, where each moral problem is worked out with detailed, and often tedious, analysis; where all intense emotion is frittered away by a ratiocinative process. Johnson, we repeat, had no natural perception nor relish for the high and excursive range of poetic fancy, and the age at which he composed his criticisms on the English poets, was far advanced beyond that when purely imaginative poetry usually affords delight.

Hence, no doubt, proceeded his capricious strictures on the odes of Gray to which we, with painful candour, advert. In criticism and in poetry, for indignation only poured forth the torrent of his song, he kept steadily in view the interests of morality and virtue: these he would not compromise for the glitter of genius, and for their maintenance of these, the main objects of his own life and labour, he praised many an author whom other more courtly critics have thought it not cruelty to ridicule. He sums up his eulogium on a poet with the reflection, that he left No line which, dying, he could wish to blot.

Johnson has also not escaped animadversion for entitling his collection The Lives of the English Poets, when he has taken so confined a range. It must be remembered, that he only professed, in the first instance, to prefix lives to the works which the booksellers chose to publish; he was, therefore, confined to a task, at which he more than once expressed his repugnance to Boswell. It should also, in fairness to his memory, be borne in mind, that he wrote, as he confesses in his preface, from scanty materials, and on various authors. It was very easy, therefore, for each successive biographer, who devoted his time to the collection of memoirs for some single individual, to point out inaccuracies in Johnson's general statements; and very natural, also for one who had contracted an affection for the subject of his labours, by continually having him present in his thoughts, to carp at all those who were not as alive to the merits, and as blind to the defects of his idol as himself. But Johnson, feeling a manly consciousness of ability, which he affected not to hide, was not dazzled by the luster of brilliant talents, and was far too honest to veil from public view the faults and failings of the sons of genius. This he did not from a sour delight in detecting and exposing the frailties of his fellow men, but from a belief that, in so doing, he was promoting the good of mankind. "It is particularly the duty," says he, "of those who consign illustrious names to posterity, to take care lest their readers be misled by ambiguous examples. That writer may justly be condemned as an enemy to goodness, who suffers fondness or interest to confound right with wrong, or to shelter the faults, which even the wisest and the best have committed, from that ignominy which guilt ought always to suffer, and with which it should be more deeply stigmatized, when dignified by its neighbourhood to uncommon worth: since we shall be in danger of beholding it without abhorrence, unless its turpitude be laid open, and the eye secured from the deception of surrounding splendour." "If nothing but the bright side of characters should be shown," he once remarked to Malone, "we should sit down in despondency, and think it utterly impossible to imitate them in any thing." It was this conscientious freedom, we believe, that has, more than any other cause, subjected the Lives of the Poets to severe censure. We readily avow this our belief, since we are persuaded that it is now generally admitted by all, but those who are influenced by an irreligious or a party spirit. We might diffuse these remarks to a wide extent, by allusions to the opinions of different authors on the Lives, and by critiques on the separate memoirs themselves; but we will not longer occupy our readers, since the literary history of the

Lives has been elsewhere so fully detailed, and is now so almost universally known. What we have already advanced, has chiefly been with a view to invite to the perusal of a work, which, for sound criticism, instructive memoir, pleasing diction, and pure morality, must constitute the most lasting monument of Johnson's fame.

Chair of Medieval English Literature and Historical Linguistics

It is the fate of those who toil at the lower employments of life, to be rather driven by the fear of evil, than attracted by the prospect of good; to be exposed to censure, without hope of praise; to be disgraced by miscarriage, or punished for neglect, where success would have been without applause, and diligence without reward.

Among these unhappy mortals is the writer of dictionaries; whom mankind have considered, not as the pupil, but the slave of science, the pioneer of literature, doomed only to remove rubbish and clear obstructions from the paths through which Learning and Genius press forward to conquest and glory, without bestowing a smile on the humble drudge that facilitates their progress. Every other author may aspire to praise; the lexicographer can only hope to escape reproach, and even this negative recompense has been yet granted to very few.

I have, notwithstanding this discouragement, attempted a dictionary of the English language, which, while it was employed in the cultivation of every species of literature, has itself been hitherto neglected; suffered to spread, under the direction of chance, into wild exuberance; resigned to the tyranny of time and fashion; and exposed to the corruptions of ignorance, and caprices of innovation.

When I took the first survey of my undertaking, I found our speech copious without order, and energetic without rules: wherever I turned my view, there was perplexity to be disentangled, and confusion to be regulated; choice was to be made out of boundless variety, without any established principle of selection; adulterations were to be detected, without a settled test of purity; and modes of expression to be rejected or received, without the suffrages of any writers of classical reputation or acknowledged authority.

Having therefore no assistance but from general grammar, I applied myself to the perusal of our writers; and noting whatever might be of use to ascertain or illustrate any word or phrase, accumulated in time the materials of a dictionary, which, by degrees, I reduced to method, establishing to myself, in the progress of the work, such rules as experience and analogy suggested to me; experience, which practice and observation were continually increasing; and analogy, which, though in some words obscure, was evident in others.

In adjusting the ORTHOGRAPHY, which has been to this time unsettled and fortuitous, I found it necessary to distinguish those irregularities that are inherent in our tongue, and perhaps coeval with it, from others which the ignorance or negligence of later writers has produced. Every language has its anomalies, which, though inconvenient, and in themselves once unnecessary, must be tolerated among the imperfections of human things, and which require only to be registered, that they may not be increased, and ascertained, that they may not be confounded: but every language has likewise its improprieties and absurdities, which it is the duty of the lexicographer to correct or proscribe.

As language was at its beginning merely oral, all words of necessary or common use were spoken before they were written; and while they were unfixed by any visible signs, must have been spoken with great diversity, as we now observe those who cannot read catch sounds imperfectly, and utter them negligently. When this wild and barbarous jargon was first reduced to an alphabet, every penman endeavoured to express, as he could, the sounds which he was accustomed to pronounce or to receive, and vitiated in writing such words as were already vitiated in speech. The powers of the letters, when they were applied to a new language, must have been vague and unsettled, and therefore different hands would exhibit the same sound by different combinations.

From this uncertain pronunciation arise in a great part the

various dialects of the same country, which will always be observed to grow fewer, and less different, as books are multiplied; and from this arbitrary representation of sounds by letters, proceeds that diversity of spelling observable in the Saxon remains, and I suppose in the first books of every nation, which perplexes or destroys analogy, and produces anomalous formations, that, being once incorporated, can never be afterward dismissed or reformed.

Of this kind are the derivatives length from long, strength from strong, darling from dear, breadth from broad, from dry, drought, and from high, height, which Milton, in zeal for analogy, writes highth; Quid te exempta juvat spinis de pluribus una; to change all would be too much, and to change one is nothing. This uncertainty is most frequent in the vowels, which are so capriciously pronounced, and so differently modified, by accident or affectation, not only in every province, but in every mouth, that to them, as is well known to etymologists, little regard is to be shown in the deduction of one language from another. Such defects are not errors in orthography, but spots of barbarity impressed so deep in the English language, that criticism can never wash them away: these, therefore, must be permitted to remain untouched; but many words have likewise been altered by accident, or depraved by ignorance, as the pronunciation of the vulgar has been weakly followed; and some still continue to be variously written, as authors differ in their care or skill: of these it was proper to enquire the true orthography, which I have always considered as depending on their derivation, and have therefore referred them to their original languages: thus I write enchant, enchantment, enchanter, after the French and incantation after the Latin; thus entire is chosen rather than entire, because it passed to us not from the Latin integer, but from the French entire.

Of many words, it is difficult to say whether they were immediately received from the Latin or the French, since at the time when we had dominions in France, we had Latin service in our churches. It is, however, my opinion, that the French generally supplied us; for we have few Latin words, among the terms of domestic use, which are not French; but many French, which are very remote from Latin.

Even in words of which the derivation is apparent, I have been often obliged to sacrifice uniformity to custom; thus I write, in compliance with a numberless majority, convey and inveigh, deceit and receipt, fancy and phantom; sometimes the derivative varies from the primitive, as explain and explanation, repeat and repetition.

Some combinations of letters having the same power are used indifferently without any discoverable reason of choice, as in choak, choke; soap, sope; jewel, fuel, and many others; which I have sometimes inserted twice, that those who search for them under either form, may not search in vain.

In examining the orthography of any doubtful word, the mode of spelling by which it is inserted in the series of the dictionary, is to be considered as that to which I give, perhaps not often rashly, the preference. I have left, in the examples, to every author his own practice unmolested, that the reader may balance suffrages, and judge between us: but this question is not always to be determined by reputed or by real learning; some men, intent upon greater things, have thought little on sounds and derivations; some, knowing in the ancient tongues, have neglected those in which our words are commonly to be sought. Thus Hammond writes fecibleness for feasibleness, because I suppose he imagined it derived immediately from the Latin; and some words, such as dependant, dependent, dependence, dependence, vary their final syllable, as one or another language is present to the writer.

In this part of the work, where caprice has long wantoned without control, and vanity sought praise by petty reformation, I have endeavored to proceed with a scholar's reverence for antiquity, and a grammarian's regard to the genius of our tongue. I have attempted few alterations, and among those few, perhaps the greater part is from the modern to the ancient practice; and I hope I may be allowed to recommend to those, whose thoughts have been perhaps employed too anxiously on verbal singularities, not to disturb, upon narrow views, or for minute propriety, the orthography of their fathers. It has been asserted, that for the law to be KNOWN, is of more importance than to be RIGHT. Change, says Hooker, is not made without inconvenience, even from worse to better. There is in constancy and stability a general and lasting advantage, which will always overbalance the slow improvements of gradual correction. Much less ought our written language to comply with the corruptions of oral utterance, or copy that which every variation of time or place makes different from itself, and imitate those changes, which will again be changed, while imitation is employed in observing them.

This recommendation of steadiness and uniformity does not proceed from an opinion, that particular combinations of letters have much influence on human happiness; or that truth may not be successfully taught by modes of spelling fanciful And erroneous: I am not yet so lost in lexicography, as to I forget that WORDS ARE THE DAUGHTERS OF EARTH, AND THAT THINGS ARE THE SONS OF HEAVEN. Language is only the instrument of science, and words are but the signs of ideas: I wish, however, that the instrument might be less apt to decay, and that signs might be permanent, like the things, which they denote.

In settling the orthography, I have not wholly neglected the pronunciation, which I have directed, by printing an accent upon the acute or elevated syllable. It will sometimes be found, that the accent is placed by the author quoted, on a different syllable from that marked in the alphabetical series; it is then to be understood, that custom has varied, or that the author has, in my opinion, pronounced wrong. Short directions are sometimes given where the sound of letters is irregular; and if they are sometimes omitted, defect in such minute observations will be more easily excused, than superfluity.

In the investigation, both of the orthography and signification of words, their ETYMOLOGY was necessarily to be considered, and they were therefore to be divided into primitives and derivatives. A primitive word, is that which can be traced no further to any English root; thus circumspect, circumvent, circumstance, delude, concave and complicate, though compounds in the Latin, are to us primitives.

Derivatives are all those that can be referred to any word in English of greater simplicity.

The derivatives I have referred to their primitives, with an accuracy sometimes needless; for who does not see that remoteness comes from remote, lovely from love, concavity from concave, and demonstrative from demonstrate? but this grammatical exuberance the scheme of my work did not allow me to repress. It is of great importance in examining the general fabrick of a language, to trace one word from another, by noting the usual modes of derivation and inflection; and uniformity must be preserved in systematical works, though sometimes at the expanse of particular propriety.

Among other derivatives I have been careful to insert and elucidate the anomalous plurals of nouns and preterits of verbs, which in the Teutonick dialects are very frequent, and though familiar to those who have always used them, interrupt and embarrass the learners of our language.

The two languages from which our primitives have been derived are the Roman and Teutonick: under the Roman I comprehend the French and provincial tongues; and under the Teutonick range the Saxon, German, and all their kindred dialects. Most of our polysyllables are Roman, and our words of one syllable are very often Teutonick.

In assigning the Roman original, it has perhaps sometimes happened that I have mentioned only the Latin, when the word was borrowed from the French, and considering myself as employed only in the illustration of my own language, I have not been very careful to observe whether the Latin word be pure or barbarous, or the French elegant or obsolete.

For the Teutonick etymologies, I am commonly indebted to Junius and Skinner, the only names which I have forborn to quote when I copied their books; not that I might appropriate their labours or usurp their honours, but that I might spare a perpetual repetition by one general acknowledgment. Of these, whom I ought not to mention but with the reverence due to instructors and benefactors, Junius appears to have excelled in extent of learning, and Skinner in rectitude of understanding. Junius was accurately skilled in all the northern languages. Skinner probably examined the ancient and remoter dialects only by occasional inspection into dictionaries; but the learning of Junius is often of no other use than to show him a track by which he may deviate from his purpose, to which Skinner always presses forward by the shortest way. Skinner is often ignorant, but never ridiculous: Junius is always full of knowledge; but his variety distracts his judgment, and his learning is very frequently disgraced by his absurdities.

The votaries of the northern muses will not perhaps easily restrain their indignation, when they find the name of Junius thus degraded by a disadvantageous comparison; but whatever reverence is due to his diligence, or his attainments, it can be no criminal degree of censoriousness to charge that etymologist with want of judgment, who can seriously derive dream from drama, because life is a drama, and a drama is a dream? and who declares with a tone of defiance, that no man can fail to derive moan from [in greek], monos, single or solitary, who considers that grief naturally loves to be alone. [Footnote: That I may not appear to have spoken too irreverently of Junius, I have here subjoined a few Specimens of his etymological extravagance.

BANISH. religare, ex banno vel territorio exigere, in exilium agere. G. bannir. It. bandire, bandeggiare. H. bandir. B. bannen. AEvi medii s criptores bannire dicebant. V. Spelm. in Bannum & in Banleuga. Quoniam vero regionum urbiumq; limites arduis plerumq; montibus, altis fluminibus, longis deniq; flexuosisq; angustissimarum viarum anfractibus includebantur, fieri potest id genus limites ban did ab eo quod [word in Greek] & [word in Greek] Tarentinis olim, sicuti tradit Hesychius, vocabantur [words in Greek], "obliquae ac minime in rectum tendentes viae." Ac fortasse quoque huc facit quod [word in Greek], eodem Hesychio teste, dicebant [words in greek] montes arduos.

Our knowledge of the northern literature is so scanty, that of words undoubtedly Teutonick the original is not always to be found in any ancient language; and I have therefore inserted Dutch or German substitutes, which I consider not as radical but parallel, not as the parents, but sisters of the English. The words which are represented as thus related by descent or cognation, do not always agree in sense; for it is incident to words, as to their authours, to degenerate from their ancestors, and to change their manners when they change their country. It is sufficient, in etymological enquiries, if the senses of kindred words be found such as may easily pass into each other, or such as may both be referred to one general idea.

The etymology, so far as it is yet known, was easily found in the volumes where it is particularly and professedly delivered; and, by proper attention to the rules of derivation, the orthography was soon adjusted. But to COLLECT the WORDS of our language was a task of greater difficulty: the deficiency of dictionaries was immediately apparent; and when they were exhausted, what was yet wanting must be sought by fortuitous and unguided excursions into books, and gleaned as industry should find, or chance should offer it, in the boundless chaos of a living speech. My search, however, has been either skilful or lucky; for I have much augmented the vocabulary.

As my design was a dictionary, common or appellative, I have omitted all words which have relation to proper names; such as Arian, Socinian, Calvinist, Benedictine, Mahometan; but have retained those of a more general nature, as Heathen, Pagan. Of the terms of art I have received such as could be found either in books of science or technical dictionaries; and have often inserted, from philosophical writers, words which are supported perhaps only by a single authority, and which being not admitted into general use, stand yet as candidates or probationers, and must depend for their adoption on the suffrage of futurity.

The words which our authors have introduced by their knowledge of foreign languages, or ignorance of their own, by vanity or wantonness, by compliance with fashion or lust of innovation, I have registered as they occurred, though commonly only to censure them, and warn others against the folly of naturalizing useless foreigners to the injury of the natives.

I have not rejected any by design, merely because they were unnecessary or exuberant; but have received those which by different writers have been differently formed, as viscid, and viscidity, viscous, and viscosity.

Compounded or double words I have seldom noted, except when they obtain a signification different from that which the components have in their simple state. Thus highwayman, woodman, and horse courser, require an explanation; but of thief like or coach driver no notice was needed, because the primitives contain the meaning of the compounds.

Words arbitrarily formed by a constant and settled analogy, like diminutive adjectives in ish, as greenish, bluish, adverbs in ly, as dully, openly, substantives in ness, as vileness, faultiness, were less diligently sought, and sometimes have been omitted, when I had no authority that invited me to insert them; not that they are not genuine and regular off springs of English roots, but because their relation to the primitive being always the same, their signification cannot be mistaken.

The verbal nouns in ing, such as the keeping of the castle, the leading of the army, are always neglected, or placed only to illustrate the sense of the verb, except when they signify things as well as actions, and have therefore a plural number, as dwelling, living; or have an absolute and abstract signification, as colouring, painting, learning.

The participles are likewise omitted, unless, by signifying rather habit or quality than action, they take the nature of adjectives; as a thinking man, a man of prudence; a pacing horse, a horse that can pace: these I have ventured to call participial adjectives. But neither are these always inserted, because they are commonly to be understood, without any danger of mistake, by consulting the verb.

Obsolete words are admitted, when they are found in authors not obsolete, or when they have any force or beauty that may deserve revival.

As composition is one of the chief characteristics of a language, I have endeavored to make some reparation for the universal negligence of my predecessors, by inserting great numbers of compounded words, as may be found under after, fore, new, night, fair, and many more. These, numerous as they are, might be multiplied, but that use and curiosity are here satisfied, and the frame of our language and modes of our combination amply discovered.

Of some forms of composition, such as that by which re is prefixed to note repetition, and un to signify contrariety or privation, all the examples cannot be accumulated, because the use of these particles, if not wholly arbitrary, is so little limited, that they are hourly affixed to new words as occasion requires, or is imagined to require them.

There is another kind of composition more frequent in our language than perhaps in any other, from which arises to foreigners the greatest difficulty. We modify the signification of many verbs by a particle subjoined; as to come off, to escape by a fetch; to fall on, to attack; to fall off, to apostatize; to break off, to stop abruptly; to bear out, to justify; to fall in, to comply; to give over, to cease; to set off, to embellish; to set in, to begin a continual tenure; to set out, to begin a course or journey; to take off, to copy; with innumerable expressions of the same kind, of which some appear wildly irregular, being so far distant from the sense of the simple words, that no sagacity will be able to trace the steps by which they arrived at the present use.

These I have noted with great care; and though I cannot flatter myself that the collection is complete, I believe I have so far assisted the students of our language, that this kind of phraseology will be no longer insuperable; and the combinations of verbs and particles, by chance omitted, will be easily explained by comparison with those that may be found.

Many words yet stand supported only by the name of Bailey, Ainsworth, Philips, or the contracted Dict. for Dictionaries subjoined; of these I am not always certain that they are read in any book but the works of lexicographers. Of such I have omitted many, because I had never read them; and many I have inserted, because they may perhaps exist, though they have escaped my notice: they are, however, to be yet considered as resting only upon the credit of former dictionaries. Others, which I considered as useful, or know to be proper, though I could not at present support them by authorities, I have suffered to stand upon my own attestation, claiming the same privilege with my predecessors of being sometimes credited without proof.

The words, thus selected and disposed, are grammatically considered; they are referred to the different parts of speech; traced, when they are irregularly inflected, through their various terminations; and illustrated by observations, not indeed of great or striking importance, separately considered, but necessary to the elucidation of our language, and hitherto neglected or forgotten by English grammarians.

That part of my work on which I expect malignity most frequently to fasten, is the explanation; in which I cannot hope to satisfy those, who are perhaps not inclined to be pleased, since I have not always been able to satisfy myself. To interpret a language by itself is very difficult; many words cannot be explained by synonymies, because the idea signified by them has not more than one appellation; nor by paraphrase, because simple ideas cannot be described. When the nature of things is unknown, or the notion unsettled and indefinite, and various in various minds, the words by which such notions are conveyed, or such things denoted, will be ambiguous and perplexed. And such is the fate of hapless lexicography, that not only darkness, but light, impedes and distresses it; things may be not only too little, but too much known, to be happily illustrated. To explain, requires the use of terms less abstruse than that which is to be explained, and such terms cannot always be found; for as nothing can be proved but by supposing something intuitively known, and evident without proof, so nothing can be defined but by the use of words too plain to admit a definition.

Other words there are, of which the sense is too subtle and evanescent to be fixed in a paraphrase; such are all those which are by the grammarians termed expletives, and, in dead languages, are suffered to pass for empty sounds, of no other use than to fill a verse, or to modulate a period, but which are easily perceived in living tongues to have power and emphasis, though it be sometimes such as no other form of expression can convey. My labour has likewise been much increased by a class of verbs too frequent in the English language, of which the signification is so loose and general, the use so vague and indeterminate, and the senses detorted so widely from the first idea, that it is hard to trace them through the maze of variation, to catch them on the brink of utter inanity, to circumscribe them by any limitations, or interpret them by any words of distinct and settled meaning; such are bear, break, come, cast, full, get, give, do, put, set, go, run, make, take, turn, throw.

If of these the whole power is not accurately delivered, it must be remembered, that while our language is yet living, and variable by the caprice of every one that speaks it, these words are hourly shifting their relations, and can no more be ascertained in a dictionary, than a grove, in the agitation of a storm, can be accurately delineated from its picture in the water. The particles are among all nations applied with so great latitude, that they are not easily reducible under any regular scheme of explication: this difficulty is not less, nor perhaps greater, in English, than in other languages. I have laboured them with diligence, I hope with success; such at least as can be expected in a task, which no man, however learned or sagacious, has yet been able to perform.

Some words there are which I cannot explain, because I do not understand them; these might have been omitted very often with little inconvenience, but I would not so far indulge my vanity as to decline this confession: for when Tully owns himself ignorant whether lessus, in the twelve tables, means a funeral song, or mourning garment; and Aristotle doubts whether [word in Greek] in the Iliad, signifies a mule, or muleteer, I may surely, without shame, leave some obscurities to happier industry, or future information.

The rigor of interpretative lexicography requires that the explanation, and the word explained, should always be reciprocal; this I have always endeavored, but could not always attain. Words are seldom exactly synonymous; a new term was not introduced, but because the former was thought inadequate: names, therefore, have often many ideas, but few ideas have many names. It was then necessary to use the proximate word, for the deficiency of single terms can very seldom be supplied by circumlocution; nor is the inconvenience great of such mutilated interpretations, because the sense may easily be collected entire from the examples.

In every word of extensive use, it was requisite to mark the progress of its meaning, and show by what gradations of intermediate sense it has passed from its primitive to its remote and accidental signification; so that every foregoing explanation should tend to that which follows, and the series be regularly concatenated from the first notion to the last.

This is specious, but not always practicable; kindred senses may be so interwoven, that the perplexity cannot be disentangled, nor any reason be assigned why one should be ranged before the other. When the radical idea branches out into parallel ramifications, how can a consecutive series be formed of senses in their nature collateral? The shades of meaning sometimes pass imperceptibly into each other; so that though on one side they apparently differ, yet it is impossible to mark the point of contact. Ideas of the same race, though not exactly alike, are sometimes so little different, that no words can express the dissimilitude, though the mind easily perceives it, when they are exhibited together; and sometimes there is such a confusion of acceptations, that discernment is wearied, and distinction puzzled, and perseverance herself hurries to an end, by crouding together what she cannot separate.

These complaints of difficulty will, by those that have never considered words beyond their popular use, be thought only the jargon of a man willing to magnify his labours, and procure veneration to his studies by involution and obscurity. But every art is obscure to those that have not learned it: this uncertainty of terms, and commixture of ideas, is well known to those who have joined philosophy with grammar; and if I have not expressed them very clearly, it must be remembered that I am speaking of that which words are insufficient to explain.

The original sense of words is often driven out of use by their metaphorical acceptations, yet must be inserted for the sake of a regular origination. Thus I know not whether ardour is used for material heat, or whether flagrant, in English, ever signifies the same with burning; yet such are the primitive ideas of these words, which are therefore set first, though without examples, that the figurative senses may be commodiously deduced.

Such is the exuberance of signification which many words have obtained, that it was scarcely possible to collect all their senses; sometimes the meaning of derivatives must be sought in the mother term, and sometimes deficient explanations of the primitive may be supplied in the train of derivation. In any case, of doubt or difficulty, it will be always proper to examine all the words of the same race; for some words are slightly passed over to avoid repetition, some admitted easier and clearer explanation than others, and all will be better understood, as they are considered in greater variety of structures and relations.

All the interpretations of words are not written with the same skill, or the same happiness: things equally easy in themselves, are not all equally easy to any single mind. Every writer of a long work commits errors, where there appears neither ambiguity to mislead, nor obscurity to confound him; and in a search like this, many felicities of expression will be casually overlooked, many convenient parallels will be forgotten, and many particulars will admit improvement from a mind utterly unequal to the whole performance.

But many seeming faults are to be imputed rather to the nature of the undertaking, than the negligence of the performer. Thus some explanations are unavoidably reciprocal or circular, as hind, the female of the stag; stag, the male of the hind: sometimes easier words are changed into harder, as burial into sepulture or interment, drier into desiccative, dryness into sic city or aridity, fit into paroxysm; for the easiest word, whatever it be, can never be translated into one more easy. But easiness and difficulty are merely relative, and if the present prevalence of our language should invite foreigners to this dictionary, many will be assisted by those words which now seem only to increase or produce obscurity. For this reason I have endeavoured frequently to join a Teutonick and Roman interpretation, as to cheer, to gladden, or exhilarate, that every learner of English may be assisted by his own tongue. The solution of all difficulties, and the supply of all defects, must be sought in the examples, subjoined to the various senses of each word, and ranged according to the time of their authors.

When first I collected these authorities, I was desirous that every quotation should be useful to some other end than the illustration of a word; I therefore extracted from philosophers principles of science; from historians remarkable facts; from chemists complete processes; from divines striking exhortations; and from poets beautiful descriptions. Such is design, while it is yet at a distance from execution. When the time called upon me to range this accumulation of elegance and wisdom into an alphabetical series, I soon discovered that the bulk of my volumes would fright away the student, and was forced to depart from my scheme of including all that was pleasing or useful in English literature, and reduce my transcripts very often to clusters of words, in which scarcely any meaning is retained; thus to the weariness of copying, I was condemned to add the vexation of expunging. Some passages I have yet spared, which may relieve the labour of verbal searches, and intersperse with verdure and flowers the dusty deserts of barren philology.

The examples, thus mutilated, are no longer to be considered as conveying the sentiments or doctrine of their authors; the word for the sake of which they are inserted, with all its appendant clauses, has been carefully preserved; but it may sometimes happen, by hasty detruncating, that the general tendency of the sentence may be changed: the divine may desert his tenets, or the philosopher his system.

Some of the examples have been taken from writers who were never mentioned as masters of elegance or models of stile; but words must be sought where they are used; and in what pages, eminent for purity, can terms of manufacture or agriculture be found? Many quotations serve no other purpose, than that of proving the bare existence of words, and are therefore selected with less scrupulousness than those which are to teach their structures and relations.

My purpose was to admit no testimony of living authors, that I might not be misled by partiality, and that none of my cotemporaries might have reason to complain; nor have I departed from this resolution, but when some performance of uncommon excellence excited my veneration, when my memory supplied me, from late books, with an example that was wanting, or when my heart, in the tenderness of friendship, solicited admission for a favorite name.

So far have I been from any care to grace my pages with modern decorations, that I have studiously endeavoured to collect examples and authorities from the writers before the restoration, whose works I regard as the wells of English undefiled, as the pure sources of genuine diction. Our language, for almost a century, has, by the concurrence of many causes, been gradually departing from its original Teutonick character, and deviating towards a Gallick structure and phraseology, from which it ought to be our endeavour to recal it, by making our ancient volumes the ground-work of stile, admitting among the additions of later times, only such as may supply real deficiencies, such as are readily adopted by the genius of our tongue, and incorporate easily with our native idioms.

But as every language has a time of rudeness antecedent to perfection, as well as of false refinement and declension, I have been cautious lest my zeal for antiquity might drive me into times too remote, and crowd my book with words now no longer understood. I have fixed Sidney's work for the boundary, beyond which I make few excursions. From the authors, which rose in the time of Elizabeth, a speech might be formed adequate to all the purposes of use and elegance. If the language of theology were extracted from Hooker and the translation of the Bible; the terms of natural knowledge from Bacon; the phrases of policy, war, and navigation from Raleigh; the dialect of poetry and fiction from Spenser and Sidney; and the diction of common life from Shakespeare, few ideas would be lost to mankind, for want of English words, in which they might be expressed.

It is not sufficient that a word is found, unless it be so combined as that its meaning is apparently determined by the tract and tenure of the sentence; such passages I have therefore chosen, and when it happened that any authour gave a definition of a term, or such an explanation as is equivalent to a definition, I have placed his authority as a supplement to my own, without regard to the chronological order, that is otherwise observed.

Some words, indeed, stand unsupported by any authority, but they are commonly derivative nouns or adverbs, formed from their primitives by regular and constant analogy, or names of things seldom occurring in books, or words of which I have reason to doubt the existence.

There is more danger of censure from the multiplicity than paucity of examples; authorities will sometimes seem to have been accumulated without necessity or use, and perhaps some will be found, which might, without loss, have been omitted. But a work of this kind is not hastily to be charged with superfluities: those quotations, which to careless or unskillful perusers appear only to repeat the same sense, will often exhibit, to a more accurate examiner, diversities of signification, or, at least, afford different shades of the same meaning: one will show the word applied to persons, another to things; one will express an ill, another a good, and a third a neutral sense; one will prove the expression genuine from an ancient author; another will show it elegant from a modern: a doubtful authority is corroborated by another of more credit; an ambiguous sentence is ascertained by a passage clear and determinate; the word, how often so ever repeated, appears with new associates and in different combinations, and every quotation contributes something to the stability or enlargement of the language. When words are used equivocally, I receive them in either sense; when they are metaphorical, I adopt them in their primitive acceptation. I have sometimes, though rarely, yielded to the temptation of exhibiting a genealogy of sentiments, by showing how one author copied the thoughts and diction of another: such quotations are indeed little more than repetitions, which might justly be censured, did they not gratify the mind, by affording a kind of intellectual history.

The various syntactical structures occurring in the examples have been carefully noted; the license or negligence with which many words have been hitherto used, has made our stile capricious and indeterminate; when the different combinations of the same word are exhibited together, the preference is readily given to propriety, and I have often endeavored to direct the choice.

Thus have I laboured by settling the orthography, displaying the analogy, regulating the structures, and ascertaining the signification of English words, to perform all the parts of a faithful lexicographer: but I have not always executed my own scheme, or satisfied my own expectations. The work, whatever proofs of diligence and attention it may exhibit, is yet capable of many improvements: the orthography which I recommend is still controvertible, the etymology which I adopt is uncertain, and perhaps frequently erroneous; the explanations are sometimes too much contracted, and sometimes too much diffused, the significations are distinguished rather with subtlety than skill, and the attention is harassed with unnecessary minuteness.

The examples are too often injudiciously truncated, and perhaps sometimes, I hope very rarely, alleged in a mistaken sense; for in making this collection I trusted more to memory, than, in a state of disquiet and embarrassment, memory can contain, and purposed to supply at the review what was left incomplete in the first transcription.

Many terms appropriated to particular occupations, though necessary and significant, are undoubtedly omitted; and of the words most studiously considered and exemplified, many senses have escaped observation.

Yet these failures, however frequent, may admit extenuation and apology. To have attempted much is always laudable, even when the enterprise is above the strength that undertakes it: To rest below his own aim is incident to every one whose fancy is active, and whose views are comprehensive; nor is any man satisfied with himself because he has done much, but because he can conceive little. When first I engaged in this work, I resolved to leave neither words nor things unexamined, and pleased myself with a prospect of the hours which I should revel away in feasts of literature, with the obscure recesses of northern learning, which I should enter and ransack; the treasures with which I expected every search into those neglected mines to reward my labour, and the triumph with which I should display my acquisitions to mankind. When I had thus enquired into the original of words, I resolved to show likewise my attention to things; to pierce deep into every science, to enquire the nature of every substance of which I inserted the name, to limit every idea by a definition strictly logical, and exhibit every production of art or nature in an accurate description, that my book might be in place of all other dictionaries whether appellative or technical. But these were the dreams of a poet doomed at last to wake a lexicographer.

I soon found that it is too late to look for instruments, when the work calls for execution, and that whatever abilities I had brought to my task, with those I must finally perform it. To deliberate whenever I doubted, to enquire whenever I was ignorant, would have protracted the undertaking without end, and, perhaps, without much improvement; for I did not find by my first experiments, that that I had not of my own was easily to be obtained: I saw that one enquiry only gave occasion to another, that book referred to book, that to search was not always to find, and to find was not always to be informed; and that thus to persue perfection, was, like the first inhabitants of Arcadia, to chace the sun, which, when they had reached the hill where he seemed to rest, was still beheld at the same distance from them.

I then contracted my design, determining to confide in myself, and no longer to solicit auxiliaries, which produced more encumbrance than assistance: by this I obtained at least one advantage, that I set limits to my work, which would in time be ended, though not completed.

Despondency has never so far prevailed as to depress me to negligence; some faults will at last appear to be the effects of anxious diligence and persevering activity. The nice and subtle ramifications of meaning were not easily avoided by a mind intent upon accuracy, and convinced of the necessity of disentangling combinations, and separating similitudes. Many of the distinctions which to common readers appear useless and idle, will be found real and important by men versed in the school philosophy, without which no dictionary shall ever be accurately compiled, or skillfully examined. Some senses however, there are, which, though not the same, are yet so nearly allied, that they are often confounded. Most men think indistinctly, and therefore cannot speak with exactness; and consequently some examples might be indifferently put to either signification: this uncertainty is not to be imputed to me, who do not form, but register the language; who do not teach men how they should think, but relate how they have hitherto expressed their thoughts.

The imperfect sense of some examples I lamented, but could not remedy, and hope they will be compensated by innumerable passages selected with propriety, and preserved with exactness; some shining with sparks of imagination, and some replete with treasures of wisdom. The orthography and etymology, though imperfect, are not imperfect for want of care, but because care will not always be successful, and recollection or information come too late for use.

That many terms of art and manufacture are omitted, must be frankly acknowledged; but for this defect I may boldly allege that it was unavoidable: I could not visit caverns to learn the miner's language, nor take a voyage to perfect my skill in the dialect of navigation, nor visit the warehouses of merchants, and shops of artificers, to gain the names of wares, tools and operations, of which no mention is found in books; what favorable accident, or easy enquiry brought within my reach, has not been neglected; but it had been a hopeless labor to glean up words, by courting living information, and contesting with the sullenness of one, and the roughness of another.

To furnish the academicians della Crusca with words of this kind, a series of comedies called la Fiera, or the Fair, was professedly written by Buonaroti; but I had no such assistant, and therefore was content to want what they must have wanted likewise, had they not luckily been so supplied.

Nor are all words which are not found in the vocabulary, to be lamented as omissions. Of the laborious and mercantile part of the people, the diction is in a great measure casual and mutable; many of their terms are formed for some temporary or local convenience, and though current at certain times and places, are in others utterly unknown. This fugitive cant, which is always in a state of increase or decay, cannot be regarded as any part of the durable materials of a language, and therefore must be suffered to perish with other things unworthy of preservation.

Care will sometimes betray to the appearance of negligence. He that is catching opportunities which seldom occur, will suffer those to pass by unregarded, which he expects hourly to return; he that is searching for rare and remote things, will neglect those that are obvious and familiar: thus many of the most common and cursory words have been inserted with little illustration, because in gathering the authorities, I forbore to copy those which I thought likely to occur whenever they were wanted. It is remarkable that, in reviewing my collection, I found the word sea unexemplified.

Thus it happens, that in things difficult there is danger from ignorance, and in things easy from confidence; the mind, afraid of greatness, and disdainful of littleness, hastily withdraws herself from painful searches, and passes with scornful rapidity over tasks not adequate to her powers, sometimes too secure for caution, and again too anxious for vigorous effort; sometimes idle in a plain path, and sometimes distracted in labyrinths, and dissipated by different intentions.

A large work is difficult because it is large, even though all its parts might singly be performed with facility; where there are many things to be done, each must be allowed its share of time and labour, in the proportion only which it bears to the whole; nor can it be expected, that the stones which form the dome of a temple, should be squared and polished like the diamond of a ring.

Of the event of this work, for which, having laboured it with so much application, I cannot but have some degree of parental fondness, it is natural to form conjectures. Those who have been persuaded to think well of my design, will require that it should fix our language, and put a stop to those alterations which time and chance have hitherto been suffered to make in it without opposition. With this consequence I will confess that I flattered myself for a while; but now begin to fear that I have indulged expectation which neither reason nor experience can justify. When we see men grow old and die at a certain time one after another, from century to century, we laugh at the elixir that promises to prolong life to a thousand years; and with equal justice may the lexicographer be derided, who being able to produce no example of a nation that has preserved their words and phrases from mutability, shall imagine that his dictionary can embalm his language, and secure it from corruption and decay, that it is in his power to change sublunary nature, and clear the world at once from folly, vanity, and affectation.

With this hope, however, academies have been instituted, to guard the avenues of their languages, to retain fugitives, and repulse intruders; but their vigilance and activity have hitherto been vain; sounds are too volatile and subtile for legal restraints; to enchain syllables, and to lash the wind, are equally the undertakings of pride, unwilling to measure its desires by its strength. The French language has visibly changed under the inspection of the academy; the stile of Amelot's translation of Father Paul is observed by Le Courayer to be un peu passe; and no Italian will maintain that the diction of any modern writer is not perceptibly different from that of Boccace, Machiavel, or Caro.

Total and sudden transformations of a language seldom happen; conquests and migrations are now very rare: but there are other causes of change, which, though slow in their operation, and invisible in their progress, are perhaps as much superior to human resistance, as the revolutions of the sky, or intumescences of the tide. Commerce, however necessary, however lucrative, as it depraves the manners, corrupts the language; they that have frequent intercourse with strangers, to whom they endeavour to accommodate themselves, must in time learn a mingled dialect, like the jargon which serves the traffickers on the Mediterranean and Indian coasts. This will not always be confined to the exchange, the warehouse, or the port, but will be communicated by degrees to other ranks of the people, and be at last incorporated with the current speech.

There are likewise internal causes equally forcible. The language most likely to continue long without alteration, would be that of a nation raised a little, and but a little above barbarity, secluded from strangers, and totally employed in procuring the conveniences of life; either without books, or, like some of the Mahometan countries, with very few: men thus busied and unlearned, having only such words as common use requires, would perhaps long continue to express the same notions by the same signs. But no such constancy can be expected in a people polished by arts, and classed by subordination, where one part of the community is sustained and accommodated by the labour of the other. Those who have much leisure to think, will always be enlarging the stock of ideas, and every increase of knowledge, whether real or fancied, will produce new words, or combinations of words. When the mind is unchained from necessity, it will range after convenience; when it is left at large in the fields of speculation, it will shift opinions; as any custom is disused, the words that expressed it must perish with it; as any opinion grows popular, it will innovate speech in the same proportion as it alters practice.

As by the cultivation of various sciences, a language is amplified, it will be more furnished with words deflected from original sense; the geometrician will talk of a courtier's zenith, or the eccentric virtue of a wild hero, and the physician of sanguine expectations and phlegmatic delays. Copiousness of speech will give opportunities to capricious choice, by which some words will be preferred, and others degraded;

vicissitudes of fashion will enforce the use of new, or extend the signification of known terms. The tropes of poetry will make hourly encroachments, and the metaphorical will become the current sense: pronunciation will be varied by levity or ignorance, and the pen must at length comply with the tongue; illiterate writers will at one time or other, by public infatuation, rise into renown, who, not knowing the original import of words, will use them with colloquial licentiousness, confound distinction, and forget propriety. As politeness increases, some expressions will be considered as too gross and vulgar for the delicate, others as too formal and ceremonious for the gay and airy; new phrases are therefore adopted, which must, for the same reasons, be in time dismissed. Swift, in his petty treatise on the English language, allows that new words must sometimes be introduced, but proposes that none should be suffered to become obsolete. But what makes a word obsolete, more than general agreement to forbear it? And how shall it be continued, when it conveys an offensive idea, or recalled again into the mouths of mankind, when it has once become unfamiliar by disuse, and unpleasing by unfamiliarity?

There is another cause of alteration more prevalent than any other, which yet in the present state of the world cannot be obviated. A mixture of two languages will produce a third distinct from both, and they will always be mixed, where the chief part of education, and the most conspicuous accomplishment, is skill in ancient or in foreign tongues. He that has long cultivated another language, will find its words and combinations crowd upon his memory; and haste and negligence, refinement and affectation, will obtrude borrowed terms and exotic expressions.

The great pest of speech is frequency of translation. No book was ever turned from one language into another, without imparting something of its native idiom; this is the most mischievous and comprehensive innovation; single words may enter by thousands, and the fabric of the tongue continue the same, but new phraseology changes much at once; it alters not the single stones of the building, but the order of the columns. If an academy should be established for the cultivation of our stile, which I, who can never wish to see dependence multiplied, hope the spirit of English liberty will hinder or destroy, let them, instead of compiling grammars and dictionaries, endeavor, with all their influence, to stop the license of translators, whose idleness and ignorance, if it be suffered to proceed, will reduce us to babble a dialect of France.

If the changes that we fear be thus irresistible, what remains but to acquiesce with silence, as in the other insurmountable distresses of humanity? It remains that we retard what we cannot repel, that we palliate what we cannot cure. Life may be lengthened by care, though death cannot be ultimately defeated: tongues, like governments, have a natural tendency to degeneration; we have long preserved our constitution, let us make some struggles for our language.

In hope of giving longevity to that which its own nature forbids to be immortal, I have devoted this book, the labour of years, to the honour of my country, that we may no longer yield the palm of philology, without a contest, to the nations of the continent. The chief glory of every people arises from its authors: whether I shall add any thing by my own writings to the reputation of English literature, must be left to time: much of my life has been lost under the pressures of disease; much has been trifled away; and much has always been spent in provision for the day that was passing over me; but I shall not think my employment useless or ignoble, if by my assistance foreign nations, and distant ages, gain access to the propagators of knowledge, and understand the teachers of truth; if my labours afford light to the repositories of science, and add celebrity to Bacon, to Hooker, to Milton, and to Boyle.

When I am animated by this wish, I look with pleasure on my book, however defective, and deliver it to the world with the spirit of a man that has endeavoured well. That it will immediately become popular I have not promised to myself: a few wild blunders, and risible absurdities, from which no work of such multiplicity was ever free, may for a time furnish folly with laughter, and harden ignorance in contempt; but useful diligence will at last prevail, and there never can be wanting some who distinguish desert; who will consider that no dictionary of a living tongue ever can be perfect, since while it is hastening to publication, some words are budding, and some falling away; that a whole life cannot be spent upon syntax and etymology, and that even a whole life would not be sufficient; that he, whose design includes whatever language can express, must often speak of what he does not understand; that a writer will sometimes be hurried by eagerness to the end, and sometimes faint with weariness under a task, which Scaliger compares to the labours of the anvil and the mine; that what is obvious is not always known, and what is known is not always present; that sudden fits of inadvertency will surprise vigilance, slight avocations will seduce attention, and casual eclipses of the mind will darken learning; and that the writer shall often in vain trace his memory at the moment of need, for that which yesterday he knew with intuitive readiness, and which will come uncalled into his thoughts tomorrow.

In this work, when it shall be found that much is omitted, let it not be forgotten that much likewise is performed; and though no book was ever spared out of tenderness to the author, and the world is little solicitous to know whence proceeded the faults of that which it condemns; yet it may gratify curiosity to inform it, that the English Dictionary was written with little assistance of the learned, and without any patronage of the great; not in the soft obscurities of retirement, or under the shelter of academic bowers, but amidst inconvenience and distraction, in sickness and in sorrow. It may repress the triumph of malignant criticism to observe, that if our language is not here fully displayed, I have only failed in an attempt which no human powers have hitherto completed. If the lexicons of ancient tongues, now immutably fixed, and comprised in a few volumes, be yet, after the toil of successive ages, inadequate and delusive; if the aggregated knowledge, and co-operating diligence of the Italian academicians, did not secure them from the censure of Beni; if the embodied critics of France, when fifty years had been spent upon their work, were obliged to change its economy, and give their second edition another form, I may surely be contented without the praise of perfection, which, if I could obtain, in this gloom of solitude, what would it avail me? I have protracted my work till most of those whom I wished to please have sunk into the grave, and success and miscarriage are empty sounds: I therefore dismiss it with frigid tranquility, having little to fear or hope from censure or from praise.

Synopsis

The story is divided into twelve books, like the *Aeneid* of Virgil. The length varies, from the longest being Book IX, with 1189 lines and the shortest, Book VII, having 640. Each book is preceded by a summary titled "The Argument". The poem follows the epic tradition of starting *in medias res* (Latin for *in the midst of things*), the background story being told in Books V-VI.

Milton's story contains two arcs: one of Satan (Lucifer) and another of Adam and Eve. Lucifer's story is a homage to the old epics of warfare. It begins *in medias res,* after Lucifer and the other rebel angels have been defeated and cast down by God into Hell. In Pandæmonium, Lucifer must employ his rhetorical ability to organize his followers; he is aided by his lieutenants Mammon and Beelzebub. Belial and Moloch are also present. At the end of the debate, Satan volunteers himself to poison the newly-created Earth. He braves the dangers of the Abyss alone in a manner reminiscent of Odysseus or Aeneas.

The other story is a fundamentally different, new kind of epic: a domestic one. Adam and Eve are presented for the first time in Christian literature as having a functional relationship while still without sin. They have passions, personalities, and sex. Satan successfully tempts Eve by preying on her vanity and tricking her with rhetoric, and Adam, seeing Eve has sinned, knowingly commits the same sin by also eating of the fruit. In this manner Milton portrays Adam as a heroic figure but also as a deeper sinner than Eve. They again have sex, but with a newfound lust that was previously not present. After realizing their error in consuming the "fruit" from the Tree of Knowledge of Good and Evil, they fight. However, Eve's pleas to Adam reconcile them somewhat. Adam goes on a vision journey with an angel where he witnesses the errors of man and the Great Flood, and he is saddened by the sin that they have released through the consumption of the fruit. However, he is also shown hope – the possibility of redemption – through a vision of Jesus Christ.

They are then cast out of Eden and an angel adds that one may find "A paradise within thee, happier farr." They now have a more distant relationship with God, who is omnipresent but invisible (unlike the previous tangible Father in the garden of Eden).

The contents of the 12 books are:

Book I: In a long, twisting opening sentence, the poet invokes the "Heavenly Muse" (the Holy Spirit) and states his theme, the Fall of Man, and his aim, to "justify the ways of God to men." (Milton 1674, 4:26). Satan, Beelzebub, and the other rebel angels are described as lying on a lake of fire, from where Satan rises up to claim hell as his own domain and delivers a rousing speech to his followers ("Better to reign in hell, than serve in heav'n").

Book II: Satan and the rebel angels debate whether or not to conduct another war on Heaven, and Beelzebub tells them of a new world being built, which is to be the home of Man. Satan decides to visit this new world, passes through the gates of Hell, past the sentries Sin and Death, and journeys through the realm of Chaos. Here, Satan is described as giving birth to Sin with a burst of flame from his forehead, as Athena was born from the head of Zeus.

Book III: God observes Satan's journey and foretells how Satan will bring about Man's Fall. God emphasizes, however, that the Fall will come about as a result of Man's own free will and excuses Himself of responsibility. The Son of God offers himself as a ransom for Man's disobedience, an offer which God accepts, ordaining the Son's future incarnation and punishment. Satan arrives at the rim of the universe, disguises himself as an angel, and is directed to Earth by Uriel, Guardian of the Sun.

Book IV: Satan journeys to the Garden of Eden, where he observes Adam and Eve discussing the forbidden Tree of Knowledge. Satan, observing their innocence and beauty hesitates in his task, but concludes that "reason just,/ Honour and empire" compel him to do this deed which he "should abhor." Satan tries to tempt Eve while she is sleeping, but is discovered by the angels. The angel Gabriel expels Satan from the Garden.

Book V: Eve awakes and relates her dream to Adam. God sends Raphael to warn and encourage Adam: they discuss free will and predestination and Raphael tells Adam the story of how Satan inspired his angels to revolt against God.

Book VI: Raphael goes on to describe further the war in Heaven and explains how the Son of God drove Satan and his minions down to Hell.

Book VII: Raphael explains to Adam that God then decided to create another world (the Earth), and he warns Adam again not to eat the fruit of the Tree of Knowledge, for "in the day thou eat'st, thou diest;/ Death is the penalty imposed, beware,/ And govern well thy appetite, lest Sin/ Surprise thee, and her black attendant Death".

Book VIII: Adam asks Raphael for knowledge concerning the stars and the heavenly orders; Raphael warns that "heaven is for thee too high/ To know what passes there; be lowly wise", and advises modesty and patience.

Book IX: Satan returns to Eden and enters into the body of a sleeping serpent. The serpent tempts Eve to eat the fruit of the Tree of Knowledge. She eats and takes some fruit for Adam. Adam realizes that Eve has been tricked, but eats of the fruit, deciding that he would rather die with Eve than live without her. At first the two become intoxicated by the fruit, and both become lustful and engage in sexual intercourse; afterwards, in their loss of innocence Adam and Eve cover their nakedness and fall into despair: "They sat them down to weep, nor only tears/ Rained at their eyes, but high winds worse within/ Began to rise, high passions, anger, hate,/ Mistrust, suspicion, discord, and shook greatly/ Their inward state of mind."

Book X: God sends his Son to Eden to deliver judgment on Adam and Eve, and Satan returns in triumph to Hell.

Book XI: The Son of God pleads with God on behalf of Adam and Eve. God declares that the couple must be expelled from the Garden, and the angel Michael descends to deliver God's judgment. Michael begins to unfold the future history of the world to Adam.

Book XII: Michael tells Adam of the eventual coming of the Messiah, before leading Adam and Eve from the Garden. Paradise has been lost. The poem ends: "The World was all before them, where to choose Their place of rest, and Providence Their guide: They hand in hand with wadding steps and slow, Through Eden took Their solitaire way Subject matter of Paradise Lost (Published in 1667) is an epic account of The Fall of Man. Milton begins his poem by invoking the aid of the (Holy) Spirit for his task, and sets forth the purpose of his song: "that... I may assert the Eternal Providence and justify the ways of God to man".

The poem then depicts Satan and his fallen angels, already expelled from heaven and burning in the fire, as they start to talk among themselves. The rest of Books I and II, are then recounted from the perspective of Satan and his minions. Satan goes on to tell how those of Hell deliberated with him as to whether or not they should war with those in heaven yet again and attempt to overthrow it. Once agreed upon, Satan struggles through Chaos from Heaven to Hell. Traditional Christians may argue that this is an unbiblical ability according to the Gospel of Luke chapter 16 in the story of the rich man and Lazarus, "...between us and you there is a great gulf fixed: so that they which would pass from hence to you cannot; neither can they pass to us, that would come from thence". Perhaps the ability to transfer from one immaterial place to another differs between composites of form and matter or soul and body (humans) and pure spirit. However, this is not even an issue in this context, even though Hell is a state of mind, "the hell within him; for within him Hell he brings, and round about him, nor from Hell one step, no more than from himself, can fly by change of place".

Later on in the poem, Satan goes on to introduce Death and Sin. Sin was birthed from the head of Satan, an allusion to the birth of the Greek god Athena. Sin is half beautiful woman and half serpent, the lower portion of her body destroyed after giving birth to Death. Hell-hounds are attached to the waist of Sin, constantly running in and out of her being re-birthed and devouring Sin's body. In book 4, Adam and Eve are introduced for the first time. Milton's idea of marriage is very much influenced in this section. Their relationship is one of inequality, but not a relation of domination or hierarchy. There is a mutual friendship between the two and they also model the ideal ruler and subject. For Milton, this marriage is political ideal just as much as it is a personal ideal. Satan also describes their personalities. Eve is described as a '"coy", flirtatious, beautiful, sex object that Adam is overwhelmed by"' or "Too much of Ornament". Adam is seen as more of an intellectual. Though there is no sin within paradise, Adam and Eve have an argument about the care of the land. Eve thinks the garden is growing too fast and that the two should split up while working to cover more ground, thus accomplishing more. Adam disagrees and says that time is not an issue for them, therefore they were meant to enjoy their work and not rush it. This disagreement would begin the stirring up their hearts, making them more vulnerable to the temptation that was to come. Adam consents to Eve's wishes and they split up during their work. Satan, as the serpent in the garden, made ready to fool Eve through the process of reduction.

In the last three chapters after the Fall, the Son of God intercedes for Adam and Eve and the Father accepts. However, he commands the angel Michael to ban Adam and Eve from the garden. In doing so, Michael gives Adam a vision of the Flood, and life and death of Christ, revealing to him the way of redemption. Adam and Eve's lives carry on but they are driven out from the Garden of Eden.

Character Analysis

Satan: Satan is the first major character introduced in the poem. He is introduced in Hell after a failed rebellion to take control of Heaven from God. Satan's desire to rebel against his creator stems from his unwillingness to accept the fact that he is a created being and that he is not self sufficient, which roots in turn from his extreme narcissism. One of the ways he tries to justify his rebellion against God is by claiming that he and the angels are self-created, claiming that the angels are "self-begot, self-raised", thereby eliminating God's authority over them as their creator. Satan's views are grossly distorted, however. Satan is narcissistic to the point of being delusional, as shown by his encounter with Sin and Death. Although they are introduced as if they are separate entities from Satan, Sin and Death can both be read as delusions of Satan's mind.Sin describes herself as sprouting out of Satan's mind at the time he conceived of his plot to overthrow God, which perhaps could be taken for the fact that she is only a part of Satan, specifically his sinful scheme to overthrow God, that he is projecting into the world.

She is described as originally having the same features as Satan, which shows the perversion of his narcissism, because Satan engages Sin in incestuous intercourse. Satan is narcissistic to the point of being aroused by his own image, and from his incest with his "daughter" Sin, Death is born. Death too, however, may be a delusion of Satan's mind, having no substance or form, no real power.

This reflects Milton's Christian theology, because Christianity sees death as having no real power also. Satan's delusion is also shown when he leaves Hell. He goes up to the gates, which fly quickly open before him. Satan sets out to portray God as a tyrant, yet here Milton shows us that the Satan is not even locked in Hell. Milton portrays Hell also as a state of Satan's mind in the opening of Book 4, talking of how Satan has "Hell within him; for within him Hell/ He brings...". Milton shows us that Satan is creating his own internal Hell by his delusions and narcissism. The fact that Satan is such a driving force within the poem has been the subject of a large amount of scholarly debate, with positions ranging anywhere from views such as that of William Blake who stated that Milton "wrote in fetters when wrote of Angels and God, and at liberty when of Devils and Hell, is because he was a true Poet and of the Devil's party without knowing it" to the critic William H. Marshall's interpretation that the poem is in fact a Christian moral tale, but that Milton fails to portray his original intent because the reader's emotional reaction to the story must be "subordinated to [his] intellectual response the explicit assertion in the final books of the Paradox of the Fortunate Fall."

Adam: Adam is the first human in Eden created by God. He is the more intellectual of the two, with Eve being more rooted in experience. Positively, Adam is a model of a good ruler, gently leading Eve during their first encounter away from her reflection, using force but not excessively. Although he and Eve are not equal in the story, Adam is not an oppressive ruler. He and Eve have a mutually dependent relationship. This illustrates Milton's views on the relationship between ruler and subject as well as husband and wife. Negatively, he like Satan shares the problem of lack of self-knowledge, but unlike Satan who is totally self-absorbed and narcissistic, Adam's problem stems from the fact that he seems to be in danger of losing sight of himself.

The cause of his loss of self is the beauty of Eve, which he complains about during his discourse with Raphael, saying that she is "Too much of Ornament". He talks anxiously of how he feels like he is becoming dependent on Eve, who conversely seems to be self-sufficient and naturally independent. Adam is distraught by this because it would seem to him that she should be the one dependent because he was created first and she was made from a part of him, and yet as it stands he is becoming obsessed with Eve almost to the point of idolizing her. There is also an element of heresy to Adam even before the Fall. He wishes to avoid confrontation with Satan completely, even to the fact of being cowardly about it, denying the idèa of the "felix culpa", that the Fall might not be a bad thing, perhaps part of God's greater plan.

Eve: Eve is the second human created, taken from one of Adam's ribs and formed into a female form of Adam.

Positively, she is the model of a good subject and wife. She consents to Adam leading her away from her reflection when they first meet, trusting Adam's authority in their relationship. She is very beautiful, so much so that she is almost a danger to herself and Adam. Her beauty not only obsesses Adam, but also herself. After she is first born, she gazes at her own reflection in a pool of water and is transfixed by her own image. Even after Adam calls out to her she returns to her image. It is not until God tells her to go to Adam that she consents to being led away from the pool.

This shows that from the beginning she is in danger of narcissism, much like Satan. She is also the first to come into contact with satanic influence; Satan worms his way into one of her dreams to tempt her. After this incident she seems to develop the independent streak that so perplexes Adam during his conversation with Raphael, wanting to go off by herself to work in the garden. She also develops the Satanic view of wanting to organize the garden, wishing to split up to get more work done, worrying that the garden is "messy" and wishing to impose some kind of order on it, which is Satan's wish as well.

She eventually does give into temptation, being the first to eat of the Tree of Knowledge of Good and Evil, effectively causing the Fall. She is not portrayed in a totally negative manner in the story, however; during her argument with Adam about whether or not they should split up, Adam says they should stay together in order to avoid temptation and implying that even to be tempted would be dishonourable to them, which is a flawed argument. Eve responds by taking a heroic stance, saying that if they would give into temptation that easily that their virtue must not have been very strong to begin with. This is not the only time Eve shows a heroic side either, despite her failings. After the Fall, Adam begins to blame her for everything that has gone wrong, acting as if she alone is the cause despite the fact that he willingly chose to sin also. Eve makes her stand here by humbly taking all the verbal abuse that Adam gives to her, instead of arguing and causing a further rift between them. By taking everything upon herself she is portrayed as Christ-figure, accepting fault that is not hers and bearing it for the sake of the future of humanity.

The Son of God: the Son of God in Paradise Lost is Christ, though he is never named explicitly as so, since He has not yet entered human form. After the Father explains to him how Adam and Eve will fall, and how the rest of humanity will be doomed to follow them in their cursed footsteps, the Son heroically proclaims that he will take the punishment for humanity. The Son gives hope to the poem because although Satan conquers humanity by successfully tempting Adam and Eve, the victory is temporary because the Son will save the human race. Interestingly enough, the Son shows a major break with orthodox religious thought on Milton's part; the accepted belief at the time was that the Trinity were all part of the one Godhead, and thus all created at the same time, and yet Milton portrays the Son as being created after the Father.

God the Father: God the Father is the creator of Eden, Heaven, Hell, and of each of the main characters in the poem. He is an all-powerful being who cannot be overthrown by even the one-third of the angels that Satan incites against Him. The poem portrays God's process of creation in the way that Milton believed it was done, that God created Heaven, Earth, Hell, and all the creatures that inhabit these separate planes from part of himself, not out of nothing. Thus according to Milton, what gives God his ultimate authority is the fact that he is the "author" of creation. Satan tries to justify his rebellion by denying this aspect of God and claiming self-creation, but he admits to himself that this is not the case, and that God "deserved no such return From me, whom he created what I was".

Milton began writing the epic in 1658, during the last years of the English Republic. The infighting among different military and political factions that doomed the Republic may show up in the Council of Hell scenes in Book II. Although he probably finished the work by 1664, Milton did not publish till 1667 on account of the Great Plague and the Great Fire.

Milton composed the entire work while completely blind, necessitating the use of paid amanuenses. The poet claimed that a divine spirit inspired him during the night, leaving him with verses that he would recite in the morning.

The 3rd Norton edition of *Paradise Lost* ignores the punctuation found in the surviving manuscript draft on the grounds that it was inserted by the printer, but this procedure has been challenged. Even into the mid-18th century a variety of publications included a wide array of spellings of even the same word within the same text.

Context

The book is influenced by the Bible, Milton's own Puritan upbringing and religious perspective, Phineas Fletcher, Edmund Spenser, and the ancient poets Virgil and Theocritus.

Milton wrote the entire work with the help of secretaries and friends, notably Andrew Marvell, after losing his sight.

Later in life, Milton wrote the much shorter *Paradise Regained*, charting the temptation of Christ by Satan, and the return of the possibility of paradise. This sequel has never had a reputation equal to the earlier poem.

Themes

Marriage

On the surface Paradise Lost appears to be a general biblical story depicting creation and the fall of Adam and Eve. Digging deeper into the plot of the poem, however, several critics have noted the relationship between Adam and Eve, and how it specifically reflects Milton's views on marriage.

Milton first presents Adam and Eve in Book 4 and the pair is viewed in impartiality. Dr. Jennifer Rust (2007) explains that the relationship between Adam and Eve is one of "... mutual dependence, not a relation of domination or hierarchy ". While the author does place Adam above Eve in regards to his intellectual knowledge, and in turn his relation to God, he also grants Eve the benefit of knowledge through experience. Hermine Van Nuis (2000), p. 50) clarifies that although there is a sense of stringency associated with the specified roles of the male and the female, each unreservedly accepts the designated role because it is viewed as an asset. Instead of believing that these roles are forced upon them, each uses the obligatory requirement as a strength in their relationship with each other. These minor discrepancies reveal the author's view on the importance of mutuality between a husband and a wife.

When examining the relationship between Adam and Eve, critics have had the tendency to accept an either Adam- or Eve-dominated point of view in relation of hierarchy and importance to God argues, however, that these positions "... overstate the independence of the characters' stances, and therefore miss the way in which Adam and Eve are entwined with each other". Milton's true vision reflects one where the husband and wife (in this instance, Adam and Eve) depend on each other and only through each other's differences are able to thrive. While most readers believe that Adam and Eve fail because of their fall from paradise, Milton would argue that the strengthening of their love for one another that results is true victory.

Although Milton does not directly mention divorce in the actual context of Paradise Lost, critics have presented solid theories on Milton's view of divorce based on inferences found within the poem. Other works by Milton have expressed that the noted English author viewed marriage as an entity separate from the church. More specifically, however, in relation to Paradise Lost, Biberman entertains the idea that "... marriage is a contract made by both the man and the woman". Based on this inference, Milton would believe that both man and woman would have equal access to divorce, as they do to marriage.

Idolatry

Owing to his Protestant views on politics and religion in 17th century England, contemporaries usually criticized Milton's ideas and considered him as something of a radical. One of Milton's greatest and most controversial arguments revolves around his concept of what is idolatrous and as critics have noted, the topic is deeply embedded in Paradise Lost.

Milton's first criticism of idolatry lies in the theory of

constructing temples and other buildings to serve as places of worship. In Book 11 of Paradise Lost, Adam tries to atone for his sins by offering to build altars to worship God and in response, the Angel Michael explains that Adam does not need to build physical objects to experience the presence of God. Joseph Lyle points to this example and further explains that "[when Milton objects to architecture, it is not a quality inherent in buildings themselves he finds offensive, but rather their tendency to act as convenient loci to which idolatry, over time, will inevitably adhere". Even if the idea is pure in nature, Milton still believes that it will unavoidably lead to idolatry simply because of the nature of humans. Instead of placing their thoughts and beliefs into God, as they should, humans tend to turn to erected objects and falsely invest their faith. While Adam attempts to build an altar for God, critics have noted that Eve is also guilty of idolatry, but in a different manner. Pitt Harding believes Eve's narcissism and obsession with herself also constitutes as idolatry. Specifically, Pitt claims that "... under the serpent's influence, Eve's idolatry and self-deification foreshadow the errors into which her "Sons" will stray". Much like Adam, Eve falsely places her faith into herself, the Tree of Knowledge, and to some extent, the Serpent, all of which do not compare to the ideal nature of God.

Furthermore, Milton makes his views on idolatry more explicit with the creation of Pandemonium and the exemplary allusion to Solomon's temple. In the beginning of Paradise Lost, as well as throughout the poem, several references are made to the rise and eventual fall of Solomon's temple. Critics elucidate that "Solomon's temple provides an explicit demonstration of how an artifact moves from its genesis in devotional practice to an idolatrous end". This example, out of the many presented, conveys Milton's views on the dangers of idolatry most clearly. Even if one builds a structure in the name of God, even the best of intentions can become immoral. In addition, critics have noted a parallel between Pandemonium and Saint Peter's Basilica, and the Pantheon as well. The majority of these similarities revolve around a structural likeness, but as Lyle explains, they play a much greater role. By linking Saint Peter's Basilica and the Pantheon to Pandemonium, an ideally false structure, the two famous buildings take on a false meaning as well. This comparison best represents Milton's Protestant views in that it rejects both the purely Catholic perspective and the Pagan perspective.

In addition to rejecting Catholicism, Milton also revolted against the idea of a monarch ruling by divine right and saw the practice as idolatrous. Barbara Lewalski concludes that the theme of idolatry in Paradise Lost "... is an exaggerated version of the idolatry Milton had long associated with the Stuart ideology of divine kingship". In the opinion of Milton, any object, human or non-human, that receives special attention that is befitting of God, is considered idolatrous.

Response and Criticism

This epic has generally been considered one of the greatest works in the English language. In the verses below the portrait in the fourth edition, John Dryden linked Milton with Homer and Virgil, suggesting that Milton encompassed and surpassed both:

"Three Poets, in three distant Ages born,
Greece, Italy, and England did adorn.
The First in loftiness of thought surpass'd;
The Next in Majesty; in both the Last.
The force of Nature cou'd no farther goe:
To make a third she joynd the former two."

Since Paradise Lost is based upon scripture, its significance in the Western canon has been thought by some to have lessened due to increasing secularism. However, this is not the general consensus, and even academics who have been labeled as secular realize the merits of the work. In William Blake's *The Marriage of Heaven and Hell,* the "voice of the devil" argues:

The reason Milton wrote in fetters when he wrote of Angels & God, and at liberty when of Devils & Hell, is because he was a true Poet and of the Devil's party without knowing it. This statement summarizes what would become the most common interpretation of the work in the twentieth century. Some critics, including C. S. Lewis and later Stanley Fish, reject this interpretation. Rather, such critics hold that the theology of *Paradise Lost* conforms to the passages of Scripture on which it is based.

The latter half of the twentieth century saw the critical understanding of Milton's epic shift to a more political and philosophical focus. Rather than the Romantic conception of the Devil as the hero of the piece, it is generally accepted that Satan is presented in terms that begin classically heroic, then diminish him until he is finally reduced to a dust-eating serpent unable even to control his own body. The political angle enters into consideration in the underlying friction between Satan's conservative, hierarchical view of the universe and the contrasting "new way" of God and the Son of God as illustrated in Book III.

In other words, in contemporary criticism the main thrust of the work becomes not the perfidy or heroism of Satan, but rather the tension between classical conservative "Old Testament" hierarchs (evidenced in Satan's worldview and even in that of the archangels Raphael and Gabriel), and "New Testament" revolutionaries (embodied in the Son of God, Adam, and Eve) who represent a new system of universal organization.

This new order is based not in tradition, precedence, and unthinking habit, but on sincere and conscious acceptance of faith and on station chosen by ability and responsibility. Naturally, this interpretation makes much use of Milton's other works and his biography, grounding itself in his personal history as an English revolutionary and social critic.

Samuel Johnson praised the poem lavishly, but conceded that "None ever wished it longer than it is".

Iconography

The history of illustrators includes, among others, John Martin, Edward Burney, Richard Westall, Francis Hayman, Bernard Lens, and John Medina. The most notable and popular illustrators include William Blake, Gustave Doré and Henry Fuseli. Salvador Dalí did fanciful illustrations for the Automobile Club. And noted surreal/visionary artist Terrance

Lindall's rendition, which was published in hardcover in 1982 and which also appeared in *Heavy Metal Magazine* around that time, is used in the Department of English at New York University to introduce students to Milton. A Toronto act entitled "Milton's Aim," which was inspired by Paradise Lost came into existence in 2006. Reviews are pending.

Cultural Significance

"Paradise Lost" has been the source of inspiration in several aspects of popular culture. A notable appearance is the musical composition The Creation by Joseph Haydn. Furthermore, classical composer Krzysztof Penderecki and metal bands Cradle of Filth and Symphony X have created musical works based upon the poem. In literature, some of William Blake's poetry was based upon the poem, and the poem is the basis for the *His Dark Materials* trilogy by Philip Pullman, of which an excerpt was included in the first novel of the series, *Northern Lights/The Golden Compass*.

The film *Se7en* includes a number of quotes of the poem. Also Death/Doom Metal band Paradise Lost was named after this piece of literature. In track "Prime Evil" from their Bicycles and Tricycles release, The Orb has Neville Jason reading various excerpts of Paradise Lost, mainly from book IV ("...close the serpent sly..."; "...Squat like a toad, close at the ear of Eve, Assaying by his devilish art to reach The organs of her fancy, and with them forge Illusions..." ; "...That bring to my remembrance from what state I fell, how glorious once above thy sphere; Till pride...threw me down Warring in Heaven against Heaven's matchless King...").In MegaMan X8- Lumine the final boss, uses an ultimate attack called Paradise Lost. In the Warhammer 40k Universe the Horus Heresy War is an epic retelling of *Paradise Lost*.

I am including Johnson's RA$SELAS in these notes on 'Restoration and Eighteenth-Century Poetry' because, although in prose, it is a 'poetic' work. First, you will find here a discussion of the novel, Second, a plan which may help you navigate it. Third, there is a guide to some of reading. Fourth, there is a list of some issues to consider, with interesting quotations.

Note that there was in the seventeenth century a group of people which was not the first 'coffee-house' group, but one of the first. It was called the Rota and it was a place for free-thinking discussion, founded by an intellectual leader of the seventeenth century, Sir James Harrington, author THE COMMONWEALTH OF OCEANA(1656). The coffee-house is a key institution in your period, its existence implying discussion and an audience for periodical writing, news and views. We think often of the theatre as a germinating institution. So was the coffee house.

The Rota met in Miles's Coffee-House, starting in 1659, the same year as Dryden wrote about the 'late Highness Oliver Lord Protector' and Milton on 'The Likeliest Means to Remove Hirelings out of the Church.' Johnson's Rasselas was published exactly 100 years later, the end of your period, when the author was fifty years old.

I mention this moment to establish that RASSELAS is a late book of your period, a range of years that is a period. There are two things relevant to RASSELAS in Harrington and the Rota: first, coffee-houses, which enabled literary journalism to flourish, and without that I think the units out of which RASSELAS is built could not have been later used - for each chapter is a bit like one issue of an early eighteenth century journal (say, THE SPECTATOR); and, second, the Rota raises the matter of discussion: RASSELAS is certainly about that.

RASSELAS is a musical work, and then show the function of its music. Three types of music could be isolated.

There is the music of Chapters 41 to 44 whose very length (their brevity) is a musical effect. Their length makes us aware of timing, and it to too life in time that the characters in the novel turn in these chapters. These are flickering chapters, their brevity making a fast passage in the book; their brevity creates a musical or kinetic effect.

There is a second style of music in the invocation at the beginning of the book (on the handout): a grand, ominous statement from authority. The authority who commands the audience to hear is himself actually never heard again in the book. The initial music is not long sustained, and this appropriate for a book which in many respects is about the small, domestic matters of life, the quotidien.

Finally, there is a type of ordered and precisely patterned type of music, like this:

The angels of affliction spread their toils alike for the virtuous and the wicked, for the mighty and the mean.

I have restrained the rage of the dog-star, and mitigated the fervours of the crab.

William Hazlitt, the Romantic literary critic, called this type of writing by Johnson a 'species of rhyming in prose... Each sentence, revolves round its centre of gravity, [and] is contained within itself like a couplet, and each paragraph forms itself into a stanza.'

If there is such music, how does it work in the book. It works as music works, that is, by inviting opposition. Music works by juxtaposition, one phase inviting the contest of another. So the sound of one type of music invites the intervention of another type of music: the precisely patterned invites the sound of imprecision and uncertainty. And this contrast is thematic, because the book the book plays between what can be securely known, what cognition can achieve, and what is incomprehensible.

'Music works by juxtaposition, one phrase or phase inviting the contest of another.' This can be illustrated by reference to Chapter 6, 'A Dissertation on the Art of Flying'.

(Think about why it is called that. I guess that Johnson was doubtful of the concept of a Dissertation'. Note the (possible) irony in Chapter 10 which has in the title 'A Dissertation upon Poetry'. Imlac delivers one, and I was proceeding to aggrandize his own profession, when the prince cried out, 'Enough! Thou hast convinced me that no human being can ever be a poet. Proceed with thy narration.')

In this chapter there is as always a remarkable lack of authorial commentary and a curt conclusion — a curtness which is, I suggest, NOT ironical, and that when we hear that the scientist (significantly called sometimes 'an artist') fails to succeed with his flying machine and 'dropped into the lake', we are coarsening the section if we smile smugly. We should not receive 'vulgar irony' here. But, if there is not commentary, there is the impact, the musical impact, of juxtaposition. So we are kept thinking by changes of modulation.

The base line of the chapter is the account by the scientist of his scientific work. And the scientific work is seriously and beautifully described. He was, scholars say, conveying the best ideas of aeronautics of the time. I like very much the science of the chapter, the reference, for example, to 'the folding continuity of the bat's wings.'

But against this is juxtaposed contrary ideas, fuelled by the ambition of the scientist, as he begins to forget that he is not proposing powers of flight in a man, but powers of flight in a machine made by man. And he begins to feel, encouraged by the patronage of his prince, that he is the ONE man who can accomplish scientific wonders — and wonders of POWER. He insists on secrecy, and some of his reasoning seems sensible. If everyone had (one recognizes the fatuity of much 'if-everyone-did-it' reasoning) a flying machine, then 'Even this valley, the retreat of princes, the abode of happiness, might be violated by the sudden descent of some of the NAKED NATIONS [my capitals] that swarm on the coast of the southern sea.' A threat indeed; but though naked they are also human — like him.

So is the chapter satirical at the expense of the scientist? Is its point 'Pride comes before a fall.' Literally Emphatically not. Pride is vividly captured within the chapter as one of several elements and in the end the scientist gets some respect for what he is — a scientist. At the end Johnson is saying that scientists do science — whose work progresses sometimes, or often, by spin-offs, or accident: 'His wings, which were of no use in the air, sustained him in the water.'

You would find it interesting to compare this part of Rasselas to Johnson on the limits of human achievement in *The Idler* (number 88), Saturday, December 22, 1759.

Music has another function in Rasselas. It induces reverie, the gateway to the dream-world, the world which is cardinally interpretable. Dreams cry out for interpretation because they are so preternaturally clear. An object seen in a dream is outlined so sharply that it must, we think, 'mean something So in this book what might in another work be merely a scene, is here a rune. Music makes us want to read into what we see. There is an example of this in Chapter 39. We hear that the chief of the Arab band which captures Pekuah believes that buildings are best preserved in places little frequented, and difficult of access: for, when once a country declines from its primitive splendor, the more inhabitants are left, the quicker ruin will be made. Walls supply stones more easily than quarries, and temples and temples will be more easily demolished to make stables of granite, and cottages of porphyry.

Is this included as 'the kind of thing an Arab chief would say', included to enhance verisimilitude? It seems more than this: the music induces in the reader a mood in which such a statement of potentially symbolic.

To the subject-matter of Rasselas. is it 'life in general'. Not quite: it is truer to say it is about the life of people like us. People who have to think; students, indeed. There is a passage in one of the journals which Johnson wrote.

The man of study suffers from a reclusive] life. When he meets with an opinion that pleases him, he catches it up with eagerness; looks only after such arguments as tend to his confirmation; or spares himself the trouble of discussion, and adopts it with very little proof; indulges it long without suspicion, and in time unites it to the general body of his knowledge, and treasures it up among incontestable truths: but when he comes into the world among men who, arguing upon dissimilar principles, have been led to different conclusions, and being place in various situations, view the same object on many sides; he finds his darling position attacked, and himself in no condition to defend it: having thought always in one train, he is in the state of a man who having fenced always with the same master, is perplexed and amazed by a new posture of his antagonist; he is entangled in unexpected difficulties, he is harassed with sudden objections, he is unprovided with solutions or replies; his surprise impedes his natural powers of reasoning, his thoughts are scattered and confounded, and he gratifies the pride of airy petulance with an easy victory.

There is indeed a 'man of study' in Rasselas, the Astronomer whose brains have been turned by solitude. he is possibly the joint-hero (though arguably this book does not go in for heroes). In his essay in The Adventurer is describing a more mundane 'man of study'. The world of this man is to a degree that of Rasselas. The novel is about thinking, or thought-talking.

If thinking and looking at things is one subject of the novel, there is another feature to its subject matter which can be defined by an absence. The book is a 'chaste' one. Not only is it lacking in eroticism (unusual for an exotic tale); it also lacks love. It is not like a Shakespeare play, but it is 'Shakespearean' in a way that Johnson understood Six years after Rasselas, in 1765, Johnson published an edition of the works of Shakespeare, in the Preface to which he says this:

Upon every other stage the universal agent is love, by whose power all good an evil is distributed, and every action quickened or retarded. To bring a lover, a lady, and a rival into the fable; to entangle them in contradictory obligations, perplex them with opposition of interest, and harass them with violence of desires inconsistent with each other; to make them meet in rapture and part in agony; to fill their mouths with hyperbolical joy and outrageous sorrow; to distress them as nothing human ever was distressed; to deliver them as nothing human was delivered is the business of the dramatist.

Shakespeare's subject is never predominantly love; likewise Rasselas is not dominated by that characteristic Western obsession, romantic love or its modern and post-modern version, sex. In Rasselas there are male and female figures, and some of they become reliant upon each other, naturally in a novel preoccupied with aloneness (of which more later). But its figures interact as people, not as excited ideas of each other. The book is refreshingly enthralling (If not about love it is, to a degree, about money, and commerce, something which academics are sometimes rather snobbish.) The novel is care, but not romance, the care in friendship between Pekuah and the Astronomer, and also the Arab who kidnaps her. It is this Arab who finds an intelligent person when he has been trained to expect no such thing of women. In this, Johnson dramatizes his dislike of what he thought of as the 'Mahometan' attitude to women, in beautiful or domestic servitude. His contrary view was shown early, in his play IRENE of 1736 written when he was twenty-seven.

Having mentioned the 'music' of the book, let me return to another aspect of its method. Three words may assist description. Epigram, or a 'pointed or antithetical expression' (1796), with this quotation the Oxford English Dictionary of a seventeenth-century usage: 'The force and virtue of an epigram is in the conclusion.' Then there is apothegm, 'a terse pointed saying, embodying an important truth in few words; a pithy or sententious maxim'. O.E.D. gives a quotation from Boswell, "Johnson suddenly uttered an apothegm at which many will start: 'Patriotism is the last refuge of a scoundrel'. Finally, there is aphorism, based on the statements of Hippocrates, best known for the enunciation of the principles of medical conduct (including the Hippocratic Oath).

> It means a definition, or concise statement, of principle. The definitions to some degree overlap, all meaning, short statements, in some way 'pregnant' or suggestive, packed with implication. Such statements can be found in Rasselas, but more broadly these statements represent a style of art to which category Rasselas belong. Aphorism, epigrams and apothegms are in the species of 'wisdom' literature, and so is Rasselas. This is not to say Rasselas is not a novel. I think it is more of a novel than is usually admitted when stress is put on its fable-like qualities. Even though its hero is a one-dimensional figure, as one-dimensional as Tin Tin and as candidly charming, it is not a book of cut-out personages. Things happen to people, not merely occur. There is pain and change. On the other hand there is not much 'irrational texture' in the book; it is indeed other-worldly, and it has some of the qualities, in an expanded form, of aphorism, epigram and apothegm. Its genre is nearer 'wisdom writing' than that

of the novel, especially in its 'transparent' form in Richardson or its garrulous form in Fielding. To make what I mean by wisdom writing, let me quote a few example of pregnant brevity for illustration, not from Johnson, but other writers, seemingly different from Johnson but hardly in their work different from Rasselas. Here are some aphorisms by Karl Kraus (1874-1936), the *Austrian satirist.*

Love and art do not embrace what is beautiful, but what is made beautiful by this embrace.

A plagiarist should be made to copy the author a hundred times.

To have talent; to be a talent: the two are always confused.

This author is so deep that it took me, the reader, a long time to get to his surface.

Now here are some from William Blake's THE MARRIAGE OF HEAVEN AND HELL, said to have been begun at the age of twelve in 1789 (about thirty years after Rasselas).

Excess of sorrow laughs; excess of joy weeps.

The most sublime act is to set another before.

If others had not been foolish, we should be so.

These are from the Bible:

The Sabbath was made for man and not man for the Sabbath (Mark: 2, 27)

Whoever gives a truthful answer kisses the lips.

This is in miniature wisdom literature, And wisdom writing often is in miniature. It certainly is didactic, but not simplistic. What is 'passed in wisdom writing is often paradoxical or puzzling, at any rate challenging, and usually linguistically challenging. By passed down I mean two things: that the statement appears to come from on high, from seer, prophet or mage passed down from the mage or seer or prophet, but also (secondly) that the statement seems to come from 'down the ages'. Wisdom statements are framed to be out of time. Observers agree that one feature of it is often a stylized archaism.

Although some wisdom writing feels as if it is passed down from a seer on high, like the tablets to Moses, one other element in it, and especially in proverbs, should be mentioned, an element that is somewhat more democratic than the expression 'passing down' suggests. Wisdom writing is democratic (and sociable) in that it invites response. proverbs especially present themselves as potential material for contradiction. For many proverbs there is a counter-proverb, so 'All the world loves a lover' can be capped with 'The course of true love ne'er ran smooth' or "The cat in gloves catches no mice' countered by 'The cat invites the mouse to a feast.' This is in miniature close to the mode of Rasselas. It is illustrated in a pivotal section of the novel.

To this pivotal section I will turn in a moment, but I would first like to say a word about not the wisdom of the book, but the wisdom in the book, about one place in which there appears to be a fount of wisdom. There are several wise people in the book whose reputation for sagacity does not survive for one reason or another. One is tempted to see the unpretentious Imlac as something of a wise man. (I think the association between him and commerce is significant.) But there is also in the book an account of wisdom of discourse as opposed to wisdom of person, and this wisdom or discourse is that of poetry. But exactly how we should take Johnson's account of this discourse is something of a puzzle (as is appropriate for 'wisdom writing')

In Chapter 10 Imlac describes how he tried to become a poet and how wonderfully significant poetry is. It has been claimed that this account of the discourse of poetry is actually Johnson's idea of poetry, not Imlac's only. It is hard to say what we should think of it. On the face of it there is a temptation to join up with Rasselas's evident boredom. After Imlac has had his say, 'Enough,' cries Rasselas, 'Thou hast convinced me that no human being can ever be a poet. Proceed with thy narration.' 'To be a poet,' said Imlac, 'is indeed very difficult. 'So difficult,' returned the prince, that I will at present hear no more of his labours.

Tell me whither you went when you had seen Persia.' One's inclined to agree with Rasselas that Imlac has possibly made a bit of a fool of himself in Chapter 10 I have a couple of suggestions about interpreting the account of poetry by Imlac and Rasselas's reaction. First, Johnson is making the point, surely, that however grand the value of poetry and its wisdom is, it can never compete with the gut-desire, the visceral wish, to hear a traveler's tale. Travel was a a key thing for Johnson: a favourite possession was a piece of the Great Wall of China. The traveler's tale is nature, not art.

Second, I think that Johnson does believe in the high value of poetry, but he is dryly saying that many people get it wrong and that perhaps Imlac is not worthy of the métier.

Third, we must remember that what Chapter 10 consists of is not poetry, or a discussion of poetry, but 'A dissertation upon poetry'. That could indeed be boring.

The mode of Rasselas is, then, wisdom writing and from the mode I would like to move for a moment back to the subject of the book and one aspect of the subject shown in Chapter Six, another dissertation, this time on 'the Art of Flying'. Everyone enjoys the end of this chapter, in which the artist or inventor who has faithfully promised to construct a flying machine for Rasselas takes off from a bluff in his machine and plops promptly into the lake.

Two things are worth noting that happen before the debacle, and one thing after it. Notice the megalomania that begins to overtake the artist, with his imaginings of world domination. Notice also his more attractive speech, when he is talking about his own work:

I have considered the structure of all volant animals, and find the folding continuity of the bat's wings most easily accommodated to the human form.

The phrasing is exquisite, exquisitely accurate: the best scientific knowledge of the moment is being used, scholars tell us, and about this Johnson is emphatically not ironical. A lack of irony here may alert one to the possibility that the ending of the chapter is not quite as ironical as it may at first appear. So the inventor's wings won't keep him in the air. But they do enable him to float in the water and effectively save his life. Johnson is surely making a point about the nature of science - that experiment can proceed crab-wise, and the spin-off discovery is not to be scorned. One failure may unpredictably lead to another success. The 'knowledge theme' of the book is beginning. I have been talking about content and now want to turn to a matter of form and content combined. I have mentioned the Astronomer, comparing him to the reclusive academic whom Johnson describes in The Adventurer. The way in which the Astronomer arrives in the story is interesting. He is someone of whom Imlac had heard, one who 'admits a few friends once a month to hear his deductions and enjoy his discoveries.' When he gets to know Imlac the Astronomer is pleased with him because Imlac seems to be a 'man of various ideas and fluent conversation.' Why does Johnson have his character Imlac find and befriend the Astronomer? It would fit equally well into the plot for Rasselas to do so on one of his forays into society. Nekayeh or Pekuah would be just as suitable discoverers of this interesting personage. But Imlac is the person who finds the Astronomer - because he rhymes with this character.

They go together because Imlac highlights one things that the Astronomer lacks. Imlac possesses fluency. He had spent time as a trader; but he is a kind of trader in life, and is in human form what is elsewhere found in geographical form, in the Nile itself, the great symbol of fluency in the novel, the phenomenon that rises and falls through it. 'Fluency' in Rasselas is set is contest with the rigidities of the Astronomer, and especially at odds with his 'imagination', a faculty 'dangerously prevalent' according to the chapter on this subject. In that chapter we are again in the world of the airplane inventor, who obsessions are now seen more darkly. That inventor had literally sent imagination out upon the wing, exploiting an imagination which is at odds with 'nature and fortune', the reliable resources. 'Fluency', with its easeful removal from one subject to another, is at odds with 'imagination' which seems another word for obsession. It is imagination which 'tyrannizes'.

It may seem strange that Johnson equates 'imagination' with the academic Astronomer in his novel. Scholars are not necessarily endowed with imagination; indeed, in the course of the nineteenth century the image of the scholar was notably one of knowledge as pedantry. The Romantic movement may have broken down the formerly prospering traditional association of the sage and mage. It is quite easy to see, however, why the scholar is chosen to epitomize the person in danger from the imagination.

The scholar is a solitary, and solitariness is a key danger in Rasselas. And here there is a link-up between this human and an intellectual concept, between psychological aloneness and intellectual insularity. The books shows the dangers of psychic solitariness and conceptual solitariness. This equation emerges at a moment, which could be called a watershed in the book.

In Chapter 23 the prince and princess set about a systematic examination of society, of public and private life. They become sociologists. In Chapter 26 Nekayeh reports back on those who lead single lives. Seldom, she says, are such people happy. In Chapter 29 she remarks how frequently marriage is unhappy. Rasselas, the typical brother, catches her out. How can both conditions be equally miserable? Both may be bad, but they cannot both be worst Nekayeh replies with dignity as befits the thinker of the two.

I did not expect, answered the princess, to hear that imputed to falsehood which is the consequence only of frailty. To the mind as to the eye, it is difficult to compare with exactness object vast in their extent, and various in their parts. Where we see or conceive the whole at once we readily note the discriminations and decide the preference: but of two systems, of which neither can be surveyed by any human being in its full compass and magnitude and multiplicity of complication, where is the wonder, that judging of the whole by parts, I am alternately affected by one and the other as either presses on my imagination.

Any knowledge, she is saying, is difficult. It is possible that the debate on marriage occurs not to give coverage of a major human institution. Possibly marriage occurs a a subject in the novel as an example, an example meant to illustrate something about the mind not the emotions, about thinking rather than hearth and home relationships. 'Marriage' paramountly can't be understood. If this is the case, this section of the book is as much about epistemology as society. It is about knowledge.

With this disagreement the young observers come up against a brick wall. At this juncture Imlac enters, at the beginning of Chapter 30, and a new phase — and new type of knowing — begins. The travelers are told by him that it is time they stopped looking and started living. The meaning of this seems obvious enough, but its exact meaning should be noted. They should live in time, Imlac is saying to them. Hitherto their knowledge has been that of the sociological snapshot. It is time for them to experience sequence. They must enter diachronic and leave synchrony. Thus and for this Imlac leads them to the Pyramids.

At the end of the 'sociology' section, the survey of the different conditions of life, which culminates with the brother-sister quarrel, Nekayeh makes us aware how hard it is to know anything. It is tempting to relate this perception to the end of the novel, to Chapter 44, 'The Conclusion, in which Nothing is Concluded'. The travelers make plans suited to their several characters and resolve that when the seasonal flood of the Nile has subsided they will execute them — though they also knew that 'of these wishes that they had formed they well knew that none could be obtained.' They return notwithstanding to whence they came. (Back to the womb?) It is Imlac who continues traveling — and with him the Astronomer whom he has effectively saved from paranoid schizophrenia. There are no conclusions, something disappointing for the young travelers, but perhaps something affirmative Imlac and the Astronomer, the men of learning who are now capable of 'fluency'. But what are we to conclude, as readers?. That knowledge, let alone material goods, cannot be relied upon? Is the ending as thoroughly skeptical as this, either sourly so, or smugly skeptical?

I do not think it is skeptical and that this is shown if we consider the subject-matter of the last phase of the book and the last conversations about the non-materiality of the soul. The travelers explore the Egyptian catacombs and see the remains of the ancient dead. A discussion arises about the nature of the soul, especially whether or not there is any material evidence for its existence. One argument is advanced that actually matter may have soul-qualities, but that these are qualities as yet unknown to human science. Perhaps there is a form of materiality as yet unknown to us. This is the sort of argument supports life on Mars because we have not yet discovered a type of creature that can have mercury in its veins and sulphur in its lungs. This argument says don't decide about extra-terrestrials because some new logic may turn up. Imlac is magisterially hard on this line of reasoning.

He who will determine... against that which he knows, because there may be something which he knows not; he that can set hypothetical possibility against acknowledged certainty, is not to be admitted among reasonable beings. All that we know of matter is, that matter is inert, senseless and lifeless; and if this conviction cannot be opposed but by referring us to something that we know not, we have all the evidence of that human intellect can admit. If that which is known may be over-ruled by that which is unknown, no being, not omniscient, can arrive at certainty.

But perhaps God has a type of logic we know not of? This is what the Astronomer asks. Imlac replies, strongly again:

It is no limitation of omnipotence... to suppose that one thing is not consistent with another, that the same proposition cannot be at once true and false, that the same number cannot be even and odd, that cogitation cannot be conferred on that which is created incapable of cogitation.

So: what is known, in spite of our limits, is known. And there is no need to attribute soul to matter to make its existence the more plausible. The existence of thought and of knowledge as we have makes plausible the idea of non-material being. 'What space does the idea of a pyramid occupy more than the idea of a grain of corn? or how can either idea suffer laceration?' The soul is therefore as real as a thought. Because some knowledge is affirmed, the end is not thoroughly skeptical.

In the last chapter, there is a final puzzle. Imlac and the

Astronomer are endowed, I suggest, with approval, from Johnson, 'driven along the stream of life without directing their course to any particular port'. They are ultimately and affirmatively 'fluent'. At the end of the book we are occasional reminded that Imlac is a poet. If at the end Imlac is 'right', or as wise as can be possible is this therefore also a vote for poetry. It is Imlac who has given the firmest and most argued idea of knowledge. Is this, then, an idea coming from a poet, implying that a poet has access to good knowledge, the 'knowledge of knowledge' that may be poetry>

Perhaps Johnson is indeed affirming the value of poetry as knowledge at the end of his quickly and unguardedly written book. Imlac and the Astronomer could be rather like Plato's poets who were, you may remember, ushered outside the walls of the good city-state. If you come to think of it, a philosopher-king, is exactly what Rasselas wanted to be: 'The prince desired a little kingdom.' Poets could only be visitors in his Abissinia. Here is some advice on reading about Rasselas.

Formal Verse Imitation and the Rhetorical Principles of Imitation in the neo-Latin Poetry of Samuel Johnson

Born in 1709, Samuel Johnson grew up with and maintained a lifelong interest in English formal verse imitation, as both poet and critic. He was familiar with its history and personally witnessed the genre's extraordinary peak in popularity in the 1730s, thanks largely to Pope's splendid Imitations of Horace, which was published to much acclaim just as Johnson was beginning his career as a professional writer. Indeed, Johnson earned his earliest literary recognition with the publication of London (1738), a verse imitation of Juvenal's Third Satire, and solidified that reputation a decade later with the publication of The Vanity of Human Wishes (1749), written in imitation of Juvenal's Tenth Satire. Moreover, Johnson maintained a lively critical interest in the genre throughout his career. From the Rambler essays (1750-52) to the Lives of the Poets (1779-81 Johnson offers an abundance of occasional commentary, most of it consistently and rather sharply critical of formal verse imitation. Less well known, even to scholars, is that Johnson's interest in verse imitation was not restricted to English. As Robert DeMaria, Jr., helpfully reminds us, Samuel Johnson was a lifelong participant in the Late Latin culture of eighteenthcentury Europe (xi). His practice as a neo-Latin poet was profoundly affected by the conventions and tradition of English verse imitation. Indeed, Johnson strove not only to emulate Pope by imitating Juvenal as Pope had imitated Horace, but also to emulate the accomplishments of such neo-Latin humanists as Buchanan, the Scaligers, Erasmus, Heinsius, and Burman. His neo-Latin imitations, as the selected readings that follow later in this essay will attest, reveal Johnson's coming to grips with classical, patristic, and neo-Latin or humanistic predecessors.

One needs to be careful, however, in discussing Johnson's Latin poetry specifically in terms of formal verse imitation. Johnson never claims, when writing Latin verse, to be writing formal verse imitation. In Latin, he never carefully updates a particular ancient poem, substituting references to modern persons and events for those that appear in the classical original. Nevertheless, he relies on many of the conventions familiar to him from his experience with the English verse imitations of such poets as Rochester, Oldham, and Pope. Sometimes, for example, he constructs a Latin poem around a series of references or allusions designed to evoke the poetry of a classical, patristic, or neo-Latin precursor. Sometimes Johnson relies on a meter associated with a particular classical or patristic genre, poet, or poem. Sometimes Johnson employs diction or subject matter in order to evoke a particular period.

Beyond the formal, poetic conventions, Johnson acquired a habit of mind-a process, of sorts-for dealing with his poetic precursors when writing English verse imitations that he also used when writing Latin poetry. The process consists of two parts. First, as Johnson writes, he enters into the moral ethos and philosophical values of the antecedent poet, striving to assume the identity and values of that poet. But then, having made this attempt at Negative Capability, Johnson begins to reassert his own identity and values, usually-but not always-in opposition to those of his model. Thus, Johnson establishes a moral and critical dialectic between himself and his Latin poetic model that mirrors the dynamics he establishes in his English verse imitations between himself and his classical predecessors.

Johnson uses all of these devices in writing his Latin verse imitations. Sometimes he organizes a neo-Latin poem around allusions to both neo-Latin and classical sources. In the case of (ProQuest Information and Learning: Foreign characters omitted) for instance, Johnson relies on a nexus of allusions to Virgil's Aeneid to create a playfully mocking contrast between the tribulations of the epic hero, Aeneas, and the Johnsonian anti-hero who has just endured the revision of the fourth edition of his Dictionary. Furthermore, in the same poem, Johnson creates a mock-heroic contrast between himself and the great humanist Joseph Scaliger, who, as he finished his Arabic lexicon, also wrote a poem-to which Johnson alludes-complaining of the tedium of dictionary-making.

In one of his most interesting exercises in neo-Latin verse imitation, Johnson updates the moral and philosophical sentiments typically found in a Horatian ode while retaining the Horatian diction and meter so that he makes Horace speak as he would were he living in eighteenth-century Europe rather than in first-century B. C. E. Rome. But, instead of making Horace speak English as John Oldham and Alexander Pope had done, Johnson has him speak as a late-eighteenth-century Latinist. Thus, in the Latin ode beginning, "Ponti Profundis," Johnson writes a Christianized version of a Horatian ode, which closes not with a celebration of Stoic self-sufficiency and an invocation of the classical gods but with a pointed reminder of humanity's dependence on a single Christian God. Johnson also Christianizes the classical in his Latin translations from the Greek Anthology, which were probably begun as a means of easing the tedium of sleepless nights during Johnson's last year of life, but which evolved into a kind of devotional exercise for the dying man.

On other occasions, Johnson uses a Latin precursor as a "screen" in order to address a subject that he was reluctant to take up in propria persona, as in his beautiful devotional poem, "Aeterne Rerum Conditor." Since religious subject matter was generally taboo for him as a poet, Johnson learned to rely on buffering models of poetic precursors when writing Latin religious poetry, much as he had done when composing his Christian response to Juvenal in the concluding section of The Vanity of Human Wishes. Finally, on occasion, Johnson adapts the style and voice of a classical precursor in order playfully to explore a subject that might otherwise seem beyond his usual poetic range. In the "Verses Addressed to Dr. Lawrence," for example, Johnson writes a delightful Ovidian-Lucretian cosmogonical poem, in which he allows himself to speculate on the origins and order of the natural world. The devoutly Christian Johnson is careful, however, to avoid personally endorsing the Epicurean materialist cosmogony that is so central to his classical sources.

These encounters between past and present in Johnson's Latin poetry are particularly fascinating because they testify to Johnson's pleasure in meeting-and sometimes confronting-his poetic precursors. For Johnson, as a philosophical and moral essentialist, the past remained historically distinct but morally accessible, and he was never shy about arguing questions of truth with other writers, even across the divide of centuries.

... ("Know Thyself") is Johnson's Latin tour de force. The poem, written in 1772, brilliantly combines complaint-and a steady soulsearching that eventually undercuts the force of that complaint-with an irony that ultimately mocks it. Chiefly through the use of classical echoes and allusions, Johnson vividly describes the anxiety and frustration he felt upon finishing the revision of the Dictionary for the fourth edition, while bringing those emotions into perspective by measuring them against objective standards. The meter Johnson chooses for his poem-heroic hexameter-helps account for this double perspective, since it was the standard Latin meter for both heroic and satiric or mock-heroic poetry. This clever dynamic helps to explain why Johnson enjoyed showing to friends a poem that modern commentators frequently have found painfully confessional:... couples its lyricism with a self-possessed, self-deprecating sense of humor.

Johnson avers that Scaliger's labor on the Arabic lexicon was indeed confining since that eminent, learned, and discerning ("sublimis, doctus, et acer"; line 6) man had mastered not only the "rough road of words" ("vocumque salebris"; line 19), but also the disciplines of history, poetry, science, and philosophy: "Qui veterum modo facta ducum, modo carmina vatum, / Gesserat et quicquid Virtus, Sapientia quicquid / Dixerat, imperiique vices, coelique meatus, / Ingentemque animo seclorum volverat orbern" ("He revolved in his mind now the deeds of ancient generals, now the verses of poets, and whatever Virtue did and Wisdom spoke: the rise and fall of empires, the motions of the heavens, and the immense cycle of the ages"; lines 8-11). By contrast, Johnson has no reason either to castigate lexicography or to celebrate the completion of his own task. Although he, too, finds himself freed from a painstaking chore-"pensum" in line 24 refers to the portion of wool weighed out to a spinner, usually a slave, for a day's workhis freedom brings no sense of relief. Instead, Johnson's liberation from work on the Dictionary serves to remind him that he remains "condemned" ("damnare"; line 52) to the inward prison of a restless temperament, an idle mind, a slothful disposition, and a troubled conscience culminates in the harrowing, introspective journey on which Johnson embarks in paragraphs five and six (lines 24-51) of the poem. Here, as Susie I. Tucker and Henry Gifford noted many years ago, the poem becomes richly allusive, resonating with echoes of, among other poems, the Aeneid, the Metamorphoses, Juvenal's Third and Tenth Satires, and Statius's Sylvae. But critics continue to be puzzled by the function, if any, of these allusions; one recent commentator, for example, criticizes them as "varied" and "random" echoes that alternate haphazardly between meaningful allusions and mere appropriations of vocabulary.' It is true that, like most neo-Latinists, Johnson enjoyed the practice of adorning his Latin poems with "tags"-words and phrases taken from classical poems that are sometimes ornamental in function, sometimes more meaningfully allusive. One can make the case, however, that Johnson organized a significant number of his allusions, which gradually shift in tone from heroic to ironic, around analogies to events in the Aeneid: just as Aeneas struggles to sustain the Trojans' morale against the onslaughts of besieging Greeks, the Juno's enmity, and the trials of a long journey, so Johnson struggles to maintain his own equanimity in the face of gnawing cares, growing anxiety, and a sense of his own squandered talents. Johnson relies most heavily on his readers' knowledge of the events of Books 1, 2, and 6 of the Aeneid. In Book 1, after his ships are overtaken by a dreadful storm that Aeolus raises at Juno's request, Aeneas sails to Carthage, where his mother, Venus, disguised as a huntress, suitably prepares him to meet Queen Dido. In Book 2, Aeneas describes for his Carthaginian hosts the sack of Troy and his narrow escape from the burning city. Finally, in Book 6, Aeneas descends to the underworld, where he observes many of the denizens of Hades and converses with the shade of his father, Anchises, who grants his son a prophetic vision of his line of illustrious progeny.

The allusions to Book 2 of the Aeneid help to explain the anxious tone and martial metaphors of paragraph five of..... When Johnson describes himself in lines 27-28 as harried ("vexat") by a relentless troop ("importuna cohors") of inescapable cares, he has begun to compare himself with Aeneas. In line 32, the comparison becomes explicit. When Johnson declares, "Omnia percurro trepidus, circum omnia lustro / Si qua usquam patent melioris semita vitae" ("In trepidation I race through all things and survey everything around me, searching everywhere for a better way of life"), he is echoing lines 564-66 of Book 2 of the Aeneid, in which Aeneas, who has just witnessed the murder of Priam, thinks in horror of the possible fate of his own family and then looks about in vain for help from his weary troops, who have either dropped to the ground in despair or fallen into the flames. Secondary allusions contribute to Johnson's comparison of himself to a combatant in the Trojan War. When Johnson, for example, refers to his sluggish existence as "tardae taedia vitae" ("the tedium of a dull life"; line 26), he is drawing on Ulysses's description of the ten years of the Trojan War in Book Thirteen of Ovid's Metamorphoses as "longi taedia belli".

With the allusions to Book 6 of the Aeneid in paragraph six, the tone changes from heroic to mock-heroic as Johnson compares the survey of his life's accomplishments to Aeneas's descent into, and survey of, the underworld. Here, the echoes grow mocking: in contrast to Aeneas, who marches hellward with "fearless steps" ("haud timidis... passibus"; Aeneid 6.263), Johnson shudders at the mere thought of the ghosts that inhabit his personal, internal Underworld: the "empty visions, fleeting shadows, and thin shapes" (lines 50-51) that flit through his mind. These visions, which symbolize the paucity of Johnson's accomplishments, contrast with Anchises's prophecy of the many achievements of Aeneas's posterity. While Aeneas is granted a vision of the greatness of his descendants, Johnson enjoys no comparable survey of the "march of [his] achievements" (line 46). Nor can Johnson boast any equivalent to the "laetos... honores" ("pleasing adornments"; line 47) with which Venus graces her son just before he first meets Dido. Echoes of Juvenal's Tenth and Third Satires and Statius's Sylvae complete the irony. The quotations from Juvenal are especially telling because Johnson had previously translated the echoed passages in The Vanity of Human Wishes and London. When an anxious Johnson looks to see "Si qua usquam pateat melioris semita vitae" ("If a better way of life should open up anywhere"; line 33), he seems to be castigating himself-in spite of his well-known reservations about Stoicism-for failing to utilize Juvenal's memorable advice on achieving peace of mind from the conclusion to Satire Ten: "Monstro quod ipse tibi possis dare; semita certe / tranquillae per virtutem patet unica vitae" ("I show what thou canst give to thyself: the only sure way to a tranquil life lies through Virtue"; lines 36364). While Juvenal confidently maintains that the path to a calm and virtuous life is open and obvious, Johnson, the famous imitator of this very poem, is forced to confess that he has not been able to find it. Likewise, when Johnson complains, "Quicquid again, quocunque ferar, conatibus obstat / Res angusta domi, et macrae penuria mentis" ("Whatever I do, wherever I go, my scanty means and the poverty of a barren mind hinder my efforts"; lines 40-41), he echoes perhaps the most famous passage in Juvenal's Third Satire, translated in London as, "Slow rises Worth, by Poverty deprest" (line 177). In telling contrast to Juvenal's speaker, who is stymied by an accidental lack of riches, Johnson admits to a more fundamental poverty of native intellectual talents. He turns his irony in upon himself further in an echo of Statius's Sylvae. When Johnson refers to his mind as "Summus... celsa dominator [in] arce" ("the mighty ruler [in] its lofty citadel"), the elaborate periphrasis mockingly dramatizes the blustery "empty force" of his mind's pretensions. In the Sylvae, by contrast, Statius uses virtually the same language to praise his patron Pollius Felix for maintaining his Epicurean detachment in the face of all-pervasive human folly. Johnson's self-mockery serves important rhetorical, moral, and psychological functions. First, it calls into question the epic proportions of the troubles depicted in paragraph five. Johnson may feel the aptness of the analogy, but do the difficulties of his lexicographical drudgery really compare with the trials of a Virgilian hero? In turn, such mockery forces Johnson to look more dispassionately at his failings, and, as the title of the poem indicates, to know himself better. The shift from subjective description to objective analysis ultimately lessens the impact of the self-recrimination that haunts much of the poem. After placing his trepidation in perspective, Johnson concludes... by laughing at himself. Indeed, Johnson seems to have enjoyed depicting himself mock-heroically. On at least one other occasion, when writing to Mrs. Thrale, Johnson playfully compares himself to Aeneas about to recount the sufferings of the Trojans to Dido. Furthermore, Isobel Grundy emphasizes that Johnson "enjoyed the implications of comparing himself in jest with Aeneas or Odysseus or Alexander". By so doing, Johnson frees himself to move from the gloomy pose of paragraph six to the laughter of the surprise ending of the poem: "Quid faciam? tenebrisne pigram damnare senectam / Restat? an accingar studiis gravioribus audax? / Aut, hoc nimium est, tandem nova lexica poscam?" ("What should I do? Is my slothful old age doomed to gloomy obscurity? Or should I boldly gird myself for more serious studies? Or if this prove too much for me, should I undertake new dictionaries?"). Perhaps Joseph Scaliger found lexicography confining, but Johnson, as Robert DeMaria, Jr., has shown, seems to have grown fond of this "harmless drudgery" because he concluded that it allowed him usefully to fill up the vacuities of his time. Indeed, two years after completing... Johnson told his Bolt Court neighbor, the Rev. Percival Stockdale, that he hoped to secure from the booksellers the job of revising Elisha Chambers's Dictionary of the Arts and Sciences, explaining, "I like that muddling work".

If Johnson builds a new moral and rhetorical context around the heroic allusions in... to emphasize his inability to measure up to epic standards, then in his Latin odes he creates a new religious context around the Horatian form of the ode in an attempt to Christianize the classical. Thus, as Alan Wiesenthal has observed about the Skye Ode beginning "Ponti Profundis," "while Johnson [the] poet can embrace the [formal elements of the] Horatian ode, Johnson the moralist must repudiate [its content]". In "Ponti Profundis," after a Horatian introduction, the speaker replaces the polytheism and Stoicism of Horace's Ode 2.16 with a celebration of the dependence of humanity on a single, Christian God. In the process, Johnson transforms the Horatian ode into a Christian hymn.

Skye is personified as a welcoming nurse ready to offer refuge to the weary traveler, battered like Johnson by autumnal storms. Initially, the speaker seems to take pleasure in describing the wild, Hebridean landscape, for he appears to accept the familiar Horatian assumption that retreat from the complexities of civilization may bring relief from care. Surely in this remote place, he tells himself, using a familiar Johnsonian metaphor, there are no emotional ambushes awaiting the traveler.

In a conventional Horatian ode, the next stanza would present the Stoic alternative. Take, for example, Horace's Ode

2.16, which Johnson recited while sailing in an open boat from Skye to Raasay during the same week that, according to Boswell, "Ponti Profundis" probably was written. The poem begins by observing the universality of the human desire for "tranquility" ("otium"): the storm-tossed mariner, the impetuous warrior, even the most wealthy and powerful of men, is compelled to pray for such peace of mind since that elusive condition is independent of one's ability to acquire material possessions. The only way to achieve lasting contentment, according to Horace, is to temper one's desires (lines 13-14), to live for the present (line 25), and to accept the will of the Fates, the "Parcae," on whose name the speaker puns, since in Latin "parca" means both "Fate" and "frugal". The passage echoes Juno's flattering invocation of Aeolus at the beginning of Book I of the Aeneid, in which she asks the god of winds to raise a storm to sink Aeneas's fleet. But Aeolus, in contrast to Johnson's Christian God, is only one of many gods, and his powers are severely limited: within fifty lines of his granting Juno's prayer, his actions are overruled by Neptune. The passage also echoes the fourth stanza (lines 13-16) of Horace's Ode 1.3, a prayer for the poet Virgil as he sets out on a voyage to Greece. Horace implores the indulgence of Notus, the South Wind, "quo non arbiter Hadriae / maior, tollere seu ponere volt freta" ("whether he elect to raise or calm the waves, since there is no mightier master of the Adriatic"). Johnson replaces the pantheon of Virgil and Horace's classical gods with a single, almighty Christian deity-"summe... solus arbiter"-who rules both the stormy seas of nature and the psychological tempests within the human breast. The image of the "tempestuous heart" ("exaestuantis pectoris") is especially effective because the adjective "exaestuans"—cognate with "estuary" and "estivate"-while usually associated with turbulent water, was sometimes used metaphorically in classical Latin to describe a distressed mind or troubled heart. By combining Horatian meter with a simple but passionate invocation of the Christian God, Johnson moves from the world of classical Latin to the prayers and hymns of the early Church Fathers. Indeed, one might say about this poem what

F. J. E. Raby says about the hymns of Saint Ambrose: "If, as regards form, [it follows classical] models, [it nevertheless remains] a true effort of original creation, in which the Christian spirit controls the artistic form, and not [a mere effort of imitation] in which the form controls the content of the verse". Johnson thus creates a subtle moral and theological rejoinder to his Horatian poetic model.

Johnson also Christianizes the classical in the process of translating poems from the Greek Anthology, a collection of about four thousand epigrams written between the seventh century B. C. E. and the tenth century C. E. Approximately one-third of these ninety-five translations are epitaphs; many of the others are elegiac, taking as their subject matter the transitoriness of life and the vanity of worldly success. In these poems, Johnson repeatedly explores the uncertainty and impermanence of human happiness: "Nil non mortale est mortalibus; one quod est hi / Praetereunt, aut hos praeterit omne bonum" ("Nothing is immortal which belongs to mortals; we pass, or are passed by, every good thing"). Even at their grimmest, however, these translations are qualified by the context of Johnson's religious faith. When he writes, "Quandoquidem passim nulla ratione feruntur / Cuncta, cinis cuncta et ludicra, cuncta nihil" ("All is laughter and ashes: since everything is brought hither randomly for no reason, everything is vain"), Johnson avoids the bleakness of classical materialism or modern nihilism by adopting the fideist position of Ecclesiastes.The very fact that "all [mundane life] is vanity" reinforces Johnson's faith in the existence of a hidden God, as the fervency and devotion of Johnson's last Latin prayers, contemporary with these translations, indicate. Indeed, the translations from the Greek Anthology and the Latin prayers complement one another in the same manner as do the "Survey" and "Prayer" sections of The Vanity of Human Wishes. Hence, although Johnson may have begun these translations, as Boswell suggests, simply as a means of alleviating the tedium of a sick man's sleepless nights during his last year of life, they developed into something much more significant: a book of spiritual exercises or meditations composed for the benefit of their dying author. Johnson models many of his verse prayers on the verse prayers and hymns of the early Church Fathers. In particular, Johnson seems to have admired the religious verse of Saint Ambrose, whose hymns he echoes in several verse prayers. As F. J. E. Raby notes, "Ambrose rejected metrical complication, chose the easy iambic dimeter, and wrote with an engaging simplicity, dignity, and fervour" (Secular Latin Poetry). Johnson most clearly captures this spirit in "Prayer (II)," which borrows its first line and its meter from an Ambrosian liturgical hymn:

Aeterne rerum conditor, Salutis aeternae dator; Felicitatis sedibus Qui nec scelestos exigis, Quoscumque scelerum poenitet; Da, Christe, poenitentiam, Veniamque, Christe, da mihi; Aegrum trahenti spiritum Succurre praesens corpori, Multo gravatam crimine Mentem benignus alleva.

Eternal author of all things, giver of eternal salvation, who drivest not away from the seats of bliss the sinful who are sorry for their sins; grant, O Christ, penitence and mercy; O Christ, grant them to me. Succor my body dragging this afflicted spirit, and raise my mind, O kindly Presence, weighed down by many sins.

Within the narrow confines of Ambrose's spare iambic dimeter, Johnson employs all of the basic rhetorical devices he commonly uses in his Latin verse prayers and then some: repetition, balance, antithesis, alliteration, rhetorical suspension; but when one reads the poem, one is struck not by the technical artistry, but by the direct and striking emotional power. How was Johnson, who was almost always reluctant to write religious verse, able in this case to overcome that taboo? The answer lies in his use of Saint Ambrose's hymn as both a model and a screen. I have discussed elsewhere Johnson's taboo against writing religious poetry. As he explains in the Life of Waller, Johnson believed that the rhetorical and mimetic qualities of poetry were hopelessly inadequate when attempting to address a God who infinitely transcends the human capacity to persuade or describe (Lives 1: 2-). But by relying on Ambrose as a model, Johnson, who tended to consider himself spiritually unworthy of addressing sacred subjects in verse, is able to capture some of the Saint's devotional power, while at the same time using Ambrose as a protective screen so that he is never compelled to step forth unassisted, as it were, and speak solely as and for himself. Johnson was, of course, familiar with this rhetorical maneuver from his work on the closing lines of The Vanity of Human Wishes, in which he freed himself to offer religious advice to his readers by speaking not in his own person but as he imagined Juvenal might, from an eighteenth-century Anglican perspective.

One of Johnson's most unusual Latin poems is the Lucretian-Ovidian cosmogonical poem, "Verses Addressed to Dr. Lawrence," written while Johnson was being treated for a serious eye ailment by his physician-friend Thomas Lawrence in the spring of. In this poem, as in "Aeterne Rerum Conditor," Johnson uses the diction and`meter of a Latin precursor as a kind of screen to explore a subject that he probably would not have approached otherwise from anything except an orthodox Christian perspective: the creation of the universe. The poem uses the same meter-heroic hexameter-and the same philosophical vocabulary as Ovid's Metamorphoses and Lucretius's De Rerum Natura, both of which address the subject of the origin of the universe from an Epicurean-materialist perspective. In the poem, the ailing Johnson sets out to entertain his doctor-naturalist friend by observing that, "It is normal for the human mind to nourish itself on the forms of Nature and it is a common passion in all to hunt out the truth by investigation, though the passions of everyone differ" ("Humanae mentis, rèrum se pascere formis, / Est proprium, et quavis captare indagine verum Omnibus unus amor, non est modus unus amoris"; lines 6-8). Johnson then divides all of humanity into two groups based on their degree of curiosity about the natural world. The first group, he explains, consists of cautious empiricists and traditionalists: "those timid people who are turned about in a narrow track; whom the senses alone lead, and custom only instructs; who are wise enough in their own eyes, content with the sensations of what they touch, see, or hear" ("Sunt qui curriculo timidi versantur in arcto, / Quos soli ducunt sensus, solus docet usus; / Qui sibi sat sapium, contend noscere quantum / Vel digiti tractant, oculus vel sentit et auris"; lines 9-). This group obviously constitutes the vast majority of human beings, but the scantness of Johnson's discussion of ther. ›nly ten lines (lines 9-)-suggests that his primary interest lies with the second group: the daring and speculative cosmogonists who are not bound by the rules of empirical observation. Indeed, Johnson devotes the remaining half of the poem, lines -, to this second group.

Here, Johnson, without any harsh or overt criticism of the philosophical position, outlines the theories of these "sons of sacred Reason" ("sanctae rationis alumni"; line), who "with great effort... invade nature, forming anew the elements of the world, mixing smooth with rough, square with round" ("magno conamine summam / Naturae invadens, mundique elementa refingens / Laevia serratis miscens, quadrata rotundis"; lines -).

Indeed, Johnson goes on to observe with more amusement than disapproval that "these are they whom no wonder surprises, nothing strange moves; while they place all things under laws they have made, and dare to fix a limit to causation" ("hi sunt quos nil mirabile turbat, / Nil movet insolitum, sub legibus omnia fictis / Dum statuunt, causisque audent prefigere metam".

Johnson's attitude in this poem toward a philosophical position that is entirely at odds with his Christian beliefs is as noteworthy as it is surprising. Typically, Johnsōn would have no time for the philosophical materialism or cosmogonical speculation of Epicurus, Lucretius, and their followers. One need or ly think of Johnson's exasperated and impatient respons: in the Life of Pope to Pope's professions of omniscience in An Essay on Man (Lives 3: 2-). But, in contrast to Jonathan Swift, who includes Epicurus the cosmogonist and his disciple Lucretius among the world's great madmen in Section IX, "A Digression Concerning the Original, the Use and Improvement of Madness in a Commonwealth," of A Tale of a Tub, Johnson displays in this poem surprising tolerance of such philosophical speculation. Why is Johnson able to discuss the philosophical materialism of the Epicureans here with such dispassion and even-dare one say-good humor? Probably because he uses the same "model and screen" approach to his subject that he employed in writing "Aeterne Rerum Conditor," except that, in this case, Johnson uses the meter and rhetoric of Ovid and Lucretius prophylactically as a buffer to protect himself from the moral contaminants of classical Epicureanism.

In other words, Johnson carefully positions himself rhetorically so that he does not speak this poem in propria persona but ventriloquially, as it were, "through" the persons of Ovid and Lucretius. Thus, by self-consciously assuming a LucretianOvidian mask, Johnson is able freely and playfully to explore the Epicureanmaterialist perspective without ever implicating himself personally in it. Interestingly, by, with the advent of the Romantic emphasis on sincerity, such rhetorical freedom would become much more difficult for writers to achieve.

Johnson's neo-Latin practice illustrates that, in the eighteenth century, verse imitation and its techniques and conventions were by no means restricted to the vernacular. Indeed, for a diminishing but still significant audience, a poet could write in Latin while drawing on three different traditions: the classical, the patristic, and the Renaissance-humanistic.

If vernacular imitations were part of an attempt by eighteenth-century poets to transcend time and space by making ancient poets speak in modern tongues, Johnson's Latin imitations exemplify the efforts of Renaissance humanists to emphasize the continuity of a cultural tradition that stretched back more than two thousand years through the medium of a language that was intended by scholars and clerics to transcend the limits of modern national and cultural boundaries. Curiously, although Johnson gave up writing verse imitations in English after The Vanity of Human Wishes in 1749, he continued to write Latin poems based on the principles of imitation until his death in 1784. In Latin, Johnson could both debate with his poetic precursors and use the rhetorical principles involved in writing verse imitations to speak through a persona on subjects that he might not otherwise have explored.

The Englishing of Juvenal

Let us begin with the matter of attribution, by far the most familiar use of computational stylistics. In the trials mentioned above, taking cases where the authorship of the texts was in no real doubt, the object was to pick out the true author of each poem from a field of twenty-five poets of the period. All told, the Delta procedure succeeded with ninety-four poems out of two hundred, even though a hundred of them were of fewer than five hundred words in length.

It succeeded with thirty-six poems out of the forty whose length exceeded fifteen hundred words. Of the twenty whose length exceeded two thousand words, it succeeded with nineteen. Since the texts to be considered in this paper range from 2766 words to 6350, the Delta procedure might therefore be used here with great confidence if it could be assumed that poets stamp their stylistic signatures as firmly on a translation as on their original work.

In reality, of course, that very question is at issue. The identifiability of the translator of a text that originates in a foreign language makes for subtle attributional problems in which different levels of stylistic versatility and different ideas of translation and imitation have a bearing. But what, precisely, is this procedure? (2) Most of the methods employed in computational stylistics rest upon multivariate statistical comparisons between some characteristics of a given specimen and those of an appropriate set of norms. For an excellent recent specimen, see Holmes.

The characteristics, which are used as statistical variables, comprise the relative frequencies of various simple phenomena such as alphabetic characters, strings of characters, whole words, or common grammatical forms. The advantage of working with whole words rests on their accessibility and their meaningfulness. They help us, in particular, to form close and fruitful inferences about the outcome of an inquiry. Whichever class of variables is chosen, it has become customary, in recent years, to allow the particular variables to "declare themselves," thus obviating, as far as possible, the danger of a predetermined outcome.

The words used, for example, might be the hundred most common in the database that provides the norms fo r a particular inquiry. In this sort of work on language, so our researches teach us, a wealth of variables, many of which may be weak discriminators, almost always offer more tenable results than a smaller number of strong ones.

The multivariate statistical instruments now most used in computational stylistics are designed to portray interrelationships of resemblance and difference across a whole set of specimens. The outcome makes it possible to form explanatory inferences bearing, for example, on the likely authorship of a given specimen. These methods, however, are unsuitable for the crude but useful task of ranking many candidates in a single, all-embracing hierarchy, thus singling out the statistically most eligible among them. Even a ranked series of aggregates or means would serve that purpose if a sound basis were available.

But, because the scores for any given specimen on the chosen set of variables will always diverge in both directions from the norms for the database, an aggregate or mean divergence will comprise an arbitrary mixture of positives and negatives.

Now while the differences between positives and negatives—high scores, say, for the in this specimen but low ones for land me—are most instructive, they are not the heart of the matter. An expression of difference, pure difference, is what we need. If all the positive and negative divergences were rendered as absolute divergences, their overall aggregate or their mean might be of interest. A delta score is just such a mean divergence.

The first step in the Delta procedure is to establish a frequency hierarchy for the most common words in a large group of suitable texts. The texts are arranged in subsets representing the work of numerous authors appropriate to the particular task in hand. With texts of a bygone era, it is usual and desirable to standardize spelling and to expand contracted forms of expression in order to reduce the influence of trivial or accidental variations. It has also been our practice, in Newcastle, to tag some of the more common homographic forms in order to distinguish the different uses of words like *so* and *that*. When the word counts have been made, the frequencies are standardized as percentages of each authorial subset so that the larger subsets do not exert an undue influence on the composition or ranking of the hierarchy.

Working on these lines, we have formed a database of verse by twenty-five poets of the English Restoration period? This set of over half a million words yielded the frequency-hierarchies used for several recent studies of authorship. (The most recent example is Burrows and Craig.) The same database yielded the norms for the Delta project. For this project, however, I have added a further range of texts.

Those to be considered in the present paper are fifteen English translations of Juvenal's Tenth Satire. They range chronologically from Henry Vaughan (1646) to Jerome Mazzaro (1965) and Peter Green (1967). Those of Evans, Green, Ramsay, and Sheridan are couched in prose, the rest in verse of one kind or another. All but one are independent of the main database. The exception is Thomas Shadwell's version (1687), retained here in order to demonstrate the need for rigor on this very point.

Table 1 represents a small Microsoft Excel worksheet. It offers a simplified version of the procedure, bringing the top twenty words of the database of Restoration verse to bear on a plain question. Can we demonstrate, by this means, that our main sample of Dryden's verse differs less from his translation of Juvenal's Tenth Satire than from The Vanity of Human Wishes? Columns A and B list the twenty most common words in descending order of their frequency in the main database. Column C shows their mean frequencies, all represented as percentages of that set while Column D shows the corresponding standard deviations. Columns E, G, and J show the scores for our sample of Dryden's verse, for his translation of Juvenal X and for The Vanity of Human Wishes respectively while Columns F, H, and K give z-scores representing their divergences from the means of the main set.

An Old Edition of Samuel Johnson's Works

Several years ago I purchased a used, two-volume edition of the complete works of Samuel Johnson. I had several reasons for doing so, one of which was to obtain a few of his works that I had had trouble finding. Among them was his early satire on Robert Walpole titled "Marmor Norfolciense," Johnson's contribution to the literary war that major writers — such as he, Jonathan Swift, and John Gay — conducted against the man who was transforming England into a commercial society run on political patronage. Another was his essay on Hermann Boerhaave, a Dutch scientist. As to that essay, I knew about Johnson's encyclopedic range of knowledge — he had once astounded Boswell by delivering a long dissertation on the craft of butchering meat — and I thought that it would be interesting to read his comments on a subject that lay outside the mainstream of his interests. My list of reading projects included the complete Rambler *essays.*

Aside from the contents, the faded grandeur of those books, when considered as physical objects, would make them visually interesting occupants of one of my bookshelves. The volumes are American first edition (1838) and leather-bound. Were they in mint condition, they would be very valuable; but their covers have deteriorated badly, some pages are torn, and all the pages are sere due to age.

I cannot identify P.R. Carrington for certain, but I think that I know who he was and some facts about him. The State Historical Society of Wisconsin's library contains a biography of Paul Carrington (1733-1818), who was a member of the first Supreme Court of Appeals of Virginia. In that book someone had placed a typewritten genealogy of the Carringtons which extends well into the nineteenth century. They were a prominent Richmond family, connected by marriage to other prominent Virginia families, such as the Peytons (this connection probably is the reason for P.R's first name) and the

Randolphs. That family included many lawyers, judges, and elected public officials. According to the genealogy, Joseph Littleberry Carrington, who was born in 1810, had a son Peyton, whose date of birth is not given, but who probably was a fairly young man in 1862. The compiler of the genealogy acknowledges the help of Peyton Carrington, no doubt Joseph's son.

An interest in genealogy seems compatible with an interest in serious works of literature. In the genealogy I found no other Carringtons from that era whose initials could have been P.R. A book about a cemetery in Richmond states that Peyton R. Carrington was ordered in 1892 to repair a wall at the Adams-Carrington burying ground but could not do so because of insufficient funds. (Those same grounds contained the remains of the brother of John Marshall, the first Chief Justice of the U.S. Supreme Court, and the remains of the grandfather of General Pickett of Pickett's Charge.) Peyton Carrington is identified in a 1904 social register as the husband of Sarah and the father of Peyton, Jr. The senior Peyton died in 1911. Those Peyton Carringtons seem to be the same person and very probably the former owner of the books I now possess.

Let us examine the inscription. First, it is important to reflect on the fact that Carrington could write his name in a book — I cannot imagine the way in which someone could place a handwritten inscription on a CD-ROM. That is another, albeit a minor, reason to be concerned about the displacement of books in our culture. When one thinks of an autographed copy of a book, one almost always thinks of the *author's* autograph. Such autographs create a magical connection between the book's owner and the book's author; owning an autographed copy — and, more obviously, asking an author to autograph a copy of a book that he or she has written — are ways to pay homage to the writer. Some collectors of autographed books are further motivated by the resulting increase in a book's value. Unluckily for me, Samuel Johnson had not autographed my books; P.R. Carrington had. Like Carrington, I sign the books, which I purchase — not to announce that it is merely one of my possessions, but that it is part of my identity. Perhaps P.R. Carrington felt the same way.

Next, Carrington wrote "Richmond, Va." On this practice, he and I differ. Perhaps I should have adopted his practice; had I written in the place of purchase for those books, which I bought in cities where I lived, I would have connected each of my books not only to a place, but also to a phase of my life. That would have allowed me to speculate later about the relationships between, on the one hand, my tastes in reading and, on the other hand, my age and the circumstances of my life when I bought each of my books. In addition, some of the books that I bought while traveling would remind me of the trip during which they were purchased or of a connection between the book and the place of purchase.

I suspect that Carrington lived all, or virtually all, of his life in Richmond. If so, the reason he chose to record the place of purchase was not one of the reasons I would have done so. Rather, he probably was asserting his pride in his city. His family's prominence — and long residence — in Richmond created some of that pride. He also might have been reacting to the Civil War: asserting his pride in Richmond and the cause that it, as the Confederacy's capital, exemplified. Perhaps he even thought that he was asserting that Richmond still existed; the Union army had not taken it during the Peninsula Campaign, although it had come close to doing so.

Finally, Carrington wrote down the year in which he bought those books. I do not do that. However, to facilitate shelving works of literature, I write in the year of publication on the first blank page of each book so that it is readily apparent. In my library, my American literature section, my British literature section, and my "other" literature section are arranged chronologically so that when I scan those shelves I learn a lesson in literary history. That "1862" in Carrington's copy astounded me, whereas, say, "1858" would not have done so. The "1862" indicated that for him life continued, and at a high intellectual level, despite the Civil War. For anyone who reads it now, that written representation of a year is a poignant reminder both of life's fragility and humankind's resilience.

Writing it was a gesture, like those that thousands of others have made throughout the centuries, attesting that they not only will endure but also will prevail.

Thus a man who lived in Richmond, Virginia, during the Civil War had spent a substantial amount of money to buy books; those volumes at that time certainly were costly. In 1862, the South was holding its own and was not yet in the desperate financial straits that were to afflict it because of its weak economy and the war's length. Nevertheless, during that year the Peninsula Campaign and the war as a whole must have made it fairly difficult, even then, to find and pay for the necessities of life. Carrington apparently either had considerable wealth and could thus purchase food, clothing, fuel, etc., as well as books, or he considered Johnson's works to be among the necessities of life. Moreover, he purchased a fine edition, probably not for show, given the exigencies of the time and place, but more likely to reflect his esteem for the contents.

Carrington probably did not think of books in some of the ways that are now common. As his purchase of those books indicates, to him their purpose was not to reinforce his own beliefs. Someone who reads books for that purpose would not spend money in Carrington's situation for books; in fact, such a person would not really need books at all. Carrington also did not reject books that opposed his beliefs. In fact, he might have known that in "Taxation no Tyranny" Johnson had written how is it that we hear the loudest *yelps* for liberty among the drivers of Negroes?"

Carrington also probably did not think that the great books—and some of Johnson's works lie on the fringe of that classification—were a monolithic block that oppressed the downtrodden and abetted the powerful. Johnson, whose household for years included an African American, whom he treated very well and looked after in his will, and for intervals included prostitutes, whom Johnson carried home on his back, and various down-and-out writers, was hardly an oppressor of the downtrodden. Moreover, his mind was too subtle and his intellectual integrity too great for him to write simplistic propaganda. No, like the other great writers, he debated himself; and the results of those self-debates join with those of other great writers to create a many-voiced commentary on the great human issues.

Because Johnson attracted him, Carrington probably read for wisdom, entertainment, and solace—Johnson's works are full of all three qualities. His moral philosophy, for example, as it is exhibited in the *Rambler* essays, is worth pondering. Some of those essays are playful, but most are incisive meditations on practical ethics. In their totality they present Johnson's views on the way in which one ought to conduct one's life.

If chronology was reversed and language was no barrier, Montaigne, who read in order to learn how to live, would have repeatedly read those essays. In his writing, Johnson entertained but did so unconventionally. His books contain occasional flashes of wit—though not nearly as many as he exhibited in his conversation as recorded by Boswell—and a few diverting narratives.

The entertainment is provided mainly by the prose style; it appeals to readers who have acquired a taste for good writing, particularly for eighteenth-century cadenced, elevated prose. More readers of that kind lived in Carrington's time than live in ours. Johnson provided solace by writing about the tribulations, large and small, that inhere in everyday life and by describing ways in which persons not only could cope with those tribulations, but also could improve themselves by withstanding them.

More specifically, why would Samuel Johnson's works be a good choice for a serious reader who lived in Richmond in 1862? Johnson's moral philosophy would have been one reason. War, like all major crises, raises and increases the complexity and importance of ethical issues. Johnson's wisdom—his understanding of the way one ought to live—and his willingness and ability to communicate that wisdom would have made him highly pertinent to a reader who was living through a war. Carrington might also have known that, regardless of the Civil War's outcome, that war would transform the South. In other words, during 1862 Carrington lived in a dying society and probably knew that he did.

Late in his life, Johnson recognized that he was living in a dying society, one in which commercial interests were displacing agrarian interests, persons were becoming less deferential to tradition and authority, and literature was moving toward the emphasis on self-expression, rather than craftsmanship, that would become full-blown during the ensuing Romantic era. In an early work titled "The Vanity of Human Wishes" he identified some of the forces that were effecting those changes. In *Lives of the Poets,* an elegiac tone prevails; Johnson reverently commemorates a literary tradition and the society that it suited as the lives faded into oblivion. (*Life of Savage,* a much earlier work than the other *Lives,* is an exception.) Most disturbingly, Johnson's frequently revealed obsession with death would have been relevant to Carrington.

Even if Carrington did not read all of the contents of the two volumes, by buying them, he gained the opportunity to read all the works by Johnson then available. Even setting aside all the persons who do not read any books at all and those who do not read any serious books, most persons, I suspect, flit from book to book and author to author, as I usually do. Reading all the works of a difficult and prolific writer is a quite different form of intellectual labor. The degree of immersion in an author's works that Carrington could have experienced—and perhaps did experience—is the kind of reading adventure that today seems unusual. Even owning all the works of such a writer is probably unusual now. The advantages of a long-term engagement with a first-rate mind are obvious enough.

Johnson's complexity and the extent to which he developed his ideas make careful and sustained concentration necessary if a reader is to understand him. Today those qualities have become more difficult to acquire as brief bursts of information, many of them accompanied by distracting visual and auditory stimuli, more frequently assault us. A person who could sit down with a copy of Johnson's works during a war—perhaps while actually hearing the sounds of war—and comprehend what he was reading amazes one. As the percentage of persons in our society who are able and willing to concentrate that tenaciously dwindles, our society becomes at risk not of the disaster of military defeat, but of the disaster of cultural deprivation.

On the basis of Carrington's books, it is also possible to make a few tentative broader generalizations. Despite his financial embarrassment in 1892, Carrington was an aristocrat in the sense that he was a member of a family that had a long record of public service in important positions, many of the members of which had probably been financially well-off and which, as his entry in the social register demonstrates, were considered socially prominent. We need to remind ourselves that during the middle of the nineteenth century—indeed, also for many centuries before that—many aristocrats were interested in intellectual matters. It is no surprise that Peyton Carrington bought, and probably read a good deal of, serious books. We need to remind ourselves of that fact also because one could plausibly argue that there are no aristocrats in this country now, and that whatever group is now a very rough equivalent of them—the rich, the powerful, or some other group—may contain few serious readers. Many members of that present group seem not to consider reading serious books to be a duty, a benefit, or even an adornment.

Carrington's books also remind us that there once was a common intellectual culture. The recent disputes about the canon and about great books annoy me not only because of the fatuity of some of the positions that have been taken during these discussions and the irrationality of some of the arguments that have been advanced, but also because they have so little relevance. Most of the participants in those disputes assume that there still is a common intellectual culture, that many persons bear it, and that it thus is important to make as satisfactory as possible the list of books that ought to be read. I think, however, that much of the common culture has dissipated. In contrast, during Carrington's time persons who considered themselves to be knowledgeable or well read (neither of which was the same as being well educated) knew many of the same things and had read many of the same authors. Among those authors was Samuel Johnson. It is not surprising that Carrington owned Johnson's works, just as it would not be surprising if he had owned *The Decline and Fall of the Roman Empire* or *Paradise Lost*. It would be surprising, though, if those two works or the complete works of Samuel Johnson were selling well today. Although Carrington's edition of Johnson was expensive, it was affordable for at least some persons, and in 1862 there probably were less expensive complete editions of Johnson. In contrast, buying Johnson's complete works today would require a good deal of money.

Carrington's books, although their condition is now poor, have survived for 145 years. They have lasted physically because they were well made, and they have lasted as a product in this stream of commerce, despite the reduced demand for such books, because some persons wanted them and no one discarded them. Books endure partly because they are not evanescent and intangible, like flickers on a television screen or on a computer monitor. Because they are tangible, their beauty can also be easily recognized and appreciated. It also has become more difficult to find, and more expensive to purchase, beautiful books.

In mint condition, Carrington's edition of Johnson must have been gorgeous to look at, and he no doubt also experienced pleasure from feeling the leather. Those secondary pleasures also are becoming rare. That, too, is unfortunate, because they add greatly to the experience of reading. Although P.R. Carrington has been dead for nearly a century, I think I know something about him because I know that he owned those books. If his library had been preserved intact and I had seen it, I would know very much about him, because I believe that a collection of books reveals a good deal about its owner. If the number of serious readers is decreasing (as seems to be the case), personal libraries will less frequently help others understand the owners of those libraries. I think that is unfortunate, not only because we will have fewer hints about persons, but because fewer persons will have been formed by books.

Despite the horrors of living in Richmond during 1862,

life there and then must have been intellectually satisfying. I find that in a way I envy P.R. Carrington. I have written about him and his books in order to connect, across a time-span of more than a century, with a fellow admirer of the works of Samuel Johnson and to create one small continuity in a world in which many of the large and important continuities are becoming disturbingly tenuous.

Reading the "Religious" Language of Samuel Johnson's Sermons

THE importance and popularity that the sermon once held in the secular as well as in the religious life of England is often underestimated today. Samuel Johnson claimed that he wrote approximately forty sermons; of these, twenty-eight are extant and have been attributed to him. The only book-length study of the sermons available to date is James Gray's Johnson's Sermons. A Study. In addition to providing a history of the composition and printing of the Sermons, Gray's study traces Johnson's attitudes on human vanity, the brevity of life, suffering, repentance, charity, domestic happiness, friendship, the Atonement, the Incarnation, rewards and punishments with parallel themes found in Rasselas, The Vanity of Human Wishes, The Idler, and The Rambler. Gray accurately argues for the integrated nature of Johnson's exhortations to right thinking and living. Moreover, Gray's study establishes numerous correlations between Johnson's Sermons and the rich English homiletic tradition. However, it does not examine Johnson's stylistic modifications of important elements within that same tradition which he found so praiseworthy. Johnson's modifications suggest his belief that religious faith is forged more by the realities of secular life and less by conventional religious ideals.

In contrast with English sermon style and especially with the metaphysical conventions dating from the seventeenth century which characterized some aspects of this style, Samuel Johnson's Sermons are remarkably free from other-worldly allusions, far-fetched symbolism, and ingenious imagery. He considered these tropes inappropriate for describing matters of religion and, more significantly, a corrupting influence on the practice of religion. Indeed, no legions of devils or choirs of angels inhabit Johnson's Sermons; they do not engage in interminable speculations on the abstract nature of the soul. The style of Johnson's Sermons always accentuates his efforts to examine the abstruse principles of religion against common human experience. By acknowledging the self-delusive propensities within human nature, the Sermons present religion as a pragmatic means to ascertain and make tolerable our basic helplessness.

Johnson's deviations in style from elements within the English sermon tradition is not an indication of his lack of esteem for the sermon as a genuine division of literature. On the contrary, his numerous observations on the English sermon reveal his appreciation of the oral, written homiletic, and literary dimensions of the genre. In a conversation concerning the posthumous sale of the Honorable Topham Beauclerk's library, Wilkes remarks on the irony that Beauclerk, a renowned rake, should have owned so many volumes of sermons: Mr. Beauclerk's great library was this season sold in London by auction. Mr. Wilkes said, he wondered to find in it such a numerous collection of sermons; seeming to think it strange that a gentleman of Mr. Beauclerk's character in the gay world, should have chosen to have many compositions of that kind. JOHNSON: Why, Sir, you are to consider that sermons make a considerable branch of English literature; so that a library must be very imperfect if it has not a numerous collection of sermons.

IN the Dictionary, Johnson's first definition for a sermon is: "A discourse of instruction pronounced by a divine for the edification of the people." The illustrative quotation, taken from Hooker, suggests both the artistic and the didactic traditions of the sermon:

As for our sermons, be they never so sound and perfect, God's words they are not, as the sermons of the prophets were; no, they are but ambiguously termed his word, because his word is commonly the subject whereof they treat, and must be the rule whereby they are framed.

However, it is not Richard Hooker but Thomas Secker, the influential Archbishop of Canterbury (1758-1768), for whom Johnson "expressed a great opinion". Archbishop Secker was a royalist, high Anglican, Tory, and a man of robust common sense. Secker's theology, like his politics and social theory, was pretty much in the main stream of eighteenth-century thought. Indeed, his first concern as Archbishop of Canterbury was to defend Christianity (synonymous for him with the Church of England) from its three perennial foes-skepticism, enthusiasm, and Roman Catholicism.

In his Eight Charges Delivered to the Clergy of the Dioceses of Oxford and Canterbury, Archbishop Secker directs that a sermon should convince by its reason and persuade by its beauty; indeed, it is these commonplace aesthetic principles which Johnson embraces as normative for a sermon to be effective. Archbishop Secker believed that much of the disregard for religion was due to the speculative content and ornate style which characterized many contemporary sermons:

> Smooth Discourses, composed partly in fine Words which they do not understand, partly in flowing Sentences which they cannot follow to the End; containing little that awakens their drowsy Attention, little that enforces on them plainly and home what they must do to be saved; leave them as ignorant and unreformed as ever, and only lull them into a fatal Security. Therefore, bring yourselves down to their level; for what suits the meanest Christian will suit the highest: Examine if they take in what you say, and change the form of it till they do. This I recommend for your first Study: and be assured, you will improve yourselves by it no less than your Hearers.

Johnson, with characteristic conviction, expressed a similar opinion when he accounted for the success of Methodist preaching:

> To insist against drunkenness as a crime, because it debases Reason, the noblest faculty of man, would be of no service to the common people; but to tell them that they may die in a fit of drunkenness, and shew them how dreadful that would be, cannot fail to make a deep impression.

While neither Johnson nor Secker genuinely entered into

sympathy with Methodist teaching and practice, both admitted that its preaching style provided great incentives for moral reformation. One of the great appeals of Archbishop Secker for Samuel Johnson, then, would have been the directive he gave his clergy to write sermons punctuated by examples from the natural rather than the supernatural world-to write with a simplified "popular eloquence" based upon practical examples rather than abstruse theological speculations. Not only does Secker appeal to Johnson's sense of propriety when he admonishes his clergy to fit the subject matter of their sermons to the audience, but he advises that this be done in a disciplined and restrained way: "But even the best qualified to exhort must keep within due Bounds; convince the Judgment before they attempt to warm the Passions..". It is precisely such a synthesis of reasoned doctrine and restrained illustration which typifies the style of Johnson's Sermons and contributes to their moral persuasiveness and literary merit.

Johnson never lowers his high literary standards when judging a sermon; yet, he is concerned with how the sermon, as a dramatic and public form of rhetoric, can make religion personal and immediate to the congregation. A sermon must not simply effect an act of intellectual assent; rather, it must engage a person's entire being with the practical concerns of moral reformation. Consequently, Johnson's Sermons often explore versions of realistically and honestly knowing human motivations through common experience which he always relates to the activity of the mind. Because he viewed reason as the most celestial faculty of human nature, Johnson devoted a major portion of his effort as a sermonist to the delineation of those conditions under which reason could play its proper role in guiding a person's ethical conduct in this life and in preparing one for the next. Johnson did not, however, believe that human affairs could be conducted wholly by the light of reason. Unless reason is supplemented by religion, the dangers of one's self-delusive nature could not be avoided. The Sermons recognize that in many circumstances reason is powerless or insufficient; nevertheless, they demonstrate that human conduct can be far more rational than it usually is, and the Sermons explain how one can make the fullest use of one's capacities for rational behavior.

Johnson's most frequent method of beginning his Sermons is to write a paragraph on some general phase of human existence which the congregation had experienced and with which it could empathize. Johnson always used the particular character of the audience or the peculiar situation for which he was writing the sermon in order to suggest morally appropriate modifications of human behavior. He never confines himself to the commonplace homiletic practice of offering consolation only through abstracted appeals to religious revelation. For example, "Sermon 23" is a pragmatic moral exemplum which denounces disobedience and wilful rebellion: Of the strife, which this day brings back to our remembrance, we may observe, that it had all the tokens of "strife" proceeding from "envy." The rage of the faction, which invaded the rights of the church and monarchy, was disproportionate to the provocation received.

Whatever one's opinion may be of the political views in the passage, Johnson is clearly shaping this sermon to the circumstances surrounding its delivery."Sermon 23" explores some of the legitimate duties of citizens as productive members of a political state. However, no less circumspect in political matters than in religious ones, Johnson, in "Sermon 23," punctures contrivance and arrives at the common sense standards of personal honesty and respect for others as best suited for pious meditation.

Johnson's sermon introductions, then, serve several rhetorical purposes: one, they effectively capture the auditor's attention through their practical concerns and common sense applications; two, they ease the secular mind into a serious consideration of the relevance of religion's answers to human questions-an approach which the modern theologian Paul Tillich, in A History of Christian Thought, describes as "the method of correlation"; and three, they emphasize Johnson's religious pragmatism by first examining human experience and thereby delaying the traditional appeal to religious revelation.

In the seventeenth century and, to a lesser extent, in the eighteenth, congregations often listened for hours to sermons placed end to end. Such congregations did not need much enticement to enter a sermon, so the preacher could plunge into the outline, confident that his listeners were receptive. Indeed, many of the standard sermon manuals of the day mandated that the outline be placed at the beginning of the sermon to help the memory of the hearer and to direct the judgment of the writer. For example, Hugh Blair's sermon, "On the Importance of Order in Conduct," begins:

In the sequel of this discourse I shall point out some of those parts of conduct wherein it is most material to virtue that order take place; and then shall conclude with showing the high advantages which attend it. Allow me to recommend to you, order in the conduct of your affairs; order in the distribution of your time; order in the management of your fortune; order in the regulation of your amusements; order in the arrangement of your society. Thus let all things be done in order. However, in his use of the outline, Samuel Johnson deviates from the traditional sermon structure and, although this may seem insignificant, it again demonstrates his sensitivity to his audience. Johnson frequently delays the outline until one-fourth of the sermon has been spent on a general and discursive consideration of the sermon's topic. He begins his sermons with a leisurely unfolding of the general topic and then introduces the outline.

An extreme example of Johnson's delay in introducing the traditional homiletic outline is "Sermon 14." The sermon is ten pages in length; the outline occurs on the sixth page after he has already made his strongest points. Johnson recognizes that the standardized method of placing the outline at the beginning of the sermon is a rigid and restricting convention; his practice de-emphasizes the outline, creates greater stylistic versatility, and stresses his religious pragmatism. It was commonplace for members of the scholar-clergy to examine selected Scriptural texts in their sermons for interesting syntactical problems or alternative translations. The ordained clergy of the day, both Established and Non-Conformist, had a strong interest in debating fine points of theology from the pulpit and made generous use of Scripture to support their contentions. For instance, the favorite court preacher during the reign of James I, Bishop Lancelot Andrewes, used linguistic analysis as a means of developing his thought; the structure of his sermons would depend on certain key words. In his sermon on Isaiah 7:14, Andrewes wrote:

> This Immanu is a compound: we may take it in sunder into nobis and cum: and so then we have three pieces. 1. El, the mighty God; 2. and anu, we, poor we, poor indeed if we have all the world beside if we have not Him to be with us; 3. and Im, which is cum and that cum is in the midst between nobis and Deus, God and us-to couple God with us; thereby to convey the things of the one to the other. ("Sermon IX")

The speculative design of this sermon vividly illustrates those defects in style which Johnson consistently maintained would baffle and overwhelm human understanding. Johnson's Sermons, on the other hand, avoid the interminable artifice exemplified in Andrewes' sermon and provide common sense correlations between religion and the experience of the congregation.

For example, Johnson's Sermons are conspicuous in their sparse use of Biblical parallels for the particular contemporary situation being examined. Johnson does not seem to be interested in relating the Biblical text closely to practical experience. He manifests a distinct preference for describing human nature in contemporary terms, for clothing misery in contemporary garb, and for using Biblical parallels almost incidentally. Where a Biblical text is useful, Johnson will take it up in his Sermons; however, he is at no pains to find Biblical justification for his presentations. He does not buttress his arguments with excessive and eclectic quotations; he does not attempt to awe his congregation with his knowledge of esoteric vocabulary.

Only on rare occasions does Johnson go into Scriptural exegesis; however, for him it consists only in an attempt to resolve possible ambiguity in the literal meaning of a quotation. In "Sermon 11," which considers the Scriptural text,

"Finally, be ye all of one mind, having compassion, one of another, love as brethren, be pitiful, be courteous", Johnson explains:

The word which is rendered having compassion, seems to include a greater latitude of signification, than the word compassion commonly obtains. Compassion is not used, but in the sense of tender regard to the unhappiness of another. But the term used by Saint Peter may mean the mutual feeling for each other, receiving the same impressions from the same things, and this sense seems to be given it by one of the translators [Castalio]. Later in the same sermon, Johnson gives two alternative translations, but since no choice is necessary in terms of his discussion, he carries the exegesis no further. Johnson's use of Scriptural revelation in his Sermons suggests that even it had to be put to the test of experience. The Sermons demonstrate that revelation is not its own sufficient judge and that to scrutinize it with the aid of pragmatic human experience does not invalidate that revelation. His Scriptural texts are those which the average churchgoer already knew; yet, he proposes to look at their concrete implications for daily life more carefully than his listeners would have had the inclination to do before. His usual technique consists in the incorporation of the Scriptural text into the delayed outline and almost invariably a repetition of the same text blended into his hortatory conclusion. For example, his Scriptural text for "Sermon 15" is taken from the book of Job: "Man that is born of woman is of few days and full of trouble". Johnson divides the sermon into two sections and grounds the Old Testament text directly in common experience: But since the mind is always of itself shrinking from disagreeable images, it is sometimes necessary to recall them; and it may contribute to the repression of many unreasonable desires, and the prevention of many faults and follies, if we frequently, and attentively consider, First, that "man born of a woman is of few days." And, secondly, "that man born of a woman is full of trouble."

The first part of "Sermon 15" is a consideration of the shortness of life and the second is a treatment of some of life's miseries. The Scriptural quotation does not require proof or illustration; it is "too evident to be denied and too clear to be mistaken". The passage from Job serves as a springboard for Johnson's astute analysis of the self-delusive propensities within human nature and it places that examination in a religious context.

It was also a common practice in the English sermon tradition, especially among metaphysical sermonists, to use exaggerated similes and metaphors, puns, and illogical antitheses as the basis for an entire sermon. A fine description of metaphysical sermon style can be found in "The Scribe Instructed" in which Robert South attacks such metaphysical sermons for

vain, luxuriant allegories, rhyming cadencies of similar words, as are such pitiful embellishments of speech, as to serve for nothing but to embase divinity... And as this can by no means be accounted divinity, so neither indeed can it pass for wit....for true wit is a severe and manly thing. Wit in divinity is nothing else, but sacred truths suitably expressed. It is not shreds of Latin or Greek, nor a Deus dixit, and a Deus benedixit, nor those little quirks... or the egress, regress, and progress, and other such stuff... that can properly be called wit. For that is not wit which consists not with wisdom.

Such techniques attempted to teach a moral truth by means of a physical symbol; the symbol selected seemed so far-fetched from the purpose that the mind would receive a shock of surprise when the preacher appeared to justify its selection by argument and by sacred authority. The language of these metaphysical sermons seems fantastic not simply because of its unusual images, but because the images come from a background of remote learning and are adopted to the contemporary sermon use by ingenious changes effected by the sermon writer. Such sermons became rhetorical counterparts to fanatical religion; enthusiasm was normative just as much in the first as in the second.

In Johnson's Sermons, on the other hand, diverting narratives, extensive and ingenious illustrations, unusual images, unrestrained similes and metaphors-poetic alternatives to theological rigor and restraint of the imagination-are never to be found. Gray astutely observes that "the paradox, the neatly turned conceit, the convoluted symbol, the far-fetched analogy" are all "conspicuously absent" from Johnson's sermon style. It is the elegant and restrained style of the Rambler which tends to predominate: extended sets of parallels; careful balance; logical antitheses; the preponderance of abstract nouns and noun clauses. Moreover, unlike the metaphysical sermonists, there is no dwelling on the physical symbol as an embodiment of spiritual truthalmost no theological sacramentalism-in Johnson's Sermons. Indeed, he deliberately seems to limit his use of figurative language, avoiding the practice of piling images on top of one another, because he is wary of the transfer of religion from dogma to the imagination. Johnson's aversion to high-flown conceit in his Sermons similarly led him to reject some forms of poetry for their affected and unnatural displays. For example, in his Life of Cowley, Johnson expressed his wellknown disdain for the heavy imagery and fine distinctions of metaphysical poetry. He found such embellishments even more inappropriate for the sermon because they distract from the didactic purpose of that genre. Johnson is always uneasy at the thought of a combination of religion and rhetoric; the use of imagery by which "the most heterogeneous ideas are yoked by violence together" is as foreign to Johnson's sermon style as it is to any stylistic expression that he employed or admired. In the Sermons, Johnson is cautious to achieve a tactful synthesis of reasoned doctrine and apt illustration; he specifically avoids numerous physical impressions on the imagination which might lure his listeners away from the concerns of grace and into the realm of chimera.

Another bond between the Rambler and the Sermons style and another deviation from the traditional style of the English sermon genre is the prevalence of secular diction throughout Johnson's sermons. Nineteen of Johnson's sermons open on a secular note; they have almost no religious terminology, no Biblical allusions, in the first paragraph. "Sermon 24" for example, proposes that a good government must be led by individuals concerned with the common good. The first sentence deals with a generally accepted secular principle; that is, government has been perverted from its original aim:

That the institutions of government owe their original, like other human actions, to the desire of happiness, is not to be denied; nor is it less generally allowed, that they have been perverted to very different ends from those which they were intended to promote. This is a truth, which it would be very superfluous to prove by authorities, or illustrate by example.

For the most part, Johnson uses religious terms when he is writing about a divine attribute such as mercy ("Sermon 2") or justice ("Sermon 3"), or when he discusses a particular phase of the liturgy, such as communion ("Sermon 9" and "Sermon 22"). For all other subjects, particularly those which deal with human behavior and relationships, he begins on the secular level and gradually moves into a religious context.

ALTHOUGH much of the style of Johnson's Sermons closely resembles his most energetic writing in the Ramblers, there is a noteworthy lack of versatility and a structural rigidness in the conclusions of his Sermons. These conclusions rely heavily on highly formalized patterns of diction which characterized the homiletic element of the sermon tradition-the diction is liturgical and often paraphrases Biblical forms of address. Johnson uses the formalized exhortation "Let us" in his Sermons rather than the more intimate "I" or "you" of the Ramblers. For example, in "Sermon 19" he ends:

Let us endeavour to reclaim vice, and to improve innocence to holiness; and remember that the day is not far distant, in which our Saviour has promised to consider our gifts to these little ones as given to himself; and that "they who have turned many to righteousness shall shine forth as the sun for ever and ever."

An important rhetorical quality-absolute restrained involvement with the subject matter-distinguishes these conclusions from the more subjective and personal endings of his Rambler essays. Moreover, on some occasions, Johnson concludes his Sermons with a traditional liturgical formula:

A uniform perseverance in these holy practices, will

produce a steady confidence in the Divine favour, and that confidence will complete his happiness. To which that we may all attain, God of his infinite mercy grant, for the merits of Jesus Christ, our Saviour; to whom, with the Father and the Holy Ghost, be ascribed, as is most due, all honour, adoration, and praise, now and ever! Amen.

After examining Johnson's imaginative adaptations of so many elements from the English sermon tradition, this unoriginal use of a formula in his sermon conclusions is striking. However, it is only after Johnson makes his vigorous arguments that he conforms to the restricting convention of a formula; as such, the standardized formula never interferes with the stylistic versatility which characterizes the main divisions in all the Sermons.

A close reading of the "religious" language of Samuel Johnson's Sermons reveals many of the rhetorical devices which characterize his Ramblers: a general introduction to the Sermons' subject-matter grounded in human experience; secular diction which stresses universal concepts over particular ones; parallelism; the disciplined use of emotional appeal and figurative devices; the delayed and in a sense "buried" outline; and the restrained use of easily comprehended Biblical quotations. These traits are important deviations from the conventions of English sermon style and accentuate Johnson's efforts to test the validity of any postulate of religion against common sense and human experience. Even when writing in the explicitly religious context of the sermon genre, Samuel Johnson could not completely anesthetize his aesthetic principles and skeptical propensities. Grounded in objective human experience, Johnson's Sermons promote a doctrine of stability which informs and empowers religion.

Bibliography

Alabama. Conecuh County. 1820 U.S. Federal Census. Federal copies of this census do not exist but the state copy exists in the Alabama State Archives. Copies of the transcript are available at the Evergreen-Conecuh County Library, Evergreen, Alabama; this transcript cites the Alabama [State] Official Archives transcript reprinted in the Alabama Historical Quarterly in 1944.

Alabama. Conecuh County. 1830 U.S. Federal Census. Micropublication M19, roll 3. 1840 U.S. Federal Census. Micropublication M704, roll 2. Washington: National Archives.

American Baptist Historical Society, letter. 25 July 1973, from Edward C. Starr, Curator, 1106 South Goodman Street, Rochester, New York 14620 to Mr. Ronald Stratton, Pittsfield, Massachusetts. Photocopy held in 2003 by Debbie Parker Wayne (Cushing, Texas).

Florida. Escambia County. 1860 U.S. Federal Census, population schedule. Micropublication M653, roll 106. Washington: National Archives.

Florida. Santa Rosa County. 1870 U.S. Federal Census. Micropublication M593, roll 133. Washington: National Archives.

Georgia. Crawford County. 1850 U.S. Federal Census, population schedule. Micropublication T6, roll 55. Washington: National Archives.